D0224949

The Anatomy of Gender

Women's Struggle for the Body

DISCARDED

70026864

UNIVERSITY COLLEGE OF THE CARIBOO LIBRARY
WILLIAM'S LAKE

20902

The Anatomy of Gender

Women's Struggle for the Body

EDITED BY

Dawn H. Currie
&
Valerie Raoul

UNIVERSITY COLLEGE OF THE CARIBOO LIBRARY,
WILLIAMS LAKE

Carleton University Press
Ottawa — Canada
1992

©Carleton University Press Inc. 1992

ISBN   0-88629-156-9 (paperback)
ISBN   0-88629-154-2 (casebound)

Printed and bound in Canada

Carleton Women's Experience Series 3

Canadian Cataloguing in Publication Data
    Main entry under title:
       Anatomy of gender

(Carleton women's experience series ; 3)
ISBN 0-88629-156-9 (paperback)
ISBN 0-88629-154-2 (casebound)

1. Feminism.   2. Sex role.   3. Women–Social conditions.   4. Sex dis-
criminations against women.   I. Currie, Dawn, 1948– .   II. Raoul, Valerie, 1941– .   III. Series

HQ1154.A685 1992   305.42   C91-090358-1

Distributed by   Oxford University Press Canada,
                 70 Wynford Drive,
                 Don Mills, Ontario,
                 Canada. M3C 1J9
                 (416) 441-2941

Cover design: Aerographics Creative Services, Ltd.

Acknowledgements

Carleton University Press gratefully acknowledges the support extended
to its publishing programme by the Canada Council and the Ontario
Arts Council.

TABLE OF CONTENTS

Section Three: Reclaiming the Female Body

Acknowledgements

This book is a product of a three-day conference entitled "Gender and the Construction of Culture and Knowledge," held at the University of British Columbia in September, 1989. Over sixty papers were presented, covering a wide variety of inter-disciplinary topics and approaches. Despite the diversity of papers, not surprisingly, the theme of "the female body" was a recurring one, whether in discussions of cultural representation or the construction of scientific knowledge and social policy. This theme was chosen for the collection presented here, which emphasizes how and why Women's Studies are part of a struggle to reclaim the female body. Most of the papers in this collection are revisions of papers presented at the conference, while a few were written specifically for this volume in order to round out the presentation and cover the most obvious gaps. All papers were previously unpublished work at the time of putting this collection together. In order to evoke the dialogue which took place, we have included discussion questions with each Chapter. "Gender and the Construction of Culture and Knowledge," an event which allowed academics engaged in Women's Studies research to share their work with colleagues and students, was the first of its kind at UBC. The enthusiasm of all involved encouraged us to put together this volume, which we hope will serve as a useful introduction to current developments in several aspects of Women's Studies.

Both the conference and this book would not have been possible without grants from the Social Sciences and Humanities Research Council of Canada, the UBC Development Fund, the Koerner Foundation, and the Faculty of Arts at UBC. We appreciate their support, which enabled 550 participants to share in lively debates arising from the sessions. We wish to thank the other members of the UBC Women's Studies Conference Committee: Kathryn McCannell, Kathy Hansen, Rose-Marie San Juan, Tannis Macbeth Williams, and our student helpers, Heidi Walsh and Joan Ouchi. We would like to thank Brian MacLean also, for his technical assistance in producing this manuscript. Finally, we extend our appreciation to Molly Wolf for her editorial assistance in the final stages.

All royalties from the sale of *The Anatomy of Gender* will go to the new Centre for Research in Women's Studies and Gender Relations at UBC which provided a subsidy towards the cost of producing this manuscript.

Foreword

As we began to put this collection together, we became increasingly aware of the enormity of the task involved in a project that has as its aim re-writing the female body. As a goal of Women's Studies, this task is made difficult because of resistance to alternative discourses within traditional academic disciplines, resistance that often springs from the pervasiveness of "common sense" wisdom about the body, particularly the female body. However, it is also difficult to produce a genuinely alternative discipline when the diversity of women's voices is masked by our tendency to concentrate on the needs of privileged women in the developed world. Women of colour, in particular, have identified ways in which white heterosexual feminists of the industrialized nations are making claims for *all* women through grand theories of patriarchy and the origins of women's oppression. Many of the gender theorists regarded as founders of the discipline of Women's Studies are now seen as trying to replace a universalizing and repressive system of patriarchal knowledge with an equally totalitarian feminist revision. As a contribution to the production of "Truth" through abstract theory, overgeneralizing and failing to regard history, Women's Studies might suppress diversity by stifling alternative voices.

We have tried to avoid speaking as members of this privileged group, but the difficulties in doing so reflect the real underrepresentation of minority women in academia. The majority of papers in *The Anatomy of Gender* are from an academic conference at which there were very few participants of Asian, Aboriginal, or other backgrounds. While this is reflected in the gaps and shortcomings of this volume, our purpose is to encourage, rather than to repress, the expression of alternatives. Academic feminists have no authority to speak for all women or to claim to know what it means to be a woman in every patriarchal culture; the project of reclaiming the female body is a collective and heterogeneous one. As editors of this project, we hope to use our relatively privileged position to help open up new possibilities and to aid in the dissemination of feminist research and writing. For this reason, we chose a diversity of styles, orientations, and disciplines when compiling this collection. We have aimed at breadth and accessibility, hoping to interest and inform those who, although not specialists, find Women's Studies important. In order to introduce readers to various areas of study, we have ordered the papers as a sequence which, we believe, represents the development of Women's Studies as a transformative discipline. From the documentation of masculinist bias to the rise of feminist resistance, Women's Studies is about the transformation of knowledge and ways of knowing.

The nature of this goal, however, means that Women's Studies is itself in a continual state of transformation. We wish to dedicate the book to our students, whose reactions to Women's Studies protect us from complacency, in the hope that they will carry on this transformation.

Dawn Currie (Anthropology and Sociology)

Valerie Raoul (French)

University of British Columbia

Vancouver, B.C.

July 1991

Contributors

Anne BROWN teaches in the French Department at the University of New Brunswick. Her research interests include feminist criticism and the work of Québécois, Acadian, and African women writers. She has published articles on contemporary Québécois authors and is currently coediting with Marjanne Gooze a book entitled *Placing Identity in International Women's Writing.*

Janet CAWLEY is Assistant Professor of Pastoral Theology at the Vancouver School of Theology and an ordained minister of the United Church of Canada. Her doctorate is in systematic theology, from Emmanuel College (Toronto School of Theology). Her areas of particular interest are feminist theology, ecclesiology, and Jungian psychology.

Dawn CURRIE is Assistant Professor at the University of British Columbia where she teaches Sociology and Women's Studies. Her special interest is feminist theory, and Dawn has published in the areas of women and law, medical sociology, and the family. She is coeditor of *Re-Thinking the Administration of Justice* (with B.D. MacLean) and of a special issue of the *Journal of Human Justice* (with Marlee Kline).

Noga GAYLE is a sociologist who teaches Women's Studies, Social Theory, Third World Issues, and Media at Capilano College, in North Vancouver. Her interests include investigations into the intersections of gender, race and class in feminist discourse, women in the Third World, and images of women in the mass media.

Rosemary HADDON has a Master's degree from the University of Victoria in Pacific and Oriental Studies, and is currently completing her PhD dissertation in the Department of Asian Studies at the University of British Columbia on "Nativist Literature (Xiangtu Wenxue) and the Poetics of Modernity." She has lived in Asia for extensive periods of time.

Barbara HERRINGER is a poet, editor, and social work educator whose work has appeared in various books and journals, including *The Radical Reviewer, Fireweed, Room of One's Own,* and *Sinister Wisdom,* as well as *Telling It: Women and Language Across Cultures* and *Living the Changes.* She is currently a Visiting Assistant Professor at the University of Victoria School of Social Work.

Kelly MAIER is a Registered Social Worker, a community activist and an MA student in Women's Studies at Simon Fraser University. Her current research interests include reproductive issues and feminist social work, especially the impact of "reproductive violations" on women. She has published relevant articles in *Affilia: Journal of Women and Social Work* and *Resources for Feminist Research*.

Daphne MARLATT, a West Coast poet and novelist, has held the Chair in Women's Studies at Simon Fraser University. Her published works include *Steveston, How Hug a Stone, Ana Historic*, and *Salvage*. She recently coedited *Telling It: Women and Language Across Cultures* (Press Gang, 1990), and was one of the founding editors of *Tessera*, a bilingual journal of feminist theory and new writing.

Kathryn McCANNELL of the School of Social Work, University of British Columbia, is senior editor of the *Canadian Journal of Mental Health*. She and Barbara Herringer are currently coediting a book on feminist social work praxis. Her research interests are in the areas of social networks, violence in families, and feminist pedagogy. She maintains a family counselling practice in Vancouver.

Claire McCARTHY is currently a social worker in the transplant program at Vancouver General Hospital. She completed her MSW at the University of British Columbia in 1989, focusing on social policy issues related to reproductive choice. She continues to be involved in a variety of feminist issues, in particular in the areas of reproductive technologies and the pro-choice movement.

Isobel McASLAN was born in Glasgow and educated in Scotland and Switzerland. After graduating from the Glasgow School of Art she worked in the U.S. and France. She now teaches in the Fine Arts Department at Kwantlen College in British Columbia. Her art work has been shown in collections in Europe, the U.S. and Canada. She has written on women in art for *Canadian Woman Studies*.

Kathy KENDALL is a criminological researcher with the Neuropsychiatric Research Unit at the University of Saskatchewan and at the Corrections Canada Regional Psychiatric Centre. She has taught in the Department of Sociology at the University of Saskatchewan. She is also involved in a number of women's organizations and in research on feminist methodology and feminism and the law.

Anne QUÉNIART teaches Sociology at the University of Québec in Montreal. She has published a book on maternity, *Le Corps paradoxal* (Éditions Saint-Martin, 1988). Her research is in the areas of women's health and alternative medicine and on images of parenthood in different social settings and for different generations.

Valerie RAOUL is Acting Head of the French Department and former co-ordinator of Women's Studies at the University of British Columbia, where she teaches courses on French and Québécois women writers and on feminist theory. She has recently completed a study of diary fiction in Québec, based on the psychoanalytic theory of narcissism in relation to gender definition. Her next project is on diaries by women in French.

Janet STOPPARD is a professor in the Psychology Department at the University of New Brunswick in Fredericton. She also teaches in the Women's Studies program and served as Women's Studies Coordinator from its inception in 1986 until 1988. Her research interests lie in the field of women's mental health, with a focus on women and depression. Currently she is Associate Dean of Graduate Studies at the University of New Brunswick.

Rosalind SYDIE is a professor in the Department of Sociology, University of Alberta. Her research interests are in the areas of gender studies, sociological theory, art, and culture. She is currently writing on the concept of artistic genius and women artists.

Winnie TOMM is coordinator of the Women's Studies Program at the University of Alberta. She has worked on the relation between emotion and reason in self-development (Spinoza, Hume, and Vasubandhu) and edited *The Effects of Feminist Approaches on Research Methodologies* (1989). She has published articles on sexuality, spirituality, ethics, and epistemology.

Betsy WARLAND has published several books of poetry. Her collection of essays and prose, *Proper Deafinitions*, was published in 1990. She was recently coeditor of *Telling It: Women and Language Across Cultures* (1990) and editor of *InVersions: Writing by Dykes, Queers and Lesbians* (1991).

Janice WILLIAMSON is a professor in the Department of English, University of Alberta. She has contributed to several feminist publications, compiled a collection of interviews with Canadian women writers (*Sounding the Difference*, 1989), coedited an anthology entitled *Canadian Women and the Peace Movement* (with Deborah Gorham, 1989), and is working on a study of the work of Daphne Marlatt.

The Anatomy of Gender: Dissecting Sexual Difference in the Body of Knowledge

Dawn H. Currie
Anthropology and Sociology
University of British Columbia

Valerie Raoul
Department of French
University of British Columbia

Equating Women with the Body

While the goal of sexual equality unifies feminist politics around the world, the question of sexual difference, and what it means in the struggle for equality, is a controversial aspect of feminist theory in the west. Prior to the 1960s, the study of sexual difference was more or less confined to the natural sciences. In the study of the social world, differences between women and men were seldom considered to be significant; if taken into account, they were seen to reflect natural rather than social processes and to justify gender inequality. As a consequence, gender divisions along sexual lines were portrayed as universally beneficial. Talcott Parsons, for example, argued that the sexual division of labour within the American family of the 1950s represented the most efficient allocation of necessary tasks, given women's childbearing potential. Labelling the husband's breadwinning and authoritative role "instrumental" and the subordinate role of the homemaking wife "expressive," he argued that these complementary roles, although different, were equally fulfilling for adult men and women.[1] Writers following this tradition warned against attempts to create more egalitarian family forms (see Berger and Berger, 1984). In almost all other spheres of social life, however, the question of sexual difference did not emerge; in the study of history, economics, politics or culture, the activities and experience of men were taken as the norm. Women and their experiences were either ignored or portrayed as deviations from the male standard (see Broverman *et al.*, 1970).

This invisibility of women and distortion of their experiences in traditional scholarship reflects the Cartesian view of knowledge that predominates in western cultures. Descartes maintained that the mind exists independently of bodily need and individual experience. He posited that, through the exercise of reason, the thinker could acquire a view of the world which transcends its point of origin. Knowledge achieved through Cartesian reason was thus called objective, in that it is severed from emotional and political considerations, and universal, in that it is able to assume a 'bird's eye' view of the social world. From this perspective the knower, like an omnipotent god, comes from 'nowhere.'

The first sustained challenge to the notion that thinkers can thus transcend their sexual identity accompanied the influx of women into universities, the official site of the (re)production of knowledge. The establishment of Women's Studies courses in the early 1970s provided a context within which the male bias of traditional scholarship could be identified and challenged. Much of this early work documented what Simone de Beauvoir had already noted:

> The terms masculine and feminine are used symmetrically only as a matter of form, as on legal paper. In actuality the relation of the sexes is not quite like that of two electrical poles, for man represents both the positive and the neutral, as is indicated by the common use of man to designate human beings in general; whereas woman represents only the negative, defined by limiting criteria, without reciprocity. (1961: xv)

This presentation of the male as both the positive and the neutral results not only from the separation of the mind and body but also from the subordination of the latter to the former. Not only is the body deemed irrelevant in the production of knowledge, it is seen as potentially subversive. In the artificial separation of mind and body, the pursuit of ordered knowledge requires repression of unruly needs and desires associated with the physicality of the body. While this applies to men and women alike, 'woman' has been associated with the body, 'man' with the mind, or reason. In cultural stereotypes as well as scientific medical practice, for example, women are seen and treated as irrationally governed by the dictates of their body whereas men are not (see Stoppard and Kendall, this volume). This view of women can be traced back to Aristotle and later through the Christian tradition. In the fourth century BC Aristotle maintained that while the function of men is to govern, that of women is to bear children. Even then, however, he claimed that in terms of reproduction "the body is from the female, it is the soul that is from the male, for the soul is the reality of the particular body. [Furthermore the] rule of the soul over the body, and of the mind and the rational element over the passionate is natural expedient; whereas the equality of the two or the rule of the inferior is always hurtful" (quoted in Sydie, 187: 3). Aristotle's work influenced Christian theologians in medieval Europe who refined this view of women. Augustine in the fifth century and Thomas Aquinas in the thirteenth continued to maintain that the function of women is to procreate, but only as a helper in the work of generation (see Mahowald, 1978; also Cawley, this volume). According to these spiritual leaders, women were not only inferior; they were the source of everything that is wrong in the world. This hostility towards women is reflected in the story of Eve, who was held responsible for the fall of humankind from an original state of grace (see McAslan, this volume). From creation onwards, women are portrayed in the Christian Bible as a threat to men's rational pursuit of salvation. Of the eight million heretics who were executed during the witchhunts of the Middle Ages, the overwhelming majority were women, who were declared to be "naturally more impressionable, and more ready to receive the influence of a disembodied spirit" because they are "feebler both in mind and body . . . All witchcraft comes from carnal lust, which is in women insatiable" (from *Hammer of Witches*, cited in Sydie 1987: 5; see Douglas, 1970a; Levack, 1987).

Although women were condemned as unreasonable, their redemption was not seen to lie in the development of their capacity to reason, which from Aristotle onwards was appropriated as a specifically masculine principle. While the sexuality of the female body was the downfall of humankind, salvation for women lay in the sacred duty of motherhood by which the Virgin Mary, giving birth without conception, epitomizes the patriarchal ideal of the asexual woman. Thus, although 'great thinkers' of the Enlightenment such as Rousseau and Hegel challenged the Church's authority in important ways, they continued to endorse Christian views of their time by maintaining that a woman's proper fate was marriage and that within the family sphere feminine piety was a 'law of nature.' This view was accepted as fact by many nineteenth-century thinkers, including the scientist Charles Darwin, who maintained that men were "more courageous, pugnacious and energetic than women, and [had] more inventive genius" (in Sydie, 1987: 6). As the public world became increasingly strife-ridden during the industrial revolution, however, women's insulation within the private sphere was seen to make them the moral guardians of the Victorian household. In the male-centred western tradition, women have been seen simultaneously as the 'devil's gateway' and the 'salvation' of humankind: in short, as a necessary evil.

Whatever positive attributes men claimed for themselves, their opposites were affixed to women. The separation of mind and body as the basis for 'objective' knowledge led to additional masculine/feminine dualities: reason or unreason, universals or particulars, subjective or objective, doing or being, culture or nature, order or disorder. A central tenet of western culture is the importance of subordinating the feminine principle to the masculine for the sake of human progress. Thus sex was not viewed simply as a matter of differentiation between men and women: through a corresponding gender system, it became an elaborately constructed rationalization of male subordination of women, maintained in part by the claim that women lacked the capacity to reason. Gender-based dualities claim for men the sphere of the abstract (culture), while they relegate women, in a less evolved state, to the level of animal-like instinct or intuition (nature). Analyzing this view, Carolyn Merchant (1980) documents how early scientific writings declared that Mind/Man, as knower, must conquer, dominate or seduce the Material/Female realm in order to gain understanding:

> Scientific method, combined with mechanical technology, would create a 'new organon,' a new system of investigation, that unified knowledge with material power. The technological discoveries of printing, gunpowder, and the magnet in the fields of learning, warfare and navigation 'help us to think about the secrets still locked in nature's bosom.' 'They [knowers] do not, like the old, merely exert a gentle guidance over nature's course; they have the power to conquer and subdue her, to shake her to her foundations.' Under the mechanical arts, 'nature betrays her secrets more fully . . . than when in enjoyment of her natural liberty.' (Francis Bacon, quoted by Merchant, 1980: 172)

The domination of nature, hence the (hetero)sexual subordination of women, was seen as justified in the interests of knowledge, of abstract 'Truth.'

Women-centred Challenges to the Construction of Patriarchal Knowledge

The legitimacy of male-centred knowledge is the hallmark of traditional scholarship in virtually every academic discipline. However, this authority of men is not simply a consequence of ruling ideas but reflects what Dorothy Smith calls "relations of ruling" that empower men while robbing women of authority by denying them a meaningful role in the making of knowledge and of culture. As Smith (1987) points out, the construction of knowledge through various means such as the media and the university reflects and coordinates relations of ruling, manages the unequal distribution of resources that maintains those in power, and presents these asymmetries symbolically as inevitable and desirable. Exclusion from the production of knowledge means that women's experiences, interests, and ways of knowing have not been represented in the official modes of thinking that organize and legitimate the social order. It also means that women have been deprived of the means to create forms of thought that define and raise social consciousness about their subordinate situation. This repression of women's knowledge of their condition underscores what Kate Millett (1970) called women's "engineered consent" to their subordination, while Dale Spender (1982) maintains that patriarchal knowledge is a "totalitarian regime." One of the first tasks for Women's Studies as a discipline has been to debunk the assumption that male-centred knowledge represents a truthful, disinterested view of the social order.

From her discipline of sociology, Smith (1987: 78–88) observes that the knower claims to construct a total perspective by combining and distilling partial views, detaching them from their origin in particular groups, classes, or localities in the social structure. In order to impart this claim of neutrality, texts are written in the abstract mode; institutionalized knowledge takes the passive voice and an externalized perspective which cannot be linked to any particular place or person. Smith calls this practice one of the "head" speaking and writing. It denies the body, the material work involved, and the general social environment. From her experience as an academic, she notes that in order for the production of texts to occur in this way, the writer must suppress sensations produced by the act of writing — the feeling of the pen in hand or the chair upon which one sits, as well as bodily sensations of hunger, fatigue, etc. — in order to operate in the abstract mode. The writer pays no attention to the manual labour of the working classes that produced the pen, the chair, etc.; nor to the domestic labour of women that feeds the body and restores it to working order; nor to the clerical work, again predominantly of women, that enables the academic — usually male — to operate in this mode. Smith emphasizes that what the Cartesian model suppresses from view are the very divisions between 'mental' and 'manual' labour and between men and women that it necessarily presupposes. Expressed in the conceptual realm as an abstract mode of presentation, men's authority and subsequent claim to reason and to knowledge reflects both class and patriarchal divisions — as well as racial ones — in the material world.[2] Because women are located in the sphere of the particular and local, because their labour (whether of production or reproduction) concerns the physical, women's experiences are among those that are suppressed in the production of abstract, universal knowledge. From this perspective, although women's struggle to claim authority as knowers occurs in the realm of ideas, values, and the production of culture, this struggle extends beyond the university to the everyday realm, in which women are excluded in practice, as well as in theory, from positions of authority.

Denial of Difference:
Liberation from the Body

In the academic community, feminist scholars from all disciplines agree that the quest for knowledge must begin by questioning male-authored views of women and notions of sex difference. The work of Women's Studies therefore begins by documenting biases in the portrayal of women in order to illustrate how the female body, when presented as a deviation from the male norm, has come to symbolize the use of sexual difference as a basis for belief in innate inferiority. The reclaiming of the female body by feminist scholars challenges the view that sexual difference is natural, revealing instead the way in which the concept of Woman is a socially constructed category. It is from this latter point of view that the term *gender* becomes important. In feminist writings and in contradistinction to malestream scholarship, the term sex designates biological differences between men and women and describes the real categories 'male' and 'female.' Gender, on the other hand, refers to those behavioural characteristics that classify individuals as 'masculine' or 'feminine' and that arise through socialization (see Oakley, 1981). The possession of the two X chromosomes and female primary and secondary sexual characteristics — of the form and reproductive function of the female body — is a biological fact. The supposed emotional and nurturing qualities of women are a socially induced difference. By separating nature from nurture, we can identify the ways in which male-biased knowledge constructs social differences and inequalities between men and women while presenting them as 'natural,' as given. For this reason, theories which reinforce traditional gender roles have been a target of feminist criticism. In particular, the biological basis of much traditional scholarship on femininity has been exposed. For example, Sigmund Freud's theory of psychosexual development, which purports to explain the passive heterosexuality of well-adjusted adult women, has been perceived instead as a normative prescription for patriarchal relations in European cultures (see Raoul, this volume). Once we see the distinction between explanation and prescription, we can reject the dictum that "anatomy is destiny" (see Friedan, 1963; Sydie, 1987; Sayers, 1982).

When patriarchal prescriptions are set aside, however, women's 'authentic nature' and potential are unknown. Recognizing that virtually all official knowledge has been constructed by men in the service of patriarchal interests, what we understand as 'woman' is revealed as a male creation. Thus Simone de Beauvoir (1945) began from the seemingly simple question: "What is a woman?" She then notes that "the fact that I ask is in itself significant. A man would never get the notion of writing a book on the peculiar situation of the human male" (1961: xv).

Germaine Greer reiterated the problem in *The Female Eunuch*:

> It is impossible to argue a case for female liberation if there is no certainty
> about the degree of inferiority or natural dependence which is unalterably
> female. That is why this book begins with the Body. We know what we
> are, but know not what we may be, or what we might have been. The
> dogmatism of science expresses the status quo as the ineluctable result of
> law: women must learn how to question the most basic assumptions about
> feminine normality in order to reopen the possibilities for development
> which have been successively locked off by conditioning. So, we begin at
> the beginning, with the sex of cells. (1970: 20)

Even in feminist theory, writers do not agree about biology's role in
women's oppression/ liberation, nor on an approach toward women and
gender relations once we are freed from current constraints. In the de-
or re-construction of Women, we have come to a central disagreement:
does sexual equality imply sameness or difference?

Although this question captured popular attention during the wom-
en's movement of the 1960s, "first wave" feminists during the nineteenth
century had already challenged political theorists who justified the exclusion of women from the rights of citizenship by appeals to natural
difference. Advocates of sexual equality had, in fact, raised the issue
centuries before. In France, as early as the fifteenth century, Christine
de Pisan, Europe's first female professional writer, rejected male definitions of femininity in her *Livre de la Cité des Dames*. Early in the
sixteenth century, Marie de Gournay (1622) wrote an essay on the equality of the sexes, and her ideas were taken up by a male writer, Poullain de
la Barre (1673). Yet in seventeenth-century England, when John Locke
challenged the rule of the monarch, maintaining that all individuals have
the right to be free and to be treated as equals, and that government
ought to be based on consent rather than coercion, he did not consider
the rights of women. Locke argued that the purpose of the state is to
protect the rights of individuals as citizens and to serve the interests
of those governed. However, when liberals promoted these progressive
ideals of the 'individual' as the basis for political democracy, they referred in fact only to male heads of families; women were not defined
as political subjects (see Okin, 1979). Jean-Jacques Rousseau invoked
nature as a justification for denying women the principles of the Enlightenment, when he declared that "Nature herself has decreed that woman,
for both herself and her children, should be at the mercy of man's judg-
ment. . . . This is the mode of life prescribed for women alike by nature
and reason" (quoted in Hunter College, 1983: 71). During the French
Revolution, Olympe de Gouges's "Déclaration des Droits de la Femme
et de la Citoyenne" led her to the guillotine, not the vote.

Not surprisingly, the first major feminist treatise in English on sexual difference, Mary Wollstonecraft's *A Vindication of the Rights of Woman* (1792), was primarily a refutation of the notion that women do not have the potential for rational and moral development. Wollstonecraft argued that women remained in a less developed state not because of nature, but because of socialization that stunts their intellectual development and prepares them for a life of servitude to men. If women appear to be incapable of reason, she maintained, this is because they have been excluded from the public arena where reason prevails and confined to the private sphere which emphasizes nonrational, sensual behaviour. Following this Sarah Grimké (1838) decried the fact that by conditioning woman to please men, patriarchy "turned her attention to personal attractions, offered her incense to her vanity, and made her the instrument of his selfish gratification, a plaything to please his eye and amuse his hours of leisure" (quoted in Donovan, 1986: 15). These writers concluded that proper education and training in critical thinking would enable women to realize their full human potential on the same terms as men. Enlightenment feminist writers thus implicitly denied sexual difference (see Donovan, 1986; Rossi, 1974; Tong, 1989). Central to their work is the argument that women's apparent lack of reason and preoccupation with the immediate and the physical occur because of unfair assessments of their abilities and potential, often embodied in law, which then become the basis for denial of access to institutions of higher learning, management of economic affairs, and exercise of the vote. In the struggle for political and legal equality, liberal feminists challenged the patriarchal view that women are irredeemably incapable of reason, emphasizing instead women's unrealized potential to achieve the male standard. Thus, although rejecting patriarchal prescriptions of femininity, they unwittingly adopted the dominant male-centered view of humanity. Included in this view is their devaluation of the specifically female functions of pregnancy and childbirth (see Eisenstein, 1990).

While not necessarily political liberals, a number of more recent "second wave" feminists similarly adopted the patriarchal evaluation of the female body as dysfunctional. Although providing one of the most developed analyses of women's oppression, Simone de Beauvoir maintained in 1947–8 that:

> the individuality of the female is opposed by the interest of the species; it is as if she were possessed by foreign forces — alienated. . . . The male finds more and more varied ways in which to employ the forces he is master of; the female feels her enslavement more and more keenly, the conflict between her own interests and the reproductive forces is heightened. . . . From birth, the species has taken possession of woman and tends to tighten its grasp. (1961: 22–3)

De Beauvoir adopted the misogynist view of menstruation as "the curse," accepting that "in truth the menstrual cycle is a burden" (*ibid.*, 24), and she saw childbirth as "a fatiguing task of no individual benefit to the woman" (*ibid.*, 26). While de Beauvoir disagreed that biology establishes a fixed and inevitable destiny for women, she did conclude that:

> In comparison with her the male seems infinitely favoured: his sexual life is not in opposition to his existence as a person, and biologically it runs an even course, without crises and generally without mishap. On the average, women live as long as men, or longer; but they are much more often ailing, and there are many times when they are not in command of themselves. (1961: 29)

While the focus of *The Second Sex* is an exploration of the social rather than the biological factors that make women the Other in a patriarchal culture, a number of writers accepted the notion that "the female is to nature as the male is to culture." Sherry Ortner (1974) maintained that, universally, women are "identified with — or, if you will, seem to be a symbol of — something that every culture devalues, something that every culture defines as being of a lower order of existence than itself." That something is nature, which is contrasted with culture as representing the ideas and technology through which "humanity attempts to assert control over nature" (1974: 71–2). Ortner maintains that this association of women with nature emerges out of their biological attributes: childbearing and childrearing, unlike men's role in procreation, make women more involved with "species life" than with the projects of culture; they place women in particularistic private roles with lower status than men's universalistic public roles; and women's traditional social roles, imposed because of bodily function, give them a different psychic structure (*ibid.*, 73–4). Within this view, then, women are seen as universally sharing an oppression based upon their reproductive potential, so that all women are seen as oppressed by men in more or less the same way. In a similar vein, Shulamith Firestone (1979: 16) argued that the fundamental dualism in western thought "sprang from the sexual division itself." Although she agrees with de Beauvoir that this difference of itself does not necessitate the development of a system of inequality, she believes that the reproductive functions of these differences do: "The biological family is an inherently unequal power distribution. The need for power leading to the development of classes arises from the psychosexual formation of each individual according to this basic imbalance. . ." (1979: 17). Firestone accepts a biological foundation for both sexual difference and the inequality of women. She claims that before the advent of birth control, women were at the mercy of their physiological makeup: menstruation, menopause, "female ills," constant pregnancy, the pain and danger of childbirth, wetnursing and the care of infants — all of these made women dependent on males. Thus reproductive difference, in her view, led directly to the first division of labour, becoming the origin of class, as well as the paradigm of caste (*ibid.*, 17). "Nature produced the fundamental inequality . . . which was later consolidated, institutionalized, in the interests of men. . . . Women were the slave class that maintained the species in order to free the other half for the business of the world" (*ibid.*, 192). In this way, Firestone directly links the oppression of women to the female body, and the struggle for women's liberation, therefore, to control of the female body through the development of reproductive technology. She concluded that the first demand of an alternative social system must be "the freeing of women from the tyranny of reproduction by every means possible, and the diffusion of the child-rearing role to the society as a whole, men as well as women" (*ibid.*, 193).

While these arguments for women's liberation through the control of their bodies were consonant with the political movement of the time for the reproductive and sexual liberation of women, most feminists do not find Firestone's vision of liberation through technologies such as extrauterine conception acceptable. Alison Jaggar (1983: 93) claims that this is due, in part, to the fact that women have been excluded from the development of technology. Other feminists note that technology (reproductive technology in particular) has been used in the past against women to reinforce male dominance. Emphasizing its catastrophic effect on both the social and the physical environment, feminist reaction against technology has stimulated a movement which emphasizes a return to, rather than a flight from, nature. Finally, Jaggar notes that this approach does not hold men responsible for the oppression of women: instead, it is female biology that is considered at fault, so that men can actually be seen as being women's protectors (*ibid.*). In the final analysis, viewing women's oppression in terms of the female body de-emphasizes the political struggle against male privilege and against socially constructed heterosexual identities for women, whereas the ideal society into which women are fully integrated, which Firestone advances, is based on an androgynous model that suppresses sexual difference.

Celebration of Difference:
Liberation through the Body

In reaction to the devaluation of the distinctly female and the hegemony of the masculinist values of reason and control through domination and negation of nature, a number of other feminist writers began to posit an alternative model for women's liberation based upon re-evaluation of the feminine. This trend can also be traced back to the eighteenth- and nineteenth-century "maternal feminists." These feminists claimed that the moral development that accompanied women's roles as guardians of the home, rather than being an impediment to reason, qualified them for the vote (see Bacchi, 1983). In "second wave" feminism, however, the notion of female moral superiority has been used to challenge rather than reaffirm the established order, including women's familial roles. Jean Baker Miller (1976) began with the premise shared by de Beauvoir and Firestone that women have always been subordinated, but she argued that the oppression of women historically is a potential source of power for women. Women's experience of oppression should not be read as entirely negative; through their confinement to childbearing and nurturing roles, women have developed positive, life-enhancing values, as well as those considered by traditionalists to be the source of inferiority. Baker Miller maintains that the characteristics which patriarchy has assigned to women are, in fact, crucial to the functioning of a healthy society. She argues that we need to reconsider the conventional division between the rational and the emotional and the emphasis that has been given to subordinating the latter by the former as the primary principle of human and societal development. Women's emotionality, reliance upon intuition, ability to express vulnerability, and tendency to cultivate co-operativeness, have led to their subservience and attendant psychological problems under conditions of inequality, but these traits represent skills that are needed for the survival of civilization:

> in the course of projecting into women's domain some of its most troublesome and problematic exigencies, male-led society may also have simultaneously, and unwittingly, delegated to women not humanity's "lowest needs" but its "highest necessities" — that is, the intense, emotionally connected cooperation and creativity necessary for human life and growth. Further, it is women who today perceive that they must openly and consciously demand them if they are to achieve even the beginnings of personal integrity. (1976: 25–6)

Baker Miller rejects the liberal notion of androgyny and argues instead that we must transcend old values and dichotomies, establishing a new psychology for women. A number of writers have taken the logic of this approach further, arguing for a new cultural and moral order based on feminine values (Gilligan, 1982, for example).

This reevaluation of the feminine gives new, positive emphasis to the specifically female experiences of sexuality, menstruation, childbirth, and lactation. Adrienne Rich, in particular, criticizes dominant views of the female body, arguing that:

female biology — the diffuse, intense sensuality radiating out from clitoris, breasts, uterus, vagina; the lunar cycles of menstruation; the gestation and fruition of life which can take place in the female body — has far more radical implications than we have yet come to appreciate. Patriarchal thought has limited female biology to its own narrow specifications. The feminist vision has recoiled from female biology for these reasons; it will, I believe, come to view our physicality as a resource, rather than a destiny. In order to live a fully human life we require not only *control* of our bodies (though control is a prerequisite); we must touch the unity and resonance of our physicality, our bond with the natural order, the corporeal ground of our intelligence. (1977: 21, emphasis in original)

Whereas previous feminist writers had accepted the patriarchal notion that motherhood in particular is a barrier to women's self-fulfillment and thus argued for its transcendence, Rich claims that motherhood *per se* is not repressive; it is the specific institution of family and motherhood in patriarchal societies which women find oppressive. Rich criticizes Firestone for accepting and reinforcing male-defined views of pregnancy as a form of victimization which necessarily entails suffering and deprivation. She maintains that, in a different social context, mothering is the source of joy and creativity for women, and concludes that we must struggle not against mothering (a potentially rewarding experience) but against the institutions that currently deny women this potential (see also Bernard, 1974). Like a number of other radical feminist writers, Rich appeals to past cultures in which the powers of female reproduction were recognized and celebrated, acknowledging that all human beings are "of woman born." Following Rich, a series of feminist writers began to rewrite the history and the experience of motherhood from this gynocentric perspective.

While writers like Rich (1977), Bernard (1974), and Chodorow (1978) have emphasized the way in which social organization and institutional arrangements give rise to distinctly masculine and feminine values, identities, and ways of knowing, Mary O'Brien (1981) links the persistence of sexually differentiated consciousness to the physicality of the reproductive body. She distinguishes between male and female "reproductive consciousness," arising from biological roles in procreation. She notes that for men, the act of copulation alienates them from their seed. They are linked to the future generation only through the notion of paternity, which is the conceptualization of a cause-and-effect relationship between copulation and childbirth; it is an abstraction, an idea that rests very specifically on theory and is not unified immediately with practice. While childbirth similarly entails the physical separation between women and the product of copulation, this alienation is mediated by the physical labour of pregnancy, childbirth, and lactation, which all affirm the connection between women and the future generation. From these differences O'Brien argues that men are driven to negate their alienation from the human race, specifically through private property[3] as a symbol of continuity — a symbol that men create and that men need but women do not (1981: 33).

On the basis of her gender-based differentiation of reproductive consciousness, O'Brien characterizes relations between the sexes as oppositional. In the same way that production gives rise to antagonisms between producers, O'Brien claims that reproduction necessarily sets up opposition between those who labour reproductively (women) and those who do not (men). From this framework, she analyzes world history as the working out of the contradictions and gender oppositions associated with reproduction, claiming that biological processes of reproduction, which are inherently female-centered, underlie human consciousness and action. It is therefore the female body and the female-centred activities of reproduction, rather than male-centered activities of cultural and material production, that form the substructure of history.

Mary Daly (1978) in particular connects the female body to the "herstory" of civilization and also to the liberation of women. For her, this reclaiming of the feminine is necessary for the affirmation of women's knowledge because:

> The kingdom of male-authored texts has appeared to be the ideal realm to be reached/entered, for we have been educated to forget that professional "knowledge" is our stolen process. . . . they rob us of everything: our myths, our energy, our divinity, our Selves. . . . Women's minds have been mutilated and muted to such a state that "Free Spirit" has been branded into them as a brand name for girdles and bras rather than as the name of our verb-ing, be-ing Selves. Such brand names brand women "Morons." Moronized, women believe that male-written texts (biblical, literary, medical, legal, scientific) are "true." (1978: 5)

Daly calls the process whereby women "see/ hear/ feel how we have been tricked by their texts" one of "exorcism, of peeling off the layers of mindbindings and cosmetics [as necessary for] movement past the patriarchally imposed sense of reality and identity" (*ibid.*, 6). This notion of exorcism goes beyond the mere assertion that women see the world differently than men. Daly emphasizes that patriarchy includes the language that we use to describe reality, drawing attention to the ways in which language reimposes the patriarchal order. She argues that, as the female self becomes "dispossessed, enspirited, she moves out of range of the passive voices and begins to hear her own Active Voice, speaking her Self in successive acts of creation. As she creates her Self, she creates new space: semantic, cognitive, symbolic, psychic, physical spaces"

(1978: 340). Following Rich (1977), Daly maintains that by "the very act of becoming more conscious of her situation in the world, a woman may feel herself coming deeper than ever into touch with her unconscious and with her body" (Rich quoted in Daly, 1978: 6). In this way, the female body is the beginning point for an epistemological revolution, which becomes possible when women learn to "think through their body" rather than through patriarchal values. Daly's writing, with its emphasis on wordplay and reappropriation/redefinition of old (formerly pejorative) terms such as "hag," or the reaffirmation of forgotten etymologies such as "spinster," comes close to the experiments in writing undertaken by French post-structuralist writers.

From Female Self to Feminine Text: The Body as Subversive

Post-structuralism rejects the fundamental assumption that there is a stable, coherent Subject capable of detached and rational inquiry into the Truth of its own existence: post-structuralists thus do not look for, or expect to find, the 'Truth' about the human condition. Rather, like Michel Foucault, they study terms, statements, texts, and other representations in order to explore how Truth is constructed. A common element in work influenced by French post-structuralist thinkers Jacques Derrida and Jacques Lacan (see Raoul, this volume) is an emphasis on language in the analysis of individual consciousness, ideologies, and social organization. Above all else, it is through language that meanings, forms of organization, and their social and political consequences are defined and contested; discourse is the site of struggle for social power. Likewise, it is where we construct our sense of self, our subjectivity. Language is no longer seen as the expression of unique individuality; rather, it constructs the individual's subjectivity in ways that are socially and culturally specific. Post-structuralism rejects the fundamental humanist assumption of Enlightenment thought: that a conscious, knowing, rational subject exists outside of discourse. From the post-structuralist position, therefore, Reason is the effect and not the cause of the symbolic order.

This emphasis upon text as the site where meaning is constructed and contested, rather than where reality is reflected, links the post-structural critique of humanism to the method of deconstruction. Deconstruction involves analysis of the ways in which meanings are made to work, particularly through the operation of 'difference' in texts. Here 'difference' in one sense refers to implicit or explicit contrast that re-presses the antithesis or negation of the established meaning in order to present a positive definition. Any unitary concept contains a repressed or negated alternative, because its meaning is constructed in opposition to its antithesis. Deconstruction thus consists of the reversal and displacement of these binary oppositions, a process that reveals the interdependence of otherwise seemingly dichotomous terms and the way in which the constructed meaning is relevant to a particular context. The categories of discourse are shown to be not natural but constructed oppositions, constructed for particular purposes within particular cultures and periods of history, whether or not writers are aware of this (Scott, 1988: 38; see also Poovey, 1988; Kendall, this volume). From this perspective, the categories of male/masculinity are constructed in opposition to those of female/femininity, in a way that requires the polar (feminine) opposites to become negative. The process is one that separates reason from emotion and calls the latter unreasonable; opposes the universal to the particular and then decries particularism; separates Subject from Object and values doing more than merely being; opposes culture to nature and order to disorder, masculine to feminine, white to black. By revealing the arbitrary hierarchies through which meaning is constructed, and by making visible the suppressed alternatives upon which meaning is dependent, deconstruction gives a new importance to previously marginal discourse. 'Feminine' becomes a privileged alternative position from which to read and discover the blind spots of male texts, as well as from which to write.

"Writing in the feminine," or "l'écriture femme" reflects the problematic position of a female subject in relation to language. Drawing upon Freudian notions of sexuality and the unconscious, a number of writers emphasize the need to develop theories of self rather than theories of society. Following Lacan, French feminists view the acquisition of language as the internalization of a patriarchal symbolic order. They see their struggle as one to destabilize the system of binary oppositions that form the basis of male-centred thought and thus link it to Derrida's use of deconstruction as "the active interrogation of logocentric texts" (Grosz, 1989: xv; see also Tong, 1989). This interrogation illuminates internal contradictions in seemingly coherent systems of thought. Writers share the common goal of developing a way in which to avoid thinking in the binary, oppositional terms that compel us to oppose male/female; nature/culture; speech/writing (Tong, 1989: 222). They see the main challenge as producing a woman's discourse, coming from the margins of the dominant male one, not only expressing but creating an 'Other' subject position. Here feminists' efforts to voice a fundamental difference have much in common with those of post-colonial writers, similarly striving to speak from outside the dominant culture.

While it is extremely difficult to challenge the symbolic order when the only words available are those issued by this order, these writers attempt to subvert dominant modes of discourse by replacing male metaphors (linearity, unity, upright solidity) by female ones of openness, fluidity, multiplicity and interweaving, and by modifying syntax and putting emphasis on the ambivalence of lexical terms. Although Tong (1989: 219) argues that deconstructionism is necessarily anti-essentialist because it rejects the search for universals, if it is used to simply revalue the feminine, it can, ironically, affirm gender-based dichotomies. This is most apparent when one considers the predominance of imagery based on the female body, specifically on the mother's body, as a threat to the single, fixed meanings of an authoritarian, phallocentric discourse. Hélène Cixous's metaphor of writing with "mother's milk" rather than with ink, for example, is striking in its reversal of the male stereotypical opposition of black and white. Further, writing is perceived as providing food (for thought) rather than serving as a phallic weapon. However seductive this subversive image may be, it plays out rather than transcends sexual differentiation.

The Body Politic:
From "Body" to Bodies

Although positively reevaluating what society has already defined as properly female, the view which advocates women's knowledge and liberation through "writing the body" affirms rather than rejects patriarchal prescriptions. Where malestream approaches to abstract knowledge remove the body from sight, in "l'écriture féminine" it is the body which assumes, with a vengeance, a subversive role. Ironically, whether we deny or celebrate sexual difference, in both cases we are accepting as given the existence of stable identities designated as male and female, masculine and feminine.[4] Neither position questions these taken-for-granted categories, a failure that leads some writers to complain that the effect of framing women's oppression in this way is merely to reaffirm dichotomous thinking. From the perspective of transcending dualisms, the task is to take the production of the categories themselves as the subject of investigation. It is primarily from this perspective that Christine Delphy (1984) argues that, although the stability of biological sex may appear to underlie the separation of and antagonism between men and women, this way of thinking itself emerged as the effect of gender-based hierarchy. She maintains that it is necessary to explain the current preoccupation with the categories of sex and gender in the context of social inequality: "gender, the respective positions of women and men, is not constructed on the (apparently) natural categories of sex (male and female), but rather . . . sex has become a pertinent fact, hence a perceived category, because of the existence of gender" (1984: 144). Biology, including the female body, is not meaningful in and of itself but only in a social context that has gender at its centre. By arguing simply to revalue the female body and all it stands for, feminist writers unwittingly help to reconstitute the patriarchal system that privileges the notion of sexual difference. For Delphy, gender-based thinking is itself problematic, and must be acknowledged as cultural and historically specific. It testifies to the pervasiveness of patriarchal ideologies in Western thought, which posit a natural hierarchical heterosexual order. More importantly, however, it draws attention to the fact that the sexed body is inseparable from discourses about it. Post-structural analyses suggest that we question the notion of an unchanging, biological/sexual identity that stands apart from our thinking about it.

In exploring the ways in which our thinking about the body is conditioned, Mary Douglas draws attention to the relationship between the literal and the metaphorical body. She observes (1966: 122) that "just as it is true that everything symbolizes the body, so it is equally true (and all the more so for that reason) that the body symbolizes everything else." She calls this social definition of the physical, and the 'physical' definition of the social, the "two bodies." What she means by the former is that although we exist physically in our bodies, we actively and physically construct and reconstruct ourselves and our bodies in accordance with social and individual norms and values, and for various purposes. Following Douglas, Anthony Synnott (1990) emphasizes that while the physical body, based on biology, is common to all, the social body is historically and culturally relative:

> We [must] discuss first the *social* construction of the body, i.e. the attribution of meanings to the body and therefore to the self: the way in which society models our construction of ourselves as tomb (Plato), temple (Paul), machine (Descartes) or self (Nietzsche, Sartre). These conceptual paradigms are no doubt of paramount significance for how people live their lives and regard themselves; but society has a very direct, immediate and physical impact upon people also. Our ideas do construct us, but so do our jobs, hobbies, lifestyles, and social roles. We are *physically* constructed by society, whether we like it or not; and in the end we are sometimes *destructed* by that same society. (Synnott, 1990: 1, emphasis original)

In the final analysis, therefore, we create a body that we then mistake as pregiven. While this creation appears to reflect the desires, goals, and values of the individual, it occurs in the context of the norms and values of a particular society: the body is a product of both self and society, literally and metaphorically.[5] The body is properly human only when it is culturally acceptable (Synnott, 1990: 11).

In traditional scholarship, this cultural transformation of the body has been a neglected topic, confined to cultural anthropologists who have documented the 'quaint' customs and body rituals of 'the primitive.' It took writers like Greer (1970), Dworkin (1974), and Daly (1978) to remind us of the ways in which women's bodies are primarily the products of cultural transformations of biology. Through cultural practice, the female body becomes the colonized terrain of heterosexual patriarchy. Germaine Greer (1970) documented the ways in which the female body in patriarchal culture is reduced to a sexual object for the pleasure and appropriation of other sexual beings, men. She equates this process with castration because, from the point of view of a woman:

> Her sexuality is both denied and misrepresented by being identified as passivity. The vagina is obliterated from the imagery of femininity in the same way that the signs of independence and vigour in the rest of her body are suppressed. The characteristics that are praised and rewarded are those of the castrate — timidity, plumpness, languor, delicacy and preciosity. (1970: 21)

In this perspective, the chief element in the cultural making of the female body is the suppression and deflection of women's potential, so that the dominant image of femininity which rules our culture and to which all women must conform is that of eunuch (see Raoul, this volume). Greer observed that this castration occurs through the masculine/feminine polarity, in which men have commandeered all the energy and streamlined it into an aggressive, conquistadorial power, reducing all heterosexual contact to a sadomasochistic pattern. Thus perverted, heterosexual relationships between men and women often involve a measure of hatred. Although in extreme cases it takes the form of loathing and disgust and inspires hideous crimes against the bodies of women, more often it is limited to ridicule and insult.

It is along these lines that Adrienne Rich (1978) admonished feminism to look as carefully at heterosexuality as it does at other patriarchal institutions, such as motherhood and the family. Although sexuality has been seen by traditionalists and feminists alike as located within the sphere of 'the natural,' Rich draws attention to heterosexuality as a forced identity[6] maintained very often by violence. In *Woman Hating* (1974) Andrea Dworkin expands upon the notion of the female body as terrain upon which hostility towards the female sex is reenacted by men. She likens the everyday practices of femininity, especially in North American culture, to preparation for patriarchal victimization:

> Pain is an essential part of the grooming process, and that is not acci-
> dental. Plucking the eyebrows, shaving under the arms, wearing a girdle,
> learning to walk in high-heeled shoes, having one's nose fixed, straighten-
> ing or curling one's hair — these things *hurt*. The pain, of course, teaches
> an important lesson: no price is too great, no process too repulsive, no
> operation too painful for the woman who would be beautiful. *The tol-*
> *erance of pain and the romanticization of that tolerance begins here*, in
> preadolescence, in socialization, and serves to prepare women for lives of
> childbearing, self-abnegation, and husband-pleasing. (1974: 133, empha-
> sis original).

Dworkin draws attention to the ways in which the cultivation of the
female as victim begins in childhood through fairytales. In adulthood,
pornography, in particular, projects the female in this role:

> Literary pornography is the cultural scenario of male/ female. It is the
> collective scenario of master/ slave. It contains cultural truth: men and
> women, grown now out of the fairy-tale landscape into the castles of erotic
> desire; woman, her carnality adult and explicit, her role as victim adult
> and explicit, her guilt adult and explicit, her punishment lived out on her
> flesh, her end annihilation — death or complete submission. (1974: 53)

While pornography perhaps illustrates most directly the way in which
women's bodies literally symbolize sex and cultural attitudes towards
(hetero)sexuality, feminist writers are beginning to explore the ways in
which the pornographic genre is central to consumer-oriented culture
(see Currie, this volume). Once incorporated into mass culture, the
insult or assault to the female body is not solely and primarily male-
authored; widespread dieting practices linked to anorexia and bulimia,
for example, indicate the extent to which women, as well as men, are
trained to be uncomfortable with the untransformed female body.

As we recognize the cultural construction of the female body, the
"society in the body," Anthony Sonnatt (1990) also reminds us of the
social body: the metaphorical body which distorts our understanding of
the physical body. He describes this latter process as somatization: the
way in which we think about our social institutions in terms of the body.
He notes that we live in the world and contemplate it through our bodies
and our senses, imposing our bodies, metaphorically, upon the universe:
clocks have hands and faces, roads have shoulders, hills have brows, and
valleys have bottoms; saws have teeth while cornstalks have ears; chairs
have arms and legs, beds have heads and feet; books have bodies, etc.
Organizations have brains; characters may be spineless or nosey, have
no guts, or be heartless. The galaxy has arms, comets have tails, and
the moon a face. Our most demonstrative terms refer to the 'private'
parts of the body and to bodily functions (1990: 13). Note, however,

that while "having balls" is generally a compliment, "to be a cunt" is an insult. Through somatization we present political, economic, ecclesiastical, and domestic institutions as somehow physical, and therefore as natural, biologically immutable, and divinely ordained. While some of these constructions are unimportant or amusing, in others the symbolism is critical: while it may not matter that roads have shoulders, it is important whether God is described as male rather than female (1990: 13; see also Cawley, this volume). The two main principles of somatic construction are hierarchy (head is to body as ruler to ruled and high to low) and gender (male is to female as ruler to ruled, high to low, head to heart). Together, these two principles interlock to create powerful equations which legitimate differentiation and hierarchy. Sonnatt concludes that:

> It is not surprising that we construct our universe based on what we know first, our bodies (*pace* Descartes); nor is it surprising that these definitions of the universe reinforce our "knowledge" of the body. What is surprising is the degree to which these ancient definitions persist, unexamined and taken for granted, and *still* determine our idea of what is *natural*. The *social* has now been reconstructed as *natural*; the cultural re-defined as biological. (1990: 15, emphasis original)

At the same time, Sonnatt emphasizes that metaphorical hierarchies rest upon social hierarchies of all kinds in the real world. The body politic is itself physically constructed and maintained by the productive labour of manual workers; it is defended by the physical work of footsoldiers; and it is directed by the mental work of bureaucrats and political leaders (see Williams, this volume). In the Foucauldian tradition, he maintains that the body politic exists to preserve, maintain, and develop human bodies. Government is a very physical matter which embodies conflicts of the seemingly natural categories of race, gender, and class (see Sydie, this volume).

As Janet Sayers (1982) points out, these 'natural' categories which appear unquestioned in many scientific theories have social histories. Social Darwinism, which claims that socially and materially advantaged groups are also the socially and biologically most fit, emerged at a time when the impoverishment of the working classes was identified as a social concern and when slavery and colonial exploitation brought Britain glory. Those in power have since applied sociobiological principles to explain all kinds of social inequalities, but primarily those of race, class, gender and sexual identity. Scientific theories about the biological inferiority of women emerged during the time when feminists were demanding equal education for women. Just as Girton College was established for women at Cambridge and plans were afoot to open Oxford to women,

Dr Henry Maudsley, an eminent British psychiatrist, declared women biologically unfit for higher education. He questioned whether they could "live laborious days of intellectual exercise and production, without injury to their functions as the conceivers, mothers, and nurses of children" (quoted in Sayers, 1982: 8; see also Kendall, this volume). In this way, ideological constructs appear as natural categories, concealing the social basis of conflicts over the production and distribution of material and human resources. The ways in which these conflicts are particularly, but not exclusively, over women's bodies are apparent in the abortion controversy, struggles over the control of new reproductive technologies, and concerns about health and child care (see Maier, Quéniart, and Mc-Cannell *et al.*, this volume). Both metaphorically and literally, the body is at the centre of political life. The relations between the metaphorical and physical body are intimate, mutually reinforcing, multidimensional and complex; they need to be dissected and reexamined if we are to avoid some of the dualistic, hierarchical, and oppressive implications of conflation between the biological and the cultural (Sonnatt, 1990: 25).

Perhaps paradoxically, by exposing the cultural matrix of categories and theoretical discourses, we also reveal the historical and cultural specificity of feminist discourses on the body. Once we recognize the political construction of 'femininity' as it informs most contemporary feminist writing on sexual difference, we can also recognize that it idealizes the white (young) female body. This means that the struggle for the body (as outlined in this book) may only be primarily relevant to white women in advanced industrial countries. Writings on the female body to date reflect the fact that white heterosexual feminists still maintain hegemony over feminism; women of colour and women of other identities have been marginalized from the production of knowledge. Many of these women reject the way in which white feminists have generalized from their experiences of oppression to make claims about the oppression of all women. The ethnocentrism underlying many interpretations of non-Western cultures as patriarchal is currently being challenged. As white academic feminists we might speculate that imperialism and colonial domination, which are central to European patriarchal cultures, create important distinctions between the bodies of relatively privileged white women and those of colonized women. If we look at the history of slavery, for example, we find that although black women, like their white counterparts, were seen as incapable of Reason, they were hardly viewed as physically frail[7] or treated as guardians of sexual morality. Exploring these kinds of questions in depth, in order to reflect the diversity of women's experiences in a genuinely global sense, is unfortunately beyond the scope of a book like this, written mostly by white feminists.

The project of producing a text such as this makes us aware of the challenges to the socially constructed hegemony of white feminism. These challenges involve more than a simply discursive debate; they demand the real inclusion of more women from all types of background in the struggle to create "women's studies" as "about women, by women, for women," acknowledging that women are not all like.

This Book:
Dissecting Sexual Difference

Although the struggle for women's liberation is not entirely equivalent to a struggle for women's bodies, equality for women cannot bypass the female body. This book is based on that premise. The struggle to reclaim the female body is a complex one, requiring analysis of the interrelationship between the cultural representation of women, through which the female body acquires meaning, and of the bodily practices affixed to claims about sexual (and racial) difference that underlie social organization and politics. Intimate connections between the literal, physical body and the body as symbol or metaphor mean that we can no longer discuss with certainty where culture ends and biology begins. This blurring of the boundaries between the natural and the cultural, between body and mind, destabilizes the foundations of traditional knowledge, making the pursuit of feminist research less straightforward and more complicated than the construction of patriarchal knowledge. What is apparent is that these boundaries, however blurred, are constructed and contested in current discourses about the female body. As an examination of this contested terrain, *The Anatomy of Gender* is a collection of feminist readings of and challenges to these discourses. The papers represent various ways in which theory and practice lead to sexual difference. By differentiating and dissecting nature and nurture, the metaphorical and literal bodies, they help us to reconnect women's minds and bodies in a way that can resist patriarchal prescriptions. Although we have only begun to dis- or uncover what this means, as women, we must know what our bodies are, what our relationship to our bodies can be, and how these are both socially and culturally constructed. From this new 'body of knowledge' we can develop bodily and political practices which are emancipatory rather than repressive. For this reason, *The Anatomy of Gender* is about both the deconstruction and the reconstruction of the female body. By highlighting ways in which dominant ideologies oppress and repress women, we hope that this book can contribute to the search for alternatives for women. At the same time, by illustrating the ways in which the representations of women in male-authored culture reappear in scientific practices, this collection of essays testifies to the importance of connecting the metaphorical and physical body, in the humanities and the social sciences. First we must deconstruct the current conflation between the social and (what we know as) the natural; then we must construct new connections, between cultural presentations of the body and the scientific discourses that govern it in our everyday lives.

To begin, papers in **Section One** critically explore the representation of women in mainstream culture. Here, feminist readings illustrate how representations of the female body do not simply reflect the 'Truth' of sexual difference but instead reflect political processes controlled historically by men. Both written and visual culture have been created by men, from the vantage point of the male Subject. Since patriarchal representations have revolved around the double standard of woman as either sexual object or chaste wife and mother, they narrow our thinking as women about the range of possibilities open for us. A further difficulty is that much of this imagery concerns the pornographic representation of women. Placing misogynist representations of the female body in their broad historical context, Isobel McAslan calls them "absurd," even by male standards: that is, they are contrary to reason and inconsistent with common sense. Documenting the pain and humiliation caused to women through practices which reflect hatred of the female body, she argues that these practices are rooted in fear. This fear evolves from ignorance and insecurity, generated by the unknown. She claims that as long as woman remains unknown on her own terms to men, men will desire to control women. Thus, reclaiming the female body is a struggle against the fear which underlies the patriarchal domination of women.

At the same time that female imagery has been obscene, male imagery has been associated with the sacred. This is most apparent when one examines the imagery of God. Janet Cawley points out that, while the Christian view of God is theoretically genderless, God is represented and perceived as male. Further, the basic structures of patriarchy are said to be ordained by God and thus part of the natural order. Given that images of the divine are also images of Self, Cawley highlights the need for female imagery of God (see also Tomm, this volume). She notes that previous religious images of women have been based largely on male projections, and can be associated with Jung's notion of the anima. Exploring female imagery in the Christian tradition, she identifies images that contradict the physical experience of women (such as those of the Virgin Mary) that deify patriarchy ("God is to the faithful as husband is to wife"), or that present God's nurturing and loving side as an exception to his normal exercise of power and coercion. Cawley concludes that we need female images of God and outlines problems that feminist believers are likely to encounter.

Similarly identifying the ways in which the female body in art has been male-authored, Rosalind Sydie links patriarchal culture to the social regulation of women. She argues that the control and confinement of women in the interest of the patriarchal state is reflected in the paintings of male artists in turbulent eighteenth-century France. The various depictions of women, as idealized love objects, as graceful goddesses and tempting mistresses, as dutiful mothers and virginal daughters, and, later, as the patriotic maternal body, reflect the social and political realities of the patriarchal state that always has cause to control the female body. Ironically, although the Revolution transformed the mother figure into "liberty leading the people," the equality towards which she led the people applied only to men: women were idealized within complementary and subservient roles. These contradictory images and political views of women — which continue into the twentieth century — highlight women's subordination to male authority and desire, confining 'good' women to socially approved roles within the family. Although this type-casting of women within artistic representation is a political process, Sydie shows how, culturally, it is portrayed and perceived as being natural.

While the papers mentioned above examine Western culture, Rosemary Haddon explores the ways in which women have been portrayed in Chinese fiction. Specifically, Haddon discusses themes which have emerged since the May Fourth Movement. Unlike the French Revolution as discussed by Sydie, this movement had more immediate consequences for the status of Chinese women. The representation of women in fiction written during this period reflects awareness on the part of Chinese writers and intellectuals (male and female) of women's struggle for full emancipation. Taking the view that fiction reflects the social and ideological order, Haddon identifies four themes as indicators of the material position of women: androcentrism, which reflects the persistence of Confucianism; liberal humanism, associated with liberationist struggles, including those for female emancipation; colonialism, as reflecting nationalist concerns; and female sexuality. These discourses provide more than insight into Chinese social life; they serve to illustrate the evolution of women's consciousness and the emergence of alternative views of the social role of women.

Usually, we tend to think of 'culture' in terms of fine art, music and published writing. However, Janice Williamson draws attention to the mass culture which permeates our everyday life in her examination of consumer culture as embodied by West Edmonton Mall. While cultural critics typically characterize this mall as a "giant stage-set for the dramas of the dollar bill," in contrast Williamson reads it as a drama of gender relations. Asking how a feminist critic might read the mall, she employs the notion of "pedestrian feminism," which conveys a double critique. First, it provides a countercultural alternative to the high modernist excavations of feminist critics, a critique which asks "how do classical theories of modernism fall short of women's modernity?" Second, the figure of the pedestrian, or the woman walker, offers a mobile position from which the feminist critic oscillates between sensory, embodied experience and detailed analysis. As a feminist pedestrian, Williamson comments on the feminization of space in the West Edmonton Mall. In looking at what the mall conceals, she reveals much: the suppression of relations of class, race, and gender. By drawing attention to the repressed subjects which disappear in the various scenarios depicted in the mall, Williamson gives new meaning to the 'fantasy' behind 'fantasyland.'

De Beauvoir maintained that one effect of male-authored culture and knowledge for women is that we confront ourselves as 'Other,' as the object of patriarchal culture. As a consequence, women's most private and personal experience — their relationship to their bodies — is mediated by cultural and political processes. The effects of male-authored culture and knowledge become more apparent when we link symbolic presentation to material practice. **Section Two** explores the practical effects of patriarchy in the fields of medicine, law, social work, and social policy. Examining the controversies surrounding menstruation, Janet Stoppard shows how the physiological functions of the female body are being increasingly medicalized, and, as a consequence, associated with assessments of women's mental as well as physical health. Although some women may welcome being able to give the name "premenstrual syndrome" to physical problems that accompany menstruation, clinical research is inconclusive regarding the nature of this 'disease.' While not denying the reality of unpleasant and unwanted changes that some women experience in association with the menstrual cycle, Stoppard identifies consequences which may be less than positive for women as a whole. Specifically, the use of the PMS construct has the effect of decontextualizing and individualizing women's problems, so that alternative, nonbiological approaches to women's well-being are less likely to be considered. In the biomedical framework, women learn to blame their bodies for unwanted, unpleasant experiences which may, in reality, be linked to their social position. Thus, Stoppard claims that PMS is an ideological construct which justifies sexist beliefs and the practices which stem from them. She argues that affirmation of women's wholeness as both biological and social beings will only be possible when PMS is no longer a plausible answer to the fundamental question, "What is wrong with women's lives?"

Also exploring the possible consequences of accepting PMS as an official category, Kathy Kendall discusses its use in the courts. While PMS has been successfully argued as a defense in a number of sensational cases, she indicates that it has been, and can continue to be, used against women. In particular, as a legal defense or when used as a mitigating factor in sentencing, PMS gives credence to misogynist claims that "women are at the mercy of their hormones." Although the PMS defence may appeal to feminists because it will benefit individual women, in the long run it can reinforce notions of women as inferior to men, legitimating discriminatory practices both within and beyond the law. Drawing on deconstruction as a method of analysis, Kendall reveals the interconnectedness of patriarchal medicine and law. These connections emerge as she explores the historical and political, rather than biological, origins of PMS as a medical and legal category. Her feminist deconstruction of PMS challenges the privileged position of patriarchal law, helping to make alternative approaches possible.

The connections between the medical and legal treatment of women are further elaborated by Kelly Maier in an examination of violations of women's reproductive rights. Maier discusses in detail two recent cases in which medical practitioners have used the rubric of the "best interests of the child" to override women's decisions concerning childbirth. Maier calls these actions to curtail women's reproductive freedom "reproductive wrongs." These wrongs reflect the growing tendency to conceptualize fetal rights as separate from and in opposition to women's rights. These debates are not about the rights of fetuses at all: they are about male control over women's reproductive bodies. The notion of maternal culpability and the practice of emphasizing the best interests of the child are ways of forcing women to accept the idealized, sacrificial model of femaleness and motherhood, while ignoring the material conditions of pregnancy and the care of children. As a social worker, Maier is particularly concerned about the ways in which this trend to counterpoise "women's rights" against "fetal rights" creates an ethical dilemma for social service professionals. From a feminist position, which advocates human rights, client self-determination, and social justice, she argues that social workers are particularly well situated to intervene on behalf of women whose voices are silenced and whose rights and bodies are violated.

The way in which notions of 'maternal culpability' and 'the best interests of the child' are forcing women to accept the idealized, sacrificial model of femaleness and motherhood is further explored by Anne

Quéniart. In her interviews with pregnant women, Quéniart found acute feelings of insecurity about pregnancy, especially during the first few months. She relates this anxiety to newly emerging discussions on the medical risks of pregnancy. The problem is that these discourses tend to highlight the behaviour of women while downplaying other social factors, such as environmental pollution or effects of the workplace. Women are only being warned about the evils of tobacco, alcohol, or their 'bad eating habits,' not about external social factors. One effect can be that women become obsessed about the 'normality' of their pregnancy. Seeking a point of reference for their experiences, they turn to the medical 'ideal type.' This causes women to pay little attention to the symptoms they experience if these symptoms are similar to those described in the medical literature, even though some may be quite worrisome, but at the same time to be frightened by symptoms that are not in fact problematic. Uncertainty is no longer tolerable, and women develop a sense of personal responsibility for processes which may in fact be out of their control. Paradoxically, this can drive women to seek reassurance at any price, even if it entails taking risks. The result is that women's experiences of pregnancy become controlled by the 'experts' who, for the large part, are men.

While papers in Section One highlight the imagery of women in visual culture, Kathryn McCannell, Clare McCarthy, and Barbara Herringer extend this theme to social policy. Just as women have been associated symbolically with reproductive roles, they are designated by the patriarchal state as economic dependents of men and mothers of children. This means that most social policy aimed at women has been designed explicitly to benefit those who depend upon them for nurturance and domestic service: husbands, children, and elderly relatives. The authors illustrate the ways in which this focus on women in relation to others, rather than on women as individuals in their own right with individual needs and concerns, occurs in Canadian social policy. Specifically, they overview reproductive choice; taxation benefits available to single women; and policies affecting women in midlife, particularly those who have never married. They conclude that as women struggle for diversity in choices and to reshape social relations, they must reclaim and rewrite the imagery of women in official policy.

Section Two highlights the importance and possibility of resistance through the development of feminist discourses and emancipating practices The papers in **Section Three** challenge male authority on what it means to be women, bringing to attention alternatives that have hitherto been suppressed and have yet to be fully explored. This final section addresses the question of making new knowledge about women possible, arising from new ways of knowing ourselves.

Although *The Anatomy of Gender* highlights the misogyny and distortions found in male-authored knowledge and culture, Dawn Currie rejects censorship as a seemingly attractive solution to the problem of offensive images of women. Examining debates concerning pornography, Currie notes that, while some writers maintain that censorship suppresses images of male hostility and helps to combat actual acts of male violence against women, others point out that it stifles alternative views on sexuality and sexual relations, including those of feminists. As feminists we seem to be faced with the dilemma of simultaneously censoring misogyny and insisting on our own freedom of speech. Currie argues, however, that this is a false choice. Setting the issue of whether we should have censorship aside, she explores whether we can have censorship as a meaningful exercise for feminists. Drawing upon semiotics more usually used in cultural analyses, she identifies the ways in which censorship fails; in fact, it can end up endorsing the very processes that feminists reject. In explaining how this contradictory effect arises, Currie maintains that it is not simply the consumption of pornography which is problematic but the conditions and relations of the production of mass culture, which, ironically, give rise to both pornography and the need for censorship. This leads to further questions about the production of culture and women's knowledge about sexuality.

In terms of producing culture and knowledge, Winnie Tomm argues that women need to assert new ways of knowing, based on integration of the rational and the emotional. Patriarchal knowledge, structured by masculine binary oppositions, sets up a false dichotomy between mind and body, accepting as valid only knowledge based on the former. Women's Studies challenge how we think about knowing, specifically about the artificial separation between mind and body. Tomm connects women's ways of knowing with sexuality, as a form of embodied social energy. Patriarchal society is organized around the male right of access to women's bodies — and therefore their consciousness — and this we must reject in order to reclaim our sexuality. As an example of how women can know themselves as subjects of independent female energy, Tomm explores goddess symbolism, specifically images of Aphrodite, as enabling women to accept their own authority.

While Tomm stresses the importance of women reclaiming their bodies, sexuality, and consciousness, Anne Brown asks how women can escape dominant, patriarchal views about themselves. She examines Québécois women writers of the Quiet Revolution. Written in a culture conditioned by Roman Catholicism and before the resurgence of feminism, a series of novels by women broke the silence on women's experiences. In an overview of these texts, Brown maintains that they present the alienation of women as resulting in large part from the sexual and procreative functions of the female body. Highlighting ways in which the female protagonists found sexuality and pregnancy repulsive in themselves, these writings illustrate how the social body constrains the way the physical body is perceived. As pessimistic as this may appear, Brown argues that the recognition of misogyny is the first step that all women must take on the journey that leads to the repossession of their bodies and to the construction of a positive self image. Thus, these novels prepared the way for the present generation of Québécois women writers.

What is often overlooked by emphases on gender is the way in which the body has racial as well as sexual characteristics. Although all gender constructions are at the same time constructions of race, the tendency has been unthinkingly to discuss the white female body as the norm to which race is 'added on.' Noga Gayle explores the invisibility of Black women in the Women's Liberation Movement in North America that results from this practice. Within the WLM, women who are not white and heterosexual have been designated as 'Other.' As such, the specifics of Black women's history and social roles remain unacknowledged, or Black women's experiences are portrayed as deviating from the dominant norms of femininity, constructed from the white female body. In raising the question of Black women's experiences, however, Gayle warns us that just as women are not a homogeneous whole, Black women are not a homogeneous group; to treat them as such negates cultural differences between these women. Like Brown, Gayle suggests that white feminists have accepted elements of dominant patriarchal culture without question, this time its racism. At the same time, Black women often have, in turn, internalized negative images and definitions of themselves as victims. She maintains that as long as Black women remain as Other, as objects of dominant culture, they will not be able to emerge from the mould in which they have been cast. She concludes by outlining the challenges that this presents for Women's Studies if our aim is to represent the diversity of women's voices and of the female body.

While Brown's overview of writers from the 1960s testifies to the fact that the struggle to reclaim the female body was then still in embryonic form, Daphne Marlatt and Betsy Warland illustrate how contemporary writers are breaking phallocentric myths and taboos. Daphne Marlatt explores the relationship between autobiography and fiction. She notes that, while the critic is concerned with how the writer represents herself, for the author the question is how to represent others. For both critic and author, it is as if a 'self' exists beyond representation, as an isolated, stable identity. Marlatt thus describes writing autobiography as "the (f) stop of act": it isolates fact as a still photo does, as a moment out of a context that goes on shifting, acting, changing after the shutter closes. Autobiography, as a mode of writing, enables women to see the context of their lives, their connection to others, and the inseparability of 'life' and fiction. She creates the term *fictionalysis*: a self-analysis that plays fictively with the primary images of one's life, a fiction that uncovers analytically that territory where fact and fiction coincide.

Betsy Warland elaborates on the creation of the female subject in her creative auto-bio-graphy, "moving parts." This autobiography includes poetic texts that Marlatt and Warland have published together and that communicate their lesbian experiences of the female body and their dual subjectivity as lovers. Here self-analysis concerns what Warland calls "the I-crises" for women: the tendency to see ourselves as a matter of what we are not, rather than as what we are and can be. If we do leave "our father's house," we place ourselves at risk of being unprotected. As Warland points out, however, this sense of security is a false one, because our most intimate protector is frequently our violator. Autobiographically, she describes how the struggle to leave home is doubly crucial and terrifying for lesbians, who are twice categorized by gender-based views of the female body. Propelled by a desire that is greater than fear, a lesbian's leaving home is described as a leap into an unnamed unknown. It is with our desire that we slowly rename everything. Through this gathering of words, as women we begin to own ourselves and become self-responsible. As Warland's auto-bio-graphy testifies, this process lasts a lifetime and is always moving, always reconnecting our parts.

The papers in this volume demonstrate that the patriarchal construction of knowledge renders the notion of a female Subject position problematic. In conclusion, Valerie Raoul takes up this problem, overviewing what has been referred to as "French feminist theory." Drawing upon Freud, but unlike many of their American counterparts who reject his work, French writers explore ways in which psychoanalytic theory can explain patriarchy and the oppression of women. De Beauvoir already argued that the Freudian notion of women as narcissistic is justified, an inevitable outcome of the definition of the feminine as Other and as object. Since no subject position is available to woman, she identifies with the desire of the male, seeing herself as the desired object. Within this system, de Beauvoir's view that women must become de-feminized — that the concept of 'woman' is in itself problematic — is entirely logical. In contrast, following the Lacanian revision of Freud, in which the Phallus (not the penis) is the ultimate signifier, a number of more recent writers focus upon the child's incorporation into the Symbolic Order, which involves separation from the (m)other. Here female bodily imagery becomes the basis for a new ontology. In the work of women psychoanalysts Luce Irigaray and Julia Kristeva, pre-Oedipal primary narcissism is reestablished as a specifically non- or pre-patriarchal state. Freud's negative assessment of specifically feminine narcissism is reversed, especially by lesbian feminists. Overall, in both lesbian and heterosexual writing, narcissism has been reevaluated as a positive way for women to develop self-esteem. Drawing upon the myth of Narcissus and Echo, Raoul identifies philosophical questions raised by this re-vision of the female subject and presentation of the female body. She notes that reclaiming the body involves two notions of the body embedded in the legal concept of *habeas corpus*: the ability to produce a body as evidence or proof; and the right of individuals to the freedom of their body, which is self-propelled and inseparable from their identity. Both of these aspects are central to the anatomy of gender and its articulation through Women's Studies.

Notes

1 For a feminist critique of Parsonian structural functionalism, see Betty Friedan's comments in *The Feminine Mystique* (1963).

2 As Kate Millett (1970: 37) notes, physicality is a class factor: those at the bottom perform the most strenuous tasks, whether they be strong or not, female or male.

3 But also other patriarchal institutions like the monogamous, heterosexual family.

4 In a similar way many writers tend to accept sexual identity as based on the existence of a stable, knowable "thing," sexuality.

5 One of the more obviously important examples here is in the case of eating disorders like anorexia nervosa and bulimia (see Currie, 1988).

6 Noting that infants — whether male or female — experience their first nurturing and loving relationship with their mother, Rich argued that women's first erotic attachment is to the same sex. Unlike boys, therefore, heterosexual attachment is not, logically speaking, "natural" for girls. This led Rich to describe heterosexuality as culturally, not biologically, "compulsory" for women.

7 Barbara Ehrenreich and Deidre English (1978) make a similar point about working-class women during the nineteenth century, when medical experts prescribed bedrest and the avoidance of physical stress for bourgeois women during their menstrual periods.

References

Bacchi, Carol Lee. 1983. *Liberation Deferred? The Ideas of the English-Canadian Suffragists, 1877–1918*. Toronto: University of Toronto Press.

Badinter, Elisabeth. 1986. *L'Un est l'autre. Des Relations entre hommes et femmes*. Paris: Denoël.

Beauvoir, Simone de. 1957/1961. *The Second Sex*. New York: Bantam.

Berger, Brigitte and Peter Berger. 1984. *The War Over the Family: Capturing the Middle Ground*. Harmondsworth: Penguin.

Bernard, Jessie. 1974. *The Future of Motherhood*. New York: Dial.

Broverman, Inge K., Donald M. Broverman, Frank E. Clarkson, Paul S. Rosenkrantz and Susan R. Vogel. 1970. "Sex-Role Stereotypes and Clinical Judgments of Mental Health," *Journal of Consulting and Clinical Psychology*, Vol. 34: 1–7.

Chodorow, Nancy. 1978. *The Reproduction of Mothering: Psychoanalysis and the Sociology of Gender*. Berkeley: University of California Press.

Currie, Dawn H. 1988. "Starvation Amidst Abundance: Female Adolescents and Anorexia." Pp. 198–215 in B.S. Bolaria and H.D. Dickinson (eds.). *The Sociology of Healthcare in Canada*. Toronto: Harcourt, Brace and Jovanovic.

Daly, Mary. 1978. *Gyn/Ecology: The Metaethics of Radical Feminism*. Boston: Beacon.

Delphy, Christine. 1984. *Close to Home*. London: Hutchinson and Company.

Donovan, Josephine. 1986. *Feminist Theory: The Intellectual Traditions of American Feminism*. New York: Ungar.

Douglas, Mary. 1966. *Purity and Danger*. New York: Praeger.

Douglas, Mary. 1970a. *Witchcraft: Confessions and Accusations*. London: Tavistock.

Douglas, Mary. 1970b. *Natural Symbols*. New York: Vintage.

Dworkin, Andrea. 1974. *Woman Hating*. New York: E.P. Dutton.

Ehrenreich, Barbara and Deidre English. 1978. *For Her Own Good — 150 Years of the Experts' Advice to Women*. Garden City, New York: Anchor-Doubleday.

Eisenstein, Zillah. 1990. *The Female Body and the Law*. Berkeley: University of California Press.

Firestone, Shulamith. 1970/1979. *The Dialectic of Sex: The Case for Feminist Revolution*. London: The Women's Press.

Friedan, Betty. 1963. *The Feminine Mystique*. New York: Norton.

Gilligan, Carol. 1982. *In A Different Voice: Psychological Theory and Women's Development*. Cambridge: Harvard University Press.

Greer, Germaine. 1970. *The Female Eunuch*. New York: McGraw-Hill.

Greer, Germaine. 1984. *Sex and Destiny. The Politics of Human Fertility*. New York: Harper and Row.

Grimké, Sarah M. 1838/1970. *Letters on the Equality of the Sexes and the Condition of Woman*. New York: Burt Franklin.

Grosz, Elizabeth. 1989. *Sexual Subversions: Three French Feminists*. Sydney: Allen and Unwin.

Hunter College, Women's Studies Collective. 1983. *Women's Realities, Women's Choices*. New York: Oxford University Press.

Jaggar, Alison M. 1983. *Feminist Politics and Human Nature*. Sussex: The Harvester Press.

Levack, Brian. 1987. *The Witch-Hunt in Early Modern Europe*. London: Longman.

Mahowald, Mary Briody (ed.). 1978. *Philosophy of Women, Classical to Current Concepts*. Indianapolis: Hackett.

Merchant, Carolyn. 1980. *The Death of Nature: Women, Ecology and the Scientific Revolution*. New York: Harper.

Miller, Jean Baker. 1976. *Toward a New Psychology of Women*. Boston: Beacon Press.

Millett, Kate. 1970. *Sexual Politics*. New York: Avon.

O'Brien, Mary. 1981. *The Politics of Reproduction*. Boston: Routledge and Kegan Paul.

Oakley, Ann. 1981. *Subject Women*. Glasgow: Fontana.

Okin, Susan Moller. 1979. *Women in Western Political Thought*. Princeton: Princeton University Press.

Ortner, Sherry. 1974. "Is Female to Male as Nature is to Culture?" Pp. 67–87 in Rosaldo and Lamphere (eds.), *Women, Culture and Society*. Stanford: Stanford University Press.

Pisan, Christine de. 1982. *The Book of the City of Ladies*. E.J. Richards. New York: Persea Books.

Poovey, Mary. 1988. "Feminism and Deconstruction," *Feminist Studies*, Vol. 14, No. 1 (spring): 51–65.

Rich, Adrienne. 1977. *Of Woman Born: Motherhood as Experience and Institution*. Toronto: Bantam.

Rich, Adrienne. 1978. "Compulsory Heterosexuality and Lesbian Existence." Pp. 416–419 in A.M. Jaggar and P.S. Rothenberg (eds.), *Feminist Frameworks*. New York: McGraw-Hill.

Rossi, Alice (ed.). 1974. *The Feminist Papers: From Adams to de Beauvoir*. New York: Bantam.

Sayers, Janet. 1982. *Biological Politics: Feminist and Anti-Feminist Perspectives*. London: Tavistock.

Scott, Joan W. 1988. "Deconstructing Equality-Versus-Difference: Or, the Uses of Post-Structural Theory for Feminists," *Feminist Studies*, Vol. 14, No. 1 (spring): 33–50.

Smith, Dorothy. 1987. *The Everyday World as Problematic: A Feminist Sociology*. Toronto: University of Toronto Press.

Spender, Dale. 1982. *Women of Ideas (And What Men Have Done to Them)*. London: Ark Paperbacks.

Sydie, Rosalind. 1987. *Natural Women, Cultured Men: A Feminist Perspective on Sociological Theory*. Toronto: Methuen.

Synnott, Anthony. 1990. "The Two Bodies: The Social Construction of Self and Society." Unpublished paper presented to the Canadian Society of Sociology and Anthropology, Victoria, British Columbia. May.

Tong, Rosemarie. 1989. *Feminist Thought: A Comprehensive Introduction*. Boulder and San Fransisco: Westview Press.

Wollstonecraft, Mary. 1792/1975. *A Vindication of the Rights of Woman*. Baltimore: Penguin.

Section One

Representation of the Female Body

Pornography or Misogyny?
Fear and the Absurd

Isobel McAslan
Fine Arts
Kwantlen College

'Pornography,' while a controversial issue, generally refers to written or visual materials deemed 'obscene' by law. Here, the term is used to designate the violent, exploitative acts performed on women's bodies throughout history. The author claims that men's irrational fear of women's physiological functions lies at the root of misogyny. This misogyny historically has expressed itself in customs and laws which today seem patently absurd, and might even seem amusing, were it not for the real suffering inflicted upon the women involved. The author reminds us, however, that absurd practices against the female body are not a thing of the past.

Definitions

Pornography is difficult to define. Dictionaries impart nothing of the reality of it, nor do they convey anything of its variety. To say that pornography is "the expression or suggestion of obscene or unchaste subjects in literature or art" (*Compact Oxford English Dictionary*, 1986) means little. Looking at the roots of the word, however, we find a clearer meaning: its first root is the Greek word "porne," which means harlot, and its second is "graphein," to write. So, harlots being women who are used sexually by men, pornography comes to have a meaning involving sex and the domination of women by men. The second root deals with the descriptions of these acts: hence, books, magazines and films, which, to paraphrase Gloria Steinem (1978), in turn intensify the 'objectification' of women. Nowhere do any of these definitions cover misogyny as part of pornographic acts.

Misogyny is apparently easy to define. Its two roots are specific: the first, from the Greek "misein," means "to hate"; the second, from the Greek "gune," means "a woman" (*Collins New English Dictionary*, 1964). Misogyny therefore means, simply, hatred of women. There have been misogynistic writings for thousands of years and these reveal much of what misogyny is; and there have been acts of hatred perpetrated on women in many forms. These acts attack the core of woman — her sex, her self. They can be subtle and insidious. They are often violent and frequently pornographic.

A desire to exert power over something, to dominate, tends to be rooted in fear. Fear evolves from ignorance and insecurity. It is generated by "The Unknown," and for thousands of years woman has been "The Unknown" to man. Men have therefore feared women, and their fear has frequently taken the form of male domination over the minds and bodies of the women in their societies. This oppression has taken various forms, ranging from the serious and the frightening to the ridiculous and the absurd.

Just as pornography is difficult to define, so is the absurd, particularly in today's terms, when it can mean anything including the norm for the basic human condition. In less philosophical terms, taking "absurd" to mean "contrary to reason and inconsistent with common sense" (Collins, 1964) comes close as a definition, but only if reason and common sense are unquestioned yardsticks from which to measure deviations. Reason, according to the *Oxford English Dictionary*, is the "ordinary thinking faculty of the human mind in its sound condition," and common sense, according to Collins, "natural sagacity." So, assuming a society where sound minds and a modicum of natural wisdom prevail, "absurd" can mean against reason and common sense.

It is the fear behind the desire for domination and power and its absurd consequences that have caused pain and humiliation to women for thousands of years, and this fear and absurdity are my focus: absurdities stemming from men's efforts to compensate for their insecurities by evolving stories and myths about women; by inventing ridiculous medical "facts" about the female body's functions; and by instituting laws and rules within society to put women firmly in the inferior position to which men wished to assign them. I should point out that I am here dealing almost exclusively with the European tradition, but these phenomena can be found elsewhere.

The Body — The Male View

Initially, the fact that woman gave birth and was, apparently, the originator of life must have engendered mixed emotions in man, awe and humility being high on the list, not to mention insecurity. She bled mysteriously and was possibly magic, another source of bafflement. Man made figurines of her — the Venus of Willendorf and the sculptures of the Cyclades are examples of these;[1] and he carved her likeness into stone — as in the Venus of Laussel. The two Venuses are great, wonderful women with massive thighs, heavy breasts and fat bellies: mother figures. They have an almost portrait-like quality to them, giving the impression of their reality as people. The Cycladic sculptures are different. They have become more stylized and therefore "distanced." They are also more sexual: the breasts are smaller and the pubic area, although simply marked out in some cases, in others is carved in explicit detail with female genitalia. These Cycladic figures were made several thousand years after the Venus ones, which leads one to suppose that somewhere between the Paleolithic and the Neolithic a connection was made about sex and the female.

Later, after man had come to the conclusion that woman did not make life all on her own, that in fact, without him it could not happen, things began to change. Woman was no longer venerated; she was no longer magic. She was impure. At times when she bled, man did not want woman near anything; and eventually this became law. In the Old Testament the Lord tells Moses that woman is unclean and that "she shall touch no hallowed thing" when she menstruates; he refers to her "infirmity" and her "separation." Interestingly, if a girl was born, the time necessary for the mother's purification was twice that required after the birth of a boy (Leviticus, 12: 1–5).

Women's menstrual activities afforded men a great deal of thought. No doubt the women wondered about it too, but it was the men who put their thoughts into written words. Aristotle believed that a menstruating woman could make a clean mirror "bloody-dark, like a cloud" (Anderson and Zinsser, 1988a: 28). Pliny, in the first century AD, went into more detail. Contact with menstrual fluid, he said:

> turns new wine sour, crops touched by it become barren, grafts die, seeds in gardens are dried up, the fruit of the trees falls off, the bright surface of mirrors in which it is merely reflected is dimmed, the edge of steel and the gleam of ivory are dulled, hives of bees die, even bronze and iron are at once seized by rust, and a horrible smell fills the air; to taste it drives dogs mad and infects their bites with an incurable poison. (*ibid.*)

Pliny also thought that women menstruated more heavily every third month, while Aristotle clung to the belief of the early physician-writers of the Hippocratic Corpus in the fourth century BC that all women menstruated at the same time of the month because they were controlled by the moon (*ibid.*). Aristotle also, rather naïvely, thought that women had fewer teeth than men, thus demonstrating a singular lack of observation.

The *Hippocratic Corpus* stated that menstrual blood wandered through the body, and that it might cause consumption if it entered the lungs. This unsubstantiated belief was later carried on in another form by Plato, who was convinced that the womb also wandered about: just as the penis becomes "maddened by the sting of lust"

> . . . the same is the case with the so-called womb or matrix of women; the animal within them is desirous of procreating children . . . and wandering in every direction through the body, closes up the passages of the breath, and by obstructing respiration, drives them to extremity, causing all varieties of disease. (*ibid.*, 29)

It must have been easy for men to look on women as inferior beings if they believed these things. Galen, in the second century AD, claimed that the reason woman was inferior was that she was "cold" (*ibid.*). According to Hippocrates men were "hot and dry" and women were "cold and moist," and Aristotle took cold to be inferior to hot. So woman, being cold, was inferior.

Not only inferior, woman was perceived as being positively dangerous. Eve and Pandora were blamed for all the wrongs of the world: Eve, created by the Jewish God, disobeyed him and made Adam eat the forbidden apple with her, and we must live with the consequences of that defiance to this day; while Pandora, created by Zeus, also disobeyed the gods and with her husband, Epimetheus, opened up her precious jar and filled the world with woe, with which we must also live to this day. Fortunately, Pandora managed to slam the lid back down before Hope got out, so we do have that. But both Eve and Pandora were disobedient women and were created as a lesson for other women. The Greek myths are peppered with terrifying women-monsters — Scylla, Echidna, Medusa and the Gorgons, the Harpies, the Sirens — all horrible and causing dread to men, sources of harm and disaster. They also gave birth to other monsters: Echidna, who was half snake herself, gave birth to the helldog Cerberus, the Hydra, the Chimæra, and Orthrus "who lay with his own mother and begot on her the Sphinx and the Numean Lion" (Graves, 1960: 4). It would not be difficult, therefore, for women themselves to feel that they were indeed lesser beings, after having these models put before them incessantly.

The Body — Trespassed

When normal women gave birth to normal children, this too could be disastrous, but for other reasons. To control the population growth abortion was not, in these early times, employed as often as infanticide. Usually the victim of infanticide was female, although not necessarily, as Reay Tannahill points out in her book *Sex in History*, for misogynist reasons, but more likely because she was a potential breeder. Conception itself was not understood at all. It was not until the seventeenth century that the ovum was 'discovered,' and even then it was thought that the egg contained a whole tiny person waiting to grow (Tannahill, 1982: 344–5).

Contraception was, of course, tried; and here things become quite revolting: the various recipes employed to avert pregnancy are filled with appalling mixtures to stuff into women's vaginas and disgusting potions to drink or eat. These recipes were written by men. Women themselves tended to prefer less nauseating herbal concoctions, many of which may have worked. In Egypt, according to the Kahun Papyrus, as cited by Tannahill (*ibid.*, 71), a mixture of crocodile dung with a paste of a substance called "auyt" was put into the vagina; or a mixture of honey and natrum; or simply a preparation of gum. The Papyrus Ebers suggested soaking a pad of lint in a mixture of acacia tips and honey and using that to block the uterus (*ibid.*, 72). The Islamic peoples used elephant dung; and the Hebrews used a sponge.

The Greeks and Romans had many inventive ideas for contraceptive devices. Apart from jumping up and down and sneezing after intercourse, which was a common method — one would presume of uncertain value — Dioscorides suggested putting pepper in the uterus. Pliny's recipes included more dung: mouse dung in the form of an ointment, or snail excrement or pigeon droppings mixed with oil or wine as a potion to be drunk. He also suggested keeping the testicles and blood of a dunghill cock under the bed, which seems to be even less likely to be effective than jumping up and down. Perhaps slightly more useful, in that it would at least suppress the sexual urges of most people, is his advice to rub the woman's loins "with blood taken from ticks on a wild black bull" (*ibid.*, 128). The effects of these recipes on a woman's physical or mental health are not recorded.

Perhaps the most ludicrous, as opposed to revolting, methods were those supposedly used by medieval women both for contraceptive purposes and to increase men's desire. These methods were recorded by churchmen. In *The Knight, the Lady and the Priest*, Georges Duby quotes Bourchard, Bishop of Worms, who "insists above all on the need to take account of female perfidy" (Duby, 1983: 65). Bourchard claimed that women kept their romantically inclined mates at bay by "anointing their [own] bodies with honey ... and then rolling in flour and using the mixture to bake cakes for their husbands" (*ibid.*, 71). Also, women were filled with "insatiable lusts" and apparently spent hours in the kitchen dreaming up ways of increasing the sexual desire of their spouses. Wives

were said to "knead the bread for their husbands with their bare but-
tocks" (*ibid*.) to make them more responsive: a feat that defies specula-
tion. According to Bourchard, women were also in the habit of mixing
their menstrual blood with their husbands' drinks,[2] and of making up
other potions with their husbands' sperm (*ibid*.). How this last item was
procured was not specified. It is true that in the Middle Ages the use of
magic was probably widespread, but whether these particular peculiar
pastimes were actually practiced or not is, in a sense, immaterial. What
is of interest is the minds of the men who could believe that women
would in fact do these things. These men where churchmen, and the
Church was the seat of misogyny. They were men whose contempt for
women was such that they would do anything in the name of the Church
to denigrate them. Their words and laws reeked of fear. Women's punishments were greater than men's, ridiculously so. For example, a man
who masturbated was given a penance of ten days of abstinence; the
punishment for a woman who masturbated "*started* at units of a year"
(*ibid*., 67–9). These men considered women as less than human. Certain
religious sects, in this instance the Cathars in the fourteenth century, believed that "the soul of a woman could not be allowed into Paradise after
her death: she had to be reincarnated as a man, however briefly, before
that could happen" (Ladurie, 1979: 194). Another Cathar comment was
that "the soul of a woman and the soul of a sow are one and the same
thing — not much" (*ibid*., 194).

The Body — Witch

Witchcraft was yet another area where men's minds ran amok, in a craze
that continued for about three hundred years. In 1486, two Dominican
monks, Heinrich Kramer and James Sprenger, published the *Malleus
Maleficarum* (*Hammer of Witches*) with the full approval of the Church
and Pope. This book was a manual for hunting witches; it was a manual
of misogyny. The *Malleus* gave detailed information on what constituted
a witch. The vast majority of witches were women because, among many
things, "they are more credulous" and have "slippery tongues." Woman
was deemed defective from the start:

> And it should be noted that there was a defect in the formation of the
> first woman, since she was formed from a bent rib, that is, a rib of the
> breast, which is bent as it were in a contrary direction to a man. And
> since through this defect she is an imperfect animal, she always deceives
> . . . (O'Faolain and Martines, 1973: 209)

Other absurdities and obscene male fantasies were listed, such as the
following, quoted by Mary Daly in *Gyn/Ecology*:

And what, then, is to be thought of those witches who . . . [by "devil's work" and "illusion"] . . . sometimes collect male organs in great numbers, as many as twenty or thirty members together, and put them in a bird's nest, or shut them up in a box, where they move themselves like living members, and eat oats and corn, as has been seen by many and is a matter of common report. (Daly, 1987: 199)

The *Malleus* also set out procedures for trying and extracting confessions from these so-called witches. It gave lists of demonic activities that witches took part in and powers that they exercised. If a cow died, or a crop failed, or sickness was prevalent, a woman was blamed for it. Of the "tests" used to prove that a woman was indeed a witch, the most common involved ordeal by water. If the woman floated, she was a witch and ought to burn; if she sank, the water had accepted her, so she was not a witch — but she was frequently dead by drowning anyway. She could not win.

One of the questions looming large in men's minds was whether she had sex with the devil. Days were spent questioning the unfortunate victims about the devil's sexual habits. The questions were the detailed and neurotic evidence of sexual repression and male fantasy. Every detail was examined: what the devil looked like when he had sex; where his semen came from; whether the act was more satisfying than with a man, and so on. Degrading and distinctly pornographic "tests" were also performed on these women:

. . . officials stripped and shaved the woman looking for the 'Devil's mark,' the spot he had touched after intercourse that neither bled nor pained when pricked with a needle. The village barber-surgeon was called in to make the test, first on the breasts and genitals . . . (Anderson and Zinsser, 1988a: 170–1)

Once these "tests" of witchcraft were "passed" the actual punishments took place. Daly cites an eyewitness account of such tortures:

There are men who in this act exceed the spirits of hell. I have seen the limbs forced asunder, the eyes driven out of the head, the feet torn from the legs, the sinews twisted from the joints, the shoulder blades wrung from their place, the deep veins swollen, the superficial veins driven in, the victim now hoisted aloft and now dropped, now revolved around, head undermost and feet uppermost. I have seen the executioner flog with the scourge, and smite with the rods, and crush with screws, and load down with weights, and stick with needles, and bind around with cords, and burn with brimstone, and baste with oil, and singe with torches. (Daly, 1987: 200)

While the witch craze was at its height, hundreds of thousands of women died. According to O'Faolain and Martines (1973: 215):

> Between 1587 and 1593 twenty-two villages in the region of Trier surrendered 368 witches to the bonfires. Two other villages survived the spasm with a female population of one each. Toulouse and its vicinage, in 1577 alone, reportedly saw the burning of 400 witches.

Tannahill (1982: 274) also notes that:

> In the single Swiss canton of Vaud, 3,371 witches died between 1591 and 1680. In the little town of Wiesensteig in Germany, 63 women were burned in the year of 1562 alone. In Obermarchtal, 54 people — seven percent of its inhabitants — went to the stake in two years, and in Oppenau 50 out of a population of 650 in only nine months.

These massacres were not the result of pornography *per se*, although the questions were lewd and the tortures and tests were frequently obscene acts in themselves. The witch craze was, for the most part, caused by fear: fear of the unknown in many forms, but mostly of women. It was men's fear of women running rampant — passing the Absurd and the Pornographic, reaching the Ultimate in death.

The Body — Virgin

Concurrent with the later stages of the witch craze, other degrading and humiliating acts were taking place in France. These were the infamous Impotence Trials, at their peak in the sixteenth and seventeenth centuries, and conducted by the Church courts. Churchmen, as we have seen, were obsessed by sexual matters. Their own repressed sexual lives led to fanatical writings and neurotic ideas about sex. They set themselves up as experts in all sexual matters and laid down rules for the sexual behaviour of lay people, whether married or single. Marriage was justified only as a way of suppressing sexual lust, and its validity therefore lay in physical consummation. Dissolution of a marriage was virtually automatic should either partner be proved impotent. The methods used for proving impotence were shameful and humiliating. The Church and the court demanded that certain tests be performed in public, among which were demonstrations of the male erection; proof of ejaculation; and, ultimately, trial by congress, during which the sexual act had to be conducted by the couple in public and observed by witnesses. In *Trial by Impotence*, Pierre Darmon provides a detailed account of these trials. While the degradation and humiliation involved were suffered by both men and women, I shall deal mainly with what the women had to endure.

Proving impotence in the male is easier than proving it in the female since women cannot, by definition, be impotent.[3] Apart from being checked for abnormalities of the "parts of shame" (Darmon, 1985: 171), the part the woman had to play was to prove whether or not intercourse had ever taken place. Much, therefore, was made of virginity. Rules for telling whether a woman was a virgin or not were evolved: once deflowered, the whites of her eyes become "lustreless" and her "gaze sadder"; the tip of her nose is "fleshier" when she is a virgin and "gaunt and cloven in she who has lost her maidenhead"; her voice sounds "harsh and deep" after she has begun "to enjoy the embraces of a man" (*ibid.*, 150).

Experiments to prove these rules were used. The woman was fed pounded wood of aloes and "if a maid, she will piss incontinently"; her neck was measured and if that measurement was equal to the length from the top of her head to her chin, she was a virgin — if it was not she was corrupted; also, virgins apparently "pissed firmer and farther" and "more clearly and finely" than did their corrupted sisters (*ibid.*). The question raised by all these incredible criteria is, how were the bases for such extraordinary beliefs established?

To prove virginity to their new husbands (for men expected purity in their wives, if not in themselves) women who were not in this condition could resort to various devices, the favourite being to soak a sponge or fill a bladder of some sort, possibly a fish's, with "blood of some beast and to insert [it] as deep as the cervix" whereupon it would burst on penetration thereby "proving" her virginity (*ibid.*, 156). Mixtures were also made up, such as "decoctions of acorn, myrtle, roses of Provins," which could contract the vaginal passage and make it seem more "virginal." In the nineteenth century, even more grim contrivances were used, such as the insertion of blood-sucking leeches or fragments of broken glass (Tannahill, 1982: 373). These subterfuges show desperation and fear: woman's fear of man and his reactions to any impurity he might find.

The Body — Exposed

Devices like these did not work for the church courts and their examinations: if a woman was not a virgin she was well and truly found out. However, a woman who was indeed a virgin might have a hard time proving it because of the methods used to determine her state. The likelihood of her being intact after the examination was small. As Darmon, quoting from the jurist Anne Robert (pseudonym of Louis Servin) in the seventeenth century, says: "What virgin could emerge intact from the hands of a midwife who has just probed her 'with a finger, or with a candle or by means of a uterine mirror'?" (1985: 153).

Darmon quotes from Anne Robert's *Quatre livres des arrests et choses jugées par la cour*, written in 1627, to describe the actual examination process of a woman as it took place during these trials. Robert says, in part:

> A maid is obliged to lie outstretched to her full length on her back, with her thighs spread to either side so that those parts of shame, that Nature has wished to conceal for the pleasure and contentment of men, are clearly visible. The midwives, matrons all, and the physicians, consider these with much attention, handling and opening them. The presiding judge adopts a grave expression and does hold back his laughter . . . The others, seeming busy, do gorge themselves on the vain and futile spectacle. The surgeon, holding an instrument that is fashioned expressly for the purpose called 'the mirror of the womb' or with a male member made of wax or other matter, explores the entrance to the cavity of Venus, opening, dilating, extending and enlarging the parts. The maid abed does feel her parts itch to such a degree that, even if she be a virgin when examined, she will not leave other than corrupted. (*ibid.*, 171)

Two hundred years later, in the nineteenth century, prostitutes were examined for venereal disease in much the same fashion. In direct contrast, the nineteenth-century middle-class woman went to the opposite extreme of intense modesty, undergoing different hells as a consequence. Gynecological examinations, for example, took place in a darkened room under a sheet where the doctor was unable to see anything or to make any proper diagnosis at all. An American professor claimed in 1852 that "women prefer to suffer the extremity of danger and pain rather than waive those scruples of delicacy which prevent their maladies from being fully explored" (in Tannahill, 1982: 352).

The Body — Gynecological

In *Of Woman Born*, Adrienne Rich outlines further gynecological and obstetrical hells. In ancient times a women in childbirth was delivered of her child by other women, unless the birth was difficult. At that point men — usually physicians or priests — were called in to "help" with the labour. This "help" took various forms, including the horrors of removing the fetus in pieces, with hooks. This method was taught by Hippocrates and Galen and was considered to be an entirely male preserve. If the mother's contractions were not strong, among other things she might "be 'shaken' in a sheet or hung from a tree" (Rich, 1986: 133). Rich also cites the prevalence of puerperal fever and the high rate of mortality resulting from it which was intensified by the emergence of the man-midwife and the male obstetricians. Conditions were so bad that many women preferred to have their babies in the gutter rather than in the hospitals which were considered as death houses. Resistance by male practitioners to any change was strong. The medical profession was appalled when Dr. Ignaz Philipp Semmelweiss suggested in 1861 that if physicians only washed their hands after examining a patient the transmission of puerperal fever could be reduced (*ibid.*, 151–5). In 1865 Joseph Lister published his proofs of asepsis and the rate of infections in general, including childbed fever, gradually began to abate by the end of the nineteenth century.

Anaesthesia to aid in childbirth was first introduced in 1847 in England. In 1852 Queen Victoria gave birth to her eighth child with its help and was delighted (Anderson and Zinsser, 1988b: 135). Unfortunately, there was outraged resistance to such aid, mostly from the clergy who complained that it would "rob God of the deep earnest cries which arise in time of trouble for help" (*ibid.*, 168). As Rich says, "the lifting of Eve's curse seemed to threaten the foundation of patriarchal religion; the cries of women in childbirth were for the glory of God the Father" (Rich, 1986: 168).

Mary Daly gives us other monstrous examples of experimentation on women's bodies, this time surgical — "sexual surgery [which] became The Man's means of restraining women" (Daly, 1979: 225). She relates, among many things, the rise to fame of J. Marion Sims, "the 'father of gynaecology' (known as 'the architect of the vagina')":

> He began his life's work 'humbly,' performing dangerous sexual surgery on black female slaves housed in a small building in his yard, but rapidly moved up the professional ladder, becoming the 'moving spirit' behind the founding of Woman's Hospital in New York, which provided him with the bodies for his brutal experimental operations. It also provided him with a theatre, in which he performed operations upon indigent women used as guinea pigs before an audience of men. (*ibid.*, 225)

Other similar acts of violence towards women were done in the name of science or medicine in the nineteenth century: clitoridectomy and cauterisation of the vulva as a cure for female masturbation; removal of the ovaries to cure "insanity." The latter was also used to keep women "tractable, orderly, industrious and cleanly" and to "elevate [their] moral sense" (*ibid.*, 228). Such acts of mutilation were, once again, the results of man's fear of woman and, particularly in the nineteenth century, of the New Woman who was beginning to embrace radical ideas which included feminism, birth control, and demands for education.

The Body — Today

As can be seen from all of this, historically, women have been demeaned and degraded in many ways, none of them called pornography: they were called justice and were carried out in the name of religion and the law and, latterly, of science and medicine. We assume that these kinds of things cannot happen now. Or can they? Throughout history men's writings have demeaned women, from the pretentious pomposity of Tertullian in the second century: "You are the devil's gateway . . . the sentence of God on your sex lives on in this age . . ." (Pagels, 1988: 63) to the bombastic ranting of the Rev. J.W. Burgon in the nineteenth century: "Inferior to us God made you; and our inferiors to the end of time you will remain" (Morris, 1978: 278). Even at the end of the nineteenth century we find absurdities such as a correspondence that ran six months in the prestigious British Medical Journal on whether "hams could be turned rancid at the touch of a menstruating woman" (Tannahill, 1982: 352). In our own time, the founder of Concern for the Family and Womanhood, David Stayt, maintains that: "The submissive female role is as nature and God intended. A woman needs and wants to be dominated by a man . . . a short spanking can work wonders" (London *Observer*, April 24, 1988), while the Rabbi Meir Yehuda Getz intoned in 1988 that: "A woman carrying a Torah is like a pig at the Wailing Wall." With no words at all, Marc Lépine shot and killed fourteen women engineering students in Montreal on December 6th, 1989 — simply because they were women.[4]

Many twentieth-century outrages against women have their origins in Big Business and advertising. Many are still based on the the menstrual mystery, the core of woman. Products are advertised that claim to "help" women overcome the "burdens" of menstruation, and, searching for answers, women fall victim to marketing ploys. Menstruation in general is still a misunderstood function of the female body and premenstrual symptoms are frequently considered something to joke about. Tampons, the prime twentieth-century item to insert into the vagina, can cause toxic shock leading to severe illness and sometimes death. Women often do not read the warnings inserted inside the packaging. Tampons are made of either rayon or cotton or both, 'purified' with heavy amounts of chlorine. Chlorine bleaching causes dioxins to form, and dioxins are now a known carcinogen. Cotton, since it is not normally used for internal consumption, also has the added twist of being grown from crops treated with pesticides. While it is possible for rayon to be processed without chlorine bleaching and while babies' diapers are being produced dioxin-free, this 'radical' idea has not been adopted by those who monopolize the production of women's sanitary items in North America.[5]

Menopausal symptoms are still considered an illness and hysterectomy is regularly suggested as the solution to both menopause and other menstrual problems. In certain cases it may, in fact, be the only solution, but in many instances there are other options. Experimentation is still taking place with drugs such as estrogen, now known to be a carcinogen. Most doctors today prescribe estrogen along with progesterone, which they claim results in a more natural balance of hormones and will counteract the carcinogenic effects of the estrogen, but this practice is relatively recent and long-term proof is still needed.[6]

The worst evidence of the estrogen-cancer link lies in the diethylstilbestrol (DES) scandals that came to light in the 1970s. DES was prescribed for some thirty years as a drug to prevent miscarriage. As many as two million women may have used it in the United States alone (Daly, 1979: 245). Unfortunately, DES gave cancer and precancerous conditions to the daughters of these women (*ibid.*). DES was withdrawn as an anti-abortion pill, and because of its alarming properties it was also banned as an additive to cattle feed. On the other hand, it continued to be in use as a morning-after pill, particularly for rape victims, in spite of the fact that the pill contains "833,000 times the amount of DES banned for human consumption in beef" (Kay Weiss, quoted in Daly, 1979: 247).

A further area of experimentation has been with intrauterine devices (IUDs). Reflecting concerns about the Pill's thrombosis-causing side effects, in the late 1960s the IUD became the alternative to hormonal contraception. Particularly infamous is the Dalkon Shield, sold in the early 1970s as "the Cadillac of IUDs." Testing of the Dalkon Shield was carried out by the same people who designed, engineered and sold it. It went on the market in January 1971 — in spite of the manufacturer's awareness that the tail string was faulty. The Shield itself was a small plastic disc about the size of a dime with little clamps around it and a wick-like tail string. It had to be medically inserted, and once in place was to be as permanent as the woman required, with no time limit. Inserting the Shield was excruciatingly painful and it frequently caused permanent pain. After inserting his tenth Dalkon Shield, one physician is quoted as calling it the "most traumatic manipulation ever perpetrated on womanhood" (in Mintz, 1985: 99). What no one other than the manufacturers knew was that, although the Shield was made of nonporous plastic, the tail was porous and thus drew bacteria up from the vagina into the normally aseptic uterus, causing infection which frequently led to horrific damage, to both the women concerned and the babies who continued to be conceived in spite of this so-called wonder device. Babies conceived while the device was in place were frequently infected and died or were horribly mutilated with permanent birth defects. Between 1971 and 1974, twenty women died. Thousands of others were left infertile and full of lesions from the infections. As of January 1990, a total of 195, 624 payable claims against manufacturers have been identified.[7] The Dalkon Shield was withdrawn from the U.S. market under pressure from the FDA in June 1974, but it continued to be used in Canada and elsewhere until April 1975. It is now being used in the Third World.

The Struggle

Battered women often come to believe that they deserve their beatings. It is only when they are removed from the source of violence and given therapy, frequently by other women and those in women's refuges, that they begin to heal and recognize their right to their own selves and the control of their bodies. As women, we have all been battered in some way, not necessarily physically, and we have all believed in our inferiority in some form: girls are not good at mathematics, women cannot drive trucks. We have all gone along with the myths.

While we cannot be removed from the source of domination and control, we can try to change it. It is a struggle: against the fear which causes this subjugation, against humiliations like pornography, and against more subtle forms of psychological violence. It is a struggle, too, against the State and the power it wields, against religions and cults that demonstrate patriarchal authority, and against laws according to which judges still give Brechtian 'Chalk Circle' judgements.[8] It is a struggle against advertising and Big Business, which are the dominant controls of the general populace, and a struggle against undue interference in our bodies by science. It is a universal struggle against continuing misunderstandings about women.

Primarily, the struggle is one *for* our bodies and our minds. It is a struggle to retain our identities as women, to be aware and free in our sexuality, to throw off the images of the "grotesque" and the "harlot" that have haunted us throughout history. It is a struggle to rid ourselves of the nightmare absurdities that have been dreamed up about us and the hurts that have been inflicted on us. It will be a long struggle. There will be differences of opinion amongst ourselves, as there are about the issue of pornography (some women advocate a new, female porn, while others wish to eliminate all of it).[9] These are simply descants to the main theme. Whatever form the struggle takes, to be successful we have to nurture our individual and collective strengths as women, and we have to believe in them — and in ourselves. With belief something can be accomplished. We need it to sustain us through the struggle. Pandora did save Hope. So, armed with Pandora's gift and our own insights and knowledge, we should be able now to do something to lessen fears and misconceptions, on both sides of the gender fence, and to create a more equal world.

Notes

1 See *Larousse Encyclopedia of Prehistoric and Ancient Art*, ed. René Huyghe. London: Hamlyn, 1966, pp. 17, 19, 194.

2 See the *Vancouver Sun*, April 26, 1990, (editorial) with reference to a party at the Merolamus Rugby Club: "the party's theme was sexism and the red vodka punch was billed as menstrual blood."

3 Darmon does refer to female impotence: "Female impotence was in the majority of cases connected with an obstruction or excessive narrowness of the vagina (impotence *ex clausura uteri aut nimia arctitudine*, as the texts called it)" (Darmon, 1985: 16).

4 The Merolamus Rugby Club (see above, 2) performed a skit parodying the Montreal massacre as part of their entertainment.

5 For more specific information see Renate Kroesa, *The Greenpeace Guide to Paper*, Greenpeace Books, 1990, pp. 34, 35.

6 Unfortunately the information available to the majority of women about these things is meagre and incomplete, usually badly designed pamphlets in the doctor's office, but for women who do search for information there are now several good books available, mostly in women's bookstores, such as Penny Wise Budoff, *No More Hot Flashes* (New York: Warner, 1984); Rosetta Reitz, *Menopause, a Positive Approach* (London: Penguin, 1984); and Sadja Greenwood, *Menopause, Naturally* (San Fransisco: 1984).

7 In conversation with Laura Jones, 24th July and 12th August, 1990. Laura Jones is part of a group of claimants against the manufacturers of the Dalkon Shield, whose mandate is to keep the issue in the public focus to see that another Dalkon Shield-type tragedy cannot happen.

8 See (a) Bertolt Brecht, *The Caucasian Chalk Circle* (1944). Part II, iv, The Story of the Judge, lines 628–94 and (b) comments by judges in the *London Sunday Times*, April 15, 1990, (i) "When a woman says no, she doesn't always mean it." "Men can't turn their emotions on and off like a tap, like some women can." (ii) It was the fault of a pregnant wife that her "healthy young husband" abused her twelve-year-old daughter.

9 See Laura Fraser (1990) "Nasty Girls," *Mother Jones*, Feb./March, page 32.

Questions

1 Is it possible that representations and acts which strike us today as "contrary to common sense" had different meanings in the past? If so, does this imply that these representations and acts are not necessarily misogynist?
2 To what extent were women historically likely to comply with or resist misogynist representations of the female body?
3 What processes other than "men's fear of the unknown" might account for misogynist practices today, especially with regard to birth control? (See Stoppard and Kendall, this volume).

References

Anderson, Bonnie S. and Judith P. Zinsser. 1988a. *A History of Their Own*, Vol. I. New York: Harper.

Anderson, Bonnie S. and Judith P. Zinsser. 1988b. *A History of Their Own*, Vol. II. New York: Harper.

Darmon, Pierre. 1985. *Trial by Impotence*. Trans. Paul Keegan. London: Chatto.

Daly, Mary. 1979. *Gyn/Ecology*. London: Women's Press.

Duby, Georges. 1983. *The Knight, the Lady and the Priest: The Making of the Modern Marriage in Medieval France*. Trans. Barbara Bray. New York: Pantheon.

Graves, Robert. 1955/1960. *The Greek Myths*: Vol. 1. London: Penguin.

Ladurie, Emmanuel LeRoy. 1979. *Montaillou: The Promised Land of Error*. Trans. Barbara Bray. New York: Vintage.

Mintz, Morton. 1985. *At Any Cost*. New York: Pantheon.

Morris, Jan (ed.). 1978. *The Oxford Book of Oxford*. Oxford: Oxford University Press.

O'Faolain, Julie and Lauro Martines (eds.). 1973. *Not in God's Image, Women in History From the Greeks to the Victorians*. New York: Harper.

Pagels, Elaine. 1988. *Adam, Eve and the Serpent*. New York: Random House.

Rich, Adrienne. 1976/1986. *Of Woman Born: Motherhood as Experience and Institution*. New York: Norton.

Steinem, Gloria. 1978. "Erotica and Pornography: A Clear and Present Difference," *Ms Magazine*, November: 53.

Tannahill, Reay. 1982. *Sex in History*. New York: Stein.

On the Way to Female Imagery of God

Janet Cawley
Vancouver School of Theology

The Christian view of God is theoretically genderless. Yet God is generally represented and perceived as male, and Christianity is closely associated with patriarchal values. Feminist Christian theologians are attempting to revise the established definitions of God to include positive female imagery. Previous female religious images have been based largely on male projections, which are illuminated by Jung's notion of the anima. Are positive female images of God possible within a Christian framework, and how might these affect the status of women in society?

God as Male

The official theologies of Christianity have always maintained that God does not have a gender: gender is a concept tied to the biology of reproduction, and since God is not thought to have a physical being, it is not possible to attribute gender to God except in a metaphorical or purely grammatical sense. Nevertheless, the personal images of God have been overwhelmingly male, both in the Bible and throughout the history of the Church. While there are some exceptions, they remain minority voices, and many ordinary believers as well as theologians defend male imagery as the only proper imagery for God.

For feminist women, this male God raises profound questions. Many have left the Christian Church, only to find that "God the Father" dominates Western culture: the basic structures of patriarchy are said to be ordained by God and thus part of the natural order, and many who have long abandoned any religious practice still hold to an image of a natural social order which has its origins in the thinking of the Church Fathers (see Daly, 1973). One does not have to be Christian or religious in any way to find the issue of female images of God rather important:

images of the divine (male and female gods and other semi-divine figures like saints and angels, which are proposed to believers as objects of worship and devotion) are also images of the Self, images which both affirm and challenge one's profoundest self-understanding and identity. I do not know who first said, "If God is male, then male is God," but this accurately expresses both the experience of women and the need for female imagery of God.

Feminist Christian theologians have been working for some years to recover and develop female imagery for God. The starting point for this project is the Bible, especially the first chapter of Genesis (Gen. 1:27), which stipulates that both male *and* female were created in the image of God, as well as Paul's statement that in Christ there is neither male nor female (Gal. 3:28). Added to these are references to God as female (see Mollenkott, 1983) and the presence and importance of women in the New Testament Church (see Fiorenza, 1983). Despite long and intense efforts by a patriarchal Church to deny, downplay, trivialize, and ignore these parts of the Bible, they keep returning to the imagination of women believers.

Feminist scholars are researching biblical and non-biblical sources of usable imagery and have expanded our understanding of the possibilities enormously. Women have been developing new liturgies which honour women as equally created in God's image and have been pressing Church authorities for justice in all areas of Church life (see Ruether, 1985). Much has been achieved; what was dismissed as a joke twenty years ago is now taken seriously in many churches. But there is also fierce resistance, and women working as feminists in the Christian churches become discouraged when the road ahead seems just as long as the one behind.

Besides the political and pastoral difficulties, other kinds of questions are being raised as feminist theology has come of age and is now self-critical. For example, it is important to explore whether some female images of God are more useful than others. Images of women in patriarchy, if applied to God, might serve the interests of patriarchal culture rather than women. For example, if God is described as female in his weaker moments, and only then, the patriarchal idea that men are strong and women are weak is reinforced, with the result that women may see themselves as God-like only in their weakness. Clearly, we need tools to help differentiate appropriate from inappropriate images. This paper is a contribution towards this goal. My contention is that the concept of *anima projection*, borrowed from the psychology of C.G. Jung, can be helpful in understanding how images of the female function within patriarchal societies such as ours. With such a tool, Christian feminists and others may be able to make better choices about female imagery for God. I will begin by exploring how images of God function in Christian theology and then go on to outline the problems which are being raised about female images for God. We will then take a careful look at the concept of *anima projection*, exploring how this concept is useful in analyzing the problems and pointing to some solutions.

Personal Images of God in Christian Theology

Female images of God should serve the same function for women as male images do for men: they should both honour the image of God in women, and challenge women to live fully out of that divine centre. It is clear that being able to conceive of God as female has implications for the rights, duties, and status of women in the church and in society at large; if God is seen as both male and female, then both (and neither) are God, and neither is any more God-like than the other. There would be no created superiority or natural dominance of one sex over the other, but an equal partnership: it is no wonder that female imagery of God arouses such passion.

Effective imagery for God, whether of persons or animals, plants or inanimate objects, works by taking everyday experience and giving it a "twist" which takes it out of the ordinary: this is how the tension between immanence and transcendence is held in the image. A good image not only invites us to imagine the ways of God in terms of our daily life but also invites us to re-imagine our daily life as the activity of God. For example, in the New Testament the coming of God's reign is said to be "like the yeast a woman took and mixed in with three measures of flour till it was leavened all through" (Luke 13:21; Matt. 13:33). Every day except the Sabbath, women took yeast and flour and made bread; no image could have been more familiar, particularly to women. The "twist" in this image, which would have surprised the original hearers, is the huge quantity of flour; three measures is nearly 50 lbs (Jeremias, 1972), enough to feed the entire village. The image invites hearers to think of the coming of the Kingdom as hidden, slow, and yet immensely powerful, like the action of yeast in dough, rather than as an obvious and sudden cataclysm. But it also invites women, at their daily task of making the family bread, to think of themselves as doing something God-like. Thus the image contains both theological and social challenge.

Problems on the Way to
Female Imagery of God

With such urgent need and a clear warrant in Scripture, feminist theologians have been hard at work, elaborating the theological base, recovering resources in the Bible, and exploring other religious traditions
for usable female imagery of God. With all this research in hand, some
fundamental questions are being raised, even about the validity of the
basic assumption, outlined above, that female imagery of God is important to women's social status. Although the idea seems obvious, the
fact remains that despite all the research into historical Goddess religions, we can establish no clear link between the cult of female gods and
equality in the social status of women, defining "equality" here as similar amounts of control over their lives for men and women. Gimbutas
(1982) has come closest to making a coherent case for a link between a
historical Goddess cult and social equality of women, but other attempts
are highly speculative. Most of the Goddess cults which have been documented indicate a comfortable coexistence of Goddess worship with the
oppression of women. It seems that when God is female, female is not
necessarily God.

Two points must be made in extenuation: first, given the general silencing of women's experience in patriarchal society, we have little record
of women's religious experience or women's cults; and second, the female
gods we know about come to us through a layer of patriarchal interpretation. There may have been all sorts of societies which lived a social
equality of men and women sanctified by female, or male and female
gods; there may have been, but we don't know about them. On the
other hand, there certainly were societies, like ancient Greece, where female gods were worshipped despite the fact that women were thought of
as inferior, deficient humans; much of the misogyny found in the Christian theological tradition comes, not from the Bible, but from the great
writers of classical Greece.

The modern experience in Christianity and other religions is also
mixed: we have little evidence that women have more control over their
lives in Hinduism (which includes devotion to female gods) than they
do in Buddhism (which does not). In western Christianity, it would be
difficult to argue that women in societies mainly Roman Catholic (which
includes devotion to the Virgin Mary and female saints) are more nearly
equal to men in controlling their life choices than are women in societies
mainly Protestant (which has rigorously excluded anything female from
God). Of course, modern Goddess worship, as well as feminist Christian and Jewish liturgies, make the link between female images of God

and the social equality of women quite specifically, but it is difficult to argue that these projects are based on historical precedent.

For Christian theology, of course, most imagery of God is drawn from the Bible, and here, too, questions arise. In the early years of feminist biblical scholarship, the main task was to recover the female imagery of God and the stories of women that are in fact in the Bible but that have been neglected or actually concealed by sexist translation and patriarchal interpretation: the catalogue is now almost complete and the results are mixed. As far as direct references to God as female are concerned, there are few of them, and most reflect cultural stereotypes about women.

The same sort of mixed evidence results from an examination of the experience of women as told in the Bible: on the one hand it is not as bad as we thought; the text is kinder to women, even to Eve, "the Mother of All Living" (Gen. 3:20), than we have been taught (Trible, 1978). But on the other hand it is worse than we feared; there are horrifying stories of violence towards women apparently condoned by God in parts of the Bible we had forgotten (Trible, 1984). Even when women are portrayed as models of faithful action in the Bible, they very often act out of a context of oppression, using the means available to the powerless; care is necessary to avoid the suggestion that "good women" are always victims whose only weapons are guile and manipulation.

The point of all this sober caution about the historical and biblical evidence is not to suggest that working on female imagery of God is wrong or pointless, but to emphasize the need for some criteria for sorting and selecting among what has become a rich field of possibilities: which female imagery of God will we choose or reject, and why? Is it possible for us to avoid imagery that disables women by deifying cultural stereotypes? Is it possible for us to choose images that challenge the social reality of patriarchy?

The Concept of Anima Projection

My contention is that the concept of *anima projection*, borrowed from Jungian psychology, helps to explain what is happening when female imagery is disabling rather than helpful, and thus can be a useful tool for distinguishing among various images we might find or create. In order to illustrate how it applies to our question, we must first describe the concept.

The concept of *projection* is common to many psychologies, and also has a certain popular currency; projection occurs when I place my own psychic contents outside myself and then fail to recognize them as my own. I become like a movie-projector looking at the screen on which I am projecting a picture; I experience the picture as coming from "out there." Since this is an unconscious transaction, I am unaware of what I am doing, though others can often see it clearly: we see it in our friends; it is the substance of sitcom plots; and we can see it in ourselves when the projection is over. Our hero turns out to be only human after all, the boss is not really a monster, the honeymoon comes to an end, and so on (see von Franz, 1980).

Projection has to do with more than confusion and misperception, painful as that can be: the real danger in projection is that, first, it creates an impersonal relationship, and second, it creates a relationship of control. As we no longer see the movie screen once the projector is working, but only the projected picture, so it is that when we project something of our own unconscious onto someone else, we no longer see that person; we obliterate their reality and cover it over with an idea or image taken from social stereotypes or our unconscious. When I am projecting, I am not relating to you as a person, but to an abstract image; therefore, I will tend not to treat you like a person; I will treat you as an interchangeable member of the category of which you are a member. People are labelled as "women" or "Jews" or "students," etc., and are subsequently treated according to a fixed image of what "they" are like. This is how the impersonal relationship created by projection leads easily to less than personal treatment of persons.

The second big danger in projection is that it creates a relationship of control: when I project some of myself onto you, I am unconsciously tied to you, and my security depends on your behaving in a way consistent with my projection; I need you to play the hero or the villain or some other role in my world. If you insist on acting like an independent person, I will at the very least feel disoriented (an unpleasant enough experience in itself) and may feel threatened, attacked, abandoned, betrayed, or worse. After all, it would take a lot more energy and courage for me to meet you as you really are, a unique individual, than it does to push you into a predetermined category.

While the projection encourages me to treat others impersonally, I react to all of their actions as if they were personally directed at me. This creates a desperate insecurity, especially when I have projected parts of myself that I fear or despise onto some person or group: if they do not accept and identify with my projection, they threaten my very identity and I will fight to keep them in their place. The choice of weapons depends on the context, but my first instinct is to try to keep the projection going. For if they resist successfully, then I may be forced to see the projection as something belonging to myself, and such knowledge would be shattering to my self-concept as a good person, a person who is certainly not like "them." Clearly when we see men reacting in terror and with violence to women who are trying to be independent persons, we are seeing men defending a projection; that brings us to the concept of anima.

The *anima* in Jungian psychology refers to those functions of a man's psyche which are seen by his unconscious as female; these functions appear as women in men's dreams and fantasies and, of course, in men's projections. The anima is not, as is sometimes assumed, "the feminine side of a man"; the anima is part of *male* psychology and is not part of female psychology. Anima images, of course, bear some relationship to actual women because they are constructed at least in part on men's personal and cultural experience, but they are structured by the male psyche in particular ways (Ulanov, 1971). It is precisely these functions in themselves which men in so many cultures despise and fear — intuition, emotion, sensuality, empathy, playfulness, and so on. The stage is set for anima projection: these unpleasant and undesirable characteristics can be projected onto women.

Given male cultural dominance, anima projection becomes not just a personal strategy, but a strategy of the whole society. Men tend to have impersonal relationships with women, relating to them as belonging to stereotypes — good wife and mother, mother-in-law, playgirl, nun, whore, nagging bitch, and so on. The other dangerous consequence of projection also follows; men who project their own anima onto women now need to control them in order to feel secure; women must fit into the stereotypes. If they attempt to escape they will be brought into line with everything from paternalistic amusement to violent beatings. Further, women may be controlled as well through religious sanctions, including imagery of God.

Anima Projection and
Female Imagery of God

According to this analysis, anima projection describes a fundamental dynamic of patriarchy, especially as it relates to the oppression of women. It seems straightforward enough to say that feminist Christians will be critical of any imagery of God that reinforces this dynamic; indeed, this is another name for the feminist criticism of much of the male imagery of God which has been used to keep women in their place. When it comes to female imagery of God the idea is a little more surprising, but still useful: clearly, it would not be helpful for women's religious consciousness simply to have anima images projected onto God; possibly, the effect would be even more alienating than male images, because we can at least recognize male images as different from our reality. In addition, as Anzaldua (1989) points out in her analysis of a patriarchal Goddess cult, men will project the "good" anima images onto the Goddess and leave women even more firmly associated with the "bad" ones.

Awareness of the pervasive and fundamental tendency to anima projection helps us to recognize imagery that *looks* female, but is disempowering for women; the point is to be critical, not necessarily to reject. It is good to have many images of God and it is not necessary for every believer to identify with every image of God; a multiplicity of images seems to be the only way to preserve monotheism from the idolatry which results from thinking we have found the one true image and can thus define God (McFague, 1987). We will probably wish to continue to use male images, even anima images, but it would be clearer to identify them for what they are, images to which men can relate directly but women only indirectly. We might hand some of these images back to men with a polite, "I think this is yours," thus helping men to reclaim parts of themselves, and sharpening women's sense of our own particularity.

Unfortunately, anima images do not come with identifying labels; we are working here in the realm of images and symbols, not definitions and signs, and so we need to look at context and intent as well as at the image itself. In this paper, I have been limiting myself to images of the divine (Gods, Goddesses, and other objects of worship and devotion). These are proposed to individuals as images of the Self, images that both affirm and challenge the person's profoundest self-understanding and identity. In this particular area, I think the concept of anima projection can help us to be critical of three kind of female images of God.

First, we can criticize images that contradict outright the physical experience of women. The most common one of these is the virgin mother, and Western Christians are most familiar with this image in the many guises of the Virgin Mary (Warner, 1976). It is important to note that Mary may be a model of many things for women — faithfulness, courage, a passion for the justice of God, etc. Even her virgin motherhood may be an appropriate model for women when the original, non-biological understanding of virgin is intended: after all, "virgin" in classical terms had little to do with sexual behaviour or lack thereof but meant autonomous, not dependent on any man, self-contained (Stroud and Thomas, 1982). However, when "virgin" is taken in a physiological sense, so that to be a virgin mother means to "achieve" motherhood without the "taint" of sexual activity, then we have an anima image (every little boy's dream, according to Oedipal theories); if this image is projected onto actual women, then it is extremely disabling, for it is literally impossible for women either to identify with it or to be challenged by it in any positive way.

Second, we can be critical of images of God which simply deify the social stereotypes of patriarchy; for example, the Church has been very fond of the analogy, "God is to the faithful as husband is to wife" (e.g. Hos. 12:12, Eph. 5:23, Rev. 21:9). Originally, these images were intended to illuminate the believers' relationship to God in terms of a well-known social relationship; they have, however, been turned upside down and now serve to deify the existing social relationship. In this area, the goal would be to avoid the suggestion that what is an appropriate relationship between a man and his anima is also an appropriate relationship between men and women, sanctified by God: it is appropriate for the male ego to take the lead over the male anima (in dreams and fantasies, as an image of psychological maturity in men); it is not appropriate for men to control women and still less to imagine that this is a social structure sanctioned by God and modelled by God.

We touch here the images of God's power, power as dominance (control over, coercion, force), and power as nurture (generation, inspiration, support). The Bible overwhelmingly reflects the patriarchal culture in which it was written, although it often seeks to mitigate the worst effects of hierarchical relationships by stressing the obligations of superior to inferior: "Wives, be subject to your husbands, as you should in the Lord. Husbands, love your wives and do not be sharp with them" (Col. 3:18ff). In order not to be part of the same phenomenon, female images of God will have to present images of nurture as images of God's power, and not as manifestations of God's "weaker side," or as an exception to God's "normal" use of coercion. Mother imagery is probably the most appropriate here, not the sentimental mother beloved of the patriarchy, but the real mother of blood, labour, and powerful care (McFague, 1987: 97–123). The Bible speaks of God as like a woman in childbirth, labouring painfully to create something new (Isa. 42:14); God's anger is like the savagery of the mother bear who has lost her cubs (Hos. 13:8); God's care is like the fiercely protective love of the mother eagle for her young (Deut. 32:11). The concept of anima projection helps us beware of the sentimental, indulgent mother who is a prop of patriarchy rather than a challenge to it.

Third, we can reject any imagery that does not challenge women to see themselves in the image of God as creative subjects of their own existence and equally responsible with men for the fate of the world; a helpful starting point here is to remember again the vigorous, active women of the Bible and not only the meek and mild ones. We need female images of God that challenge women without putting them down; anima projections cannot do this for women because a man's ego properly protects and contains his anima — it is only one part of his psyche and cannot act responsibly for the whole. The God who is reduced to a cherished inner emotional experience, kept carefully from contact with the dirty world, reserved for special moments, is very like the little wife who is kept in the cosy domestic sphere and is told not to bother her pretty head about politics, money, and such unpleasant realities of a man's life. Some of the Victorian images of Jesus make him into an "effeminate" man, too sensitive, too good, too delicate for the real world: it would be a thrill to "walk in the garden alone" with him, as the popular Victorian religious song said, but you couldn't take him downtown to the office.

Probably the best antidote to this kind of anima imagery is a robust imagery of Wisdom and the Spirit: these, along with the Glory of God, are grammatically feminine words in Hebrew and are sometimes expressed as female (generally in the Books of Proverbs and the Wisdom of Solomon). As Ruether points out (1983: 59), "many early Christian texts refer to the Spirit as female," and a number of modern liturgies are recovering this practice. The Spirit is particularly important because she is a wild and sovereign force, often upsetting the conventional order, including the gender order of patriarchy. Deborah, by the inspiration of the Spirit was prophet, judge and military leader in Israel (Judg. 4-5). In the primitive Christian churches, the Spirit bestowed gifts without regard to gender, so that women performed a full range of functions alongside men (Rom. 16:1-16). Awareness of anima projection can help us avoid the suggestion that the inner experience of God, especially for women, is somehow opposed to engagement with the world.

Conclusion

The concept of *anima projection* is helpful in analyzing what is going on when we meet confusing female images of God, images that, despite their feminine dress, seem disabling to women. When we understand that men image some of their own psychological functions as female, we can see why these anima images feel so foreign to us; they truly are not images of women's psyche and cannot function as images of God for us. Anima images like the asexual mother, the subordinate submissive woman, and the delicate, unworldly maiden, should be rejected as images of woman-in-the-image-of-God and as images of God.

Our images of God are in dialogical relationship with our images of ourselves and each other: on the one hand, we project onto God our understanding of what it means to be a person and to relate to other persons; on the other hand, our images of God become the standard for personhood and relationship. Any particular religious tradition, composed of stories and theology and cultic practices, sets a critical framework for imagery, but these elements are also in a dialogical relationship with the culture around them and that culture's understanding of personhood and relationship. There is no question but that the Christian tradition became deeply embedded in the sexism of patriarchy and that real female images could not be applied to God, because female was inferior, even bad. The question remains whether Christianity is essentially and inevitably patriarchal and sexist. One of the ways to test answers to this question is to see if female imagery of God can be integrated into the ongoing tradition; in that project, the concept of anima projection may help us avoid inappropriate imagery.

Questions

1 What are the implications of perceiving "God" as female, as opposed to male or as genderless?
2 What specific problems face women seeking to combine feminism with Christianity?
3 Many militant feminists are opposed to all religious beliefs. Why is this the case?
4 Is the categorization of "spirituality" as a female quality justified or not? On what grounds?

References

Anzaldua, Gloria. 1989. "Entering into the Serpent." Pp. 77–86 in Plaskow and Christ (eds.), *Weaving the Visions: New Patterns in Feminist Spirituality*. San Francisco: Harper and Row.

Daly, Mary. 1973. *Beyond God the Father: Toward a Philosophy of Women's Liberation*. Boston: Beacon Press.

Fiorenza, Elizabeth Schüssler. 1983. *In Memory of Her: A Feminist Theological Reconstruction of Christian Origins*. New York: Crossroad Publishers.

Gimbutas, Marija. 1982. *The Goddesses and Gods of Old Europe, 6500–3500 BC: Myths and Cult Images*. Berkeley: University of California Press.

Jeremias, Joachim. 1972. *The Parables of Jesus*. London: SCM Press.

McFague, Sallie. 1987. *Models of God: Theology for an Ecological, Nuclear Age*. Philadelphia: Fortress Press.

Mollenkott, Virginia Ramey. 1987. *The Divine Feminine: The Biblical Imagery of God as Female*. New York: Crossroad Publishers.

Ruether, Rosemary Radford. 1983. *Sexism and God-Talk: Toward a Feminist Theology*. Boston: Beacon Press.

Ruether, Rosemary Radford. 1985. *Woman-Church: Theology and Practice of Feminist Liturgical Communities*. San Francisco: Harper and Row.

Stroud, Joanne and Thomas, Gail (eds.). 1982. *Images of the Untouched: Virginity in Psyche, Myth and Community*. Dallas: Spring Publications.

Trible, Phyllis. 1978. *God and the Rhetoric of Sexuality*. Philadelphia: Fortress Press.

Trible, Phyllis. 1984. *Texts of Terror: Literary-Feminist Readings of Biblical Narratives*. Philadelphia: Fortress Press.

Ulanov, Ann Belford. 1971. *The Feminine in Jungian Psychology and in Christian Theology*. Evanston: Northwestern University Press.

von Franz, Marie-Louise. 1980. *Projection and Re-collection in Jungian Psychology: Reflections of the Soul*. La Salle: Open Court Publications.

Warner, Marina. 1976. *Alone of All Her Sex: The Myth and Cult of the Virgin Mary*. London: Pan Books.

Wehr, Demaris S. 1988. *Jung and Feminism: Liberating Archetypes*. London: Routledge.

References to scripture are taken from *The New Jerusalem Bible*. 1985. New York: Doubleday.

The Female Body in Eighteenth-Century Art

R.A. Sydie
Department of Sociology
University of Alberta

The depiction of female figures in eighteenth-century French art conveys changing attitudes to the female body in society, reflecting shifts in political ideology. In the early rococo period, Watteau and Boucher show charming self-preoccupied young girls whose bodies serve to arouse the jaded gaze of the aristocratic male voyeur. In the middle part of the century, the new emphasis on "sensibility" and feminine virtue produces images of dutiful mothers and virginal daughters representing a bourgeois ideal of domestic bliss, as portrayed by Chardin and Greuze. As the century ends, the mother figure is transformed into a source of nourishment for revolutionary fervour, to become later, in retrospect, "Liberty leading the people," ironically proclaiming equality for men while accepting a "complementary" subservience for women.

The Social Regulation of Women

In her *Memoirs*, Madame Vigée-Lebrun states that in pre-Revolutionary society women reigned supreme while after the Revolution "it was very difficult to convey an adequate idea of the urbanity, the gracious ease and pleasant manners, which gave so much charm to Paris society . . . The gallantry of which I talk . . . has completely vanished" (1927: 112). Other authors, such as the Goncourt brothers, also viewed pre-Revolutionary France as a sort of "paradise" for women, at least for upper-class women. The evidence for the privileged life of French women is, however, contradictory. On the one hand the almost exclusive celebration of love in the rococo art of the first part of the century and the important role played by many upper-class women as facilitators and participants in the intellectual and artistic life of the period seems to suggest that women had a far greater impact on social life in general than had been the case in previous periods. In contrast, but of equal significance, the emphasis in later years on a cult of sensibility that stressed the importance of natural impulses and innate feelings over the artifices of reason gave women, by virtue of their supposedly more "natural" physiology and psychology, moral superiority over men. Yet sensibility was exercised in the domestic realm, and the role of wife and mother was the highest calling for any woman.

Whether women acted as *salonnières*, as skilled *coquettes* who obtained power through their seduction of influential men, or as domestic heroines, the appropriate role for women fueled an important and continuous debate, especially amongst Enlightenment thinkers, that revolved around the question of women's nature. It was considerations of women's nature, especially women's sexual nature, that produced a contradictory mixture of celebration and condemnation of women. In the debate, a central concern was the nature of a social and political order that must encompass the "naturally" disorderly woman. It was the female body as an erotic, sexual body that was problematic and that was deemed to require containment in the interest of social order.

Concern with the body, especially the female body, is not a new phenomenon in the various Western discourses on social order and harmony. As Douglas (1982: 70) has remarked, the body is "always treated as an image of society" so that there "can be no natural way of considering the body that does not involve at the same time a social dimension." The body is not a neutral, biological entity, and the body that is taken as the norm for social order is gendered. More specifically, in the formation of states, the regulation of the female sexual body has always presented a problem. Lerner (1986: 140) points out that "the sexual regulation of women underlies the formation of classes and is one of the foundations upon which the state rests." Seen as a modification or deviation from the norm, nothing makes the female body more problematic to the order and harmony of society than its sexuality. Women's "nature" has been generally understood as more instinctual and emotional than men's and consequently their sexuality has been perceived as more unbridled and dangerous than that of men. As such, the regulation of women was, of necessity, more stringent than that required for men.

Women's sexuality and reproductive capacity are difficult to control absolutely unless women are, for example, enclosed in harems. Control of women is difficult not only because women's nature supposedly predisposes them to unrestrained sexual expression, but also because women are a resource for men in their relations with each other. Women's sexuality and reproductive capacity may be appropriated by men as property, but this also means that a man's power and position can be challenged through the seduction of his woman. This problem of controlling female sexuality and reproductive capacity finds expression in the conception of the female body as a disorderly body. Whether it is the malignity of the menses or the hysterical uterus, the female body is potentially a wild and dangerous thing, a threat to the patriarchal order. Consequently, in the organization and maintenance of the patriarchal State, with or without a monarch, the control and containment of women is a critical issue.

A subtext of the French political debates of the eighteenth century over the nature of the State is the consideration of the means by which women may be regulated and controlled. The issue is exemplified in the various depictions of the female body in eighteenth-century art. Paintings are not "neutral vehicles which 'express' social meaning" (Nead, 1988: 8) but they do refer to and mediate the social world of which they are a part. The depiction of the female body is an important sign around which social and political relationships can be represented. Pollock (1988: 32) claims that "woman" signifies social order and the female body is "therefore to be understood as having to be produced ceaselessly across a range of social practices and institutions and the meanings for it are constantly being negotiated in those signifying systems of culture, for instance film or painting." The female body as "sign" is particularly important in the art of eighteenth-century France. Rococo art in the first part of the period depicts the female body as the erotic object of aristocratic sensuality. This style is gradually challenged by the maternal body of bourgeois sentimentality and later by the Revolutionary and patriotic body of which Delacroix's *Liberty Leading the People* (Louvre) is a prime example.

The depiction of the female body as a symbolic referent for gender and state relations will be the focus of this paper. Here the painters Watteau, Boucher, Chardin, and Greuze will be central. The work of these artists is seen to exemplify significant conceptions of women's place in the pre-Revolutionary period in France. Whether as graceful goddess, tempting mistress, dutiful mother, or "natural" daughter, the depiction of the female embodied an ideal form of female subordination in the interest of order and harmony in the patriarchal State.

Graceful Goddesses and Tempting Mistresses

Because the female body has been associated with disorder, for a considerable period of time the depiction of the female nude in Western art was rare and often unflattering. Clark (1956: 403) indicates that in the Gothic depiction of the nude, both male and female, "Christian dogma had eradicated the image of bodily beauty":

> the unclothed figures of the early Middle Ages are more shamefully naked, are undergoing humiliations, martyrdoms, or tortures. Above all, it was in this condition that man suffered his cardinal misfortune, the Expulsion from Paradise; and this was the moment in the Christian story of his first consciousness of the body, "They knew that they were naked." While the Greek nude began with the heroic body proudly displaying itself in the palaestra, the Christian nude began with the huddled body cowering in consciousness of sin.

The revival of the classical tradition governing the depiction of the nude occurs during the Renaissance, but it is generally the nude male that is the subject of interest to artists. It is not until the seventeenth century that the depiction of the female nude becomes more prevalent. One of the popular depictions of the female nude was in the form of Venus. The celebration of the female as ideal love object was, however, problematic because of the danger and disorder the female represents as an object of male desire. It was during the late Renaissance that the problem of Venus was resolved with the idea of two Venuses, *Venus Coelestis* and *Venus Naturalis*. The distinction was a way of purifying the depiction of the female body, of elevating it from the sensual to the celestial.

The taming of the sexuality of the female temptress and her transformation into a graceful goddess, who is also a pliant and erotically stimulating mistress, is central to the western art tradition, and nowhere is it more fully realized than in rococo art (Clark, 1956: 109). Rococo art is essentially aristocratic art. Its appeal, its content, and its meaning revolve around the ideal lifestyle of the wealthy aristocrat who sees the world as existing for his, and her, pleasure.[1] The world depicted by Antoine Watteau (1684–1721) is one in which aristocrats play with grace and ease in arcadian settings. Watteau's *fête galante* was about love, its numerous faces and the search for it, and in his depiction of women it is they who seem to hold the key to the perfection of mutual love. According to Mullins (1985: 206), Watteau's art is unusual in its depiction of women in that, although they are objects, "they have hearts that must be won; . . . they are mistresses of themselves and not of the men around them. Exquisitely pretty they may be, . . . but it is not their bodies that Watteau tries to capture in paint; it is their feelings." Indeed, Watteau "takes women seriously — usually more seriously than he takes men" who court women and who "indulge in absurd antics" in trying to find the key to a woman's heart (Mullins, 1985: 210).

Women seem to hold the key to love in Watteau's work, and men play court to women as representatives of celestial Venus. In this respect,

Watteau's work mirrors the conventions of aristocratic gender relations. It was only as representations of Venus that women had access to power and influence, and it was generally rather as mistress than as spouse that Watteau's elegantly dressed woman could find the mutual love she sought. In the first part of the eighteenth century, aristocratic as well as wealthy bourgeois women did not necessarily expect to find love or sexual fulfillment within marriage. Marriages were usually arranged "with an eye to family advantage rather than the personal happiness of the spouses" (Fairchilds, 1984: 98). As long as marriage was a matter of impersonal dynastic considerations, love and sexual pleasure belonged to extramarital relations. Both men and women sought romantic and sexual satisfaction outside marriage, but for women the stakes were higher, given their reproductive vulnerability. It is not surprising that women appear to control the game of love in Watteau's works; it is essential that they do so.

The idyllic existence portrayed in Watteau's work, including the role of women as arbiters of romantic love, was, in practice, less than ideal for the majority of women. It was only wealthy and aristocratic women who had some leeway in their sexual relations outside marriage, as part of the manners and style expected of a privileged caste. Madeleine de Scudéry, one of the *habitués* of the first salon established by the Marquise de Rambouillet in the previous century, outlined the meaning of the aristocratic game of love. For the aristocrat, love is not a "simple passion," as it is for others, but a necessity, so that "all men must be lovers, all ladies must be loved. Indifference is not allowed" (quoted in Stanton, 1980: 136). In fact the code of *galanterie* ritualized the behaviour expected of the lover, of which the "faithful submission to a dominant, demanding female" was the key. However, the submission is a game and carries no threat of sexual subjection for the male. In fact, Stanton (1980: 139) suggests that for aristocratic men "love represents an indispensable stage in the construction of the self-as-art, and woman an instrumentality of competence in the *art de plaire*." Women remained, then, objects for the sexual and social display of men.[2]

The feminine world celebrated in Watteau's work is a courtly ritual that may enable women to assume a semblance of power but only within the confines of a code of manners constructed and controlled by men. As Fox-Genovese (1984: 7) points out, the growth of absolutism "promoted a tendency toward a sharp delineation of women's status, at least at the upper levels of society. The most notable feature was surely the explicit patriarchalism of royal law . . . royal law distinctly fostered primogeniture (normally male) in particular and men's dominance of property and the family unit in general." Women who took seriously the idea that they could contribute to public life or that they were the equals of men were problematic — that is, disorderly. Even the women who ran salons were more often facilitators for the display of masculine wit and intelligence than significant contributors to the debates about social and political change so central to the pre-Revolutionary period.[3]

Watteau's work looks back to the *ancien régime* ideal of aristocratic existence. More representative of the taste of the pre-Revolutionary wealthy groups was the work of François Boucher (1703–1770). His work is expressive of the sexual tensions and contradictions of aristocratic sexuality. In Boucher's work the female body is tamed and made an erotic object of masculine desire. When Walters (1978: 204) suggests that "Rococo is the art of striptease," Boucher's work comes to mind. His depictions of the female nude are designed to excite "by coyness, by pretense of modesty" the eye of the masculine spectator. Watteau's pretty and exquisitely turned-out women are graceful goddesses brought to earth. In contrast, Boucher's women are always in some state of undress, if not entirely nude, and represent, by their provocative poses and passivity, the ideal mistress.

Rococo art may be about women, and may be "feminine" in its decorative, frivolous and extravagant style, but the content of that art is designed for the pleasure of men. Part of the association of the rococo with the "feminine" label is the fact that women played a significant role in commissioning, buying, and even producing such art. Madame de Pompadour was an important patron of the arts and Boucher was one of her favourite painters. Rice (1984: 246) points out that Madame de Pompadour had a particularly important influence on the collaboration between fine art and the minor or applied arts that was a feature of the mid-eighteenth-century art scene.

> The artists patronized by Madame de Pompadour worked collaboratively on architecture, designs for interiors, tapestries, porcelains, and painted decorations. Descriptions of the total environments conceived by Pompadour and executed with the help of teams of artists at the château de Bellevue and her other residences almost defy the imagination. (*ibid.*)

However, the involvement of women in the arts did not change the phallocentric style and content of rococo art.[4] As Walters (1978: 208) suggests, women's involvement reinforced the "gracious and accommodating femininity" exemplified by Madame de Pompadour, so that although rococo art celebrates women, it also "reminds her that her true empire is to please."

Boucher's goddess/mistresses are, in Levy's (1966: 104) view, "warmed by love or lust, and made always girls before they are goddesses." In fact, the various mythological subjects are "increasingly only different wrappings for the same offering, guaranteed not to interfere with the contemplation of the woman even if she is supposed to be *Diana after the Hunt*" (Levy: 104). The Boucher nude is the ideal mistress — beautiful, young, always ready and available, but simple and undemanding, her sole reason for existence being the pleasure of her male owner.

The owner/voyeur of the Boucher nude is an aristocrat with time and money to expend on the satisfaction of his erotic desires. The object of desire — the Boucher nude — is not, however, aristocratic. Watteau's graceful goddess, who might well be of the same status as her lover, is now replaced by the tempting mistress whose lower status allows her male owner more certain control over her sexuality. These tempting mistresses can reassure men of their superiority and control over the sexuality of women even in the emasculated society of Versailles, and even in the face of challenges from women of their own rank and status. Describing Boucher's *Birth of Venus*, Levy (1966: 205) evokes Venus as "a ravishingly pretty, demure girl, half-shy of the commotion of which she is the centre." This Venus is "reality idealized, divinely blonde and slender, touched with a voluptuous vacancy, a lack of animation, which perhaps only increase her charm."[5] Such a woman would not run a salon renowned for its intelligent and stimulating conversation; neither would she be concerned with women's rights, as increasing numbers of upper-class women were as the century progressed. Boucher's Venus presented no challenge; she simply existed for the pleasure of her male.

The idea that only the gaze of the owner is permitted and only his desire gives meaning to the work is, however, a fantasy and possibly a precarious one. Walters (1978: 208) finds a contradiction in Boucher's work; "the girls exist for men's pleasure, but at the same time, they are narcissistically withdrawn into their wholly feminine world of flowers and doves and pretty children." In fact, in Walters's view, the paucity of men in Boucher's work "echoes the fantasies of the woman whose life is centred on a man, but who in revenge never really looks at him, allows him no independent life at all" (1978: 208). For example, in Boucher's *Pan and Syrinx*, "we only see the head and shoulders of the god pushing hopefully through the reeds; the true lovers are the two identical girls, petite and curvy, who lie facing one another. They are not particularly startled by the lustful god, and clearly no male is necessary to their pleasure" (Walters, 1978: 209). Nevertheless, the narcissism of Boucher's nudes does not obscure the fact that they are male possessions, and the absorption of the women in themselves or each other is illustrated for the voyeuristic pleasure of the male owner.

The basic reality of eighteenth-century gender relations is that women are possessions of men. However, as the century progresses, male control over women is thought to be threatened, especially male control over women's sexuality and reproductive capacity. As Browne (1987:19) indicates, in the eighteenth century, especially during periods of political uncertainty, "many people saw a strong symbolic link between female rebellion and political upheaval." Increasingly women — at least upper-class women — appear to challenge male authority, and the frank eroticism attributed to women in much rococo art was dangerously disturbing when contemplated as a mirror of real life. Unregulated female sexuality was the ultimate threat to social order, and the extra-marital licence of the aristocracy, combined with the suggestive symbols of rococo art, seemed to signal to many observers that control and regulation of women were imperative for the reform of a corrupt society.

The control and regulation of women's sexuality and reproductive capacity were framed in the promotion of the domestic woman, the dutiful mother. In the later part of the *ancien régime*, "Conjugal domesticity and motherhood were gradually seen to offer the perfect molds within which to reconfine female sexuality and female authority" (Fox-Genovese, 1984: 16). As an art critic, Diderot was particularly offended by rococo art, and in his comments on the Salons of the 1760s he singled out Boucher as symbolic of the decadence of the rococo: "La dégradation du goût, de la couleur, de la composition, des caractères, de l'expression, du dessin, a suivi pas à pas la dépravation des moeurs"[6] (quoted in Bukdahl, 1979: 57). Diderot willingly admitted the delight that Boucher's work might evoke: "un vice si agréable, c'est une extravagance si inimitable et si rare! Il y a tant d'imagination, d'effet, de magie et de facilité"[7] (quoted in Bukdahl, 1979: 175). But these were, in his view, an abuse of artistic talent.

Behind Diderot's critique of Boucher and other rococo artists was the idea that the licentious Boucher nudes were "against nature." The eroticism of the rococo female was seen to be a corruption of the innate modesty, delicacy, and sensibility of women and, by extension, a root cause of the corruption and decadence of contemporary society. More tasteful and more "true to nature" were the depictions of dutiful mothers and innocent virgins found in the genre works of Chardin and Greuze, two of Diderot's favourite painters.

Dutiful Mothers and Virginal Daughters

Diderot's artistic preferences were a part of the mid-eighteenth century taste for simplicity, honesty, and dignity, seen in the rejection of the artificial manners and tastes of an aristocratic society. Life lived in accordance with "nature" was family life, in which gender relations of female subordination to male authority were "naturally" organized. The

domestic "truth to nature" was regarded as the foundation for the rejuvenation of the State.

Jean-Jacques Rousseau is perhaps the most significant proponent of
the "natural" differences between the sexes and the need to discard artificial constraints for the virtuous life lived in conformity with natural
impulses. The virtuous life is critically dependent upon the recognition
of the biological differences between the sexes, and most especially upon
the constraining nature of women's reproductive capacity which "naturally" leads to moral and political difference.[8] The "book of nature" laid
out the blueprint for harmonious gender relations as "naturally" relations
of difference, and science seemed to confirm these "natural" differences.
As Schiebinger (1987: 68) illustrates, "The *Encyclopédie* article of 1765
on the 'skeleton' devoted half its text to a comparison of the male and
female skeleton. In great detail the differences are laid out between the
male and female skull, spine, clavicle, sternum, cocyx, and pelvis. The
article ends with one prescriptive phrase: 'all of these facts prove that
the destiny of women is to have children and to nourish them.'" A physician, Pierre Roussel, argued in 1775 that the differences between men
and women were not the result of custom or education (and therefore
amenable to change) but were "as innate and as enduring as the bones
of the body" (Schiebinger, 1987: 68). Interestingly, Rousseau's recommendations for domestic and social reform found a ready audience even
among those whose marital and maternal practices his works attacked
— the aristocracy and the wealthy bourgeoisie. As Schama (1989: 155)
points out; "if the old regime was subverted by the cult of Sensibility,
then much of the damage . . . was self-inflicted. *The Marriage Contract*
(by Greuze), which actually represented a Protestant ceremony with a
notary standing in for a priest, and which stood as the exact antithesis of grandiose dynastic marriages at Versailles, was bought by Louis
XV's Minister of Arts, the Marquis de Marigny." The Marquis's sister,
Madame de Pompadour, "organized the first performance of Rousseau's
opera *The Village Soothsayer* at Fontainebleau in 1752" (Schama, 1989:
155).

The art of Jean-Baptiste Chardin (1699–1779) and Jean-Baptiste
Greuze (1725–1805) addresses the cult of sensibility. In Chardin's work,
orderly domestic scenes of family peace and contentment are the basic themes. The domestic virtues that were considered the particular
province of women — frugality, piety, humility, sobriety, and love —
were celebrated as the means for domestic harmony and, by extension,
social harmony. Chardin's genre pictures delighted Diderot, not simply
because of their content but also because of his technique. In the Salon critique of 1765, Diderot calls Chardin "un grand magicien" in his

handling of volume and line as well as "le premier coloriste du Salon, et peut-être un des premiers coloristes de la peinture"[9] (quoted in Bukdahl, 1980: 1, 191).

Chardin's work owed some of its popularity to its similarity with Dutch genre paintings. The political organization of the Dutch Republic was attractive to some eighteenth-century liberals. Both Diderot and Montesquieu saw the Dutch Republic as the example of "wealth, freedom of goods and persons and the homely dignities that stood in damning contrast to the court of Versailles" (Schama, 1989: 96). Like much of the Dutch genre work, Chardin's domestic scenes reflect:

> a puritan, perhaps almost more truly Quaker, life that is depicted in simple, windowless rooms, dark and sheltered interiors in which nothing more is happening than the preparing or serving meals, the education or amusement of children. The appeal is in the restriction: an emphasis on plain living and clean linen — linen, not silk. (Levy, 1966: 142)

The appeal is to bourgeois virtue in contrast to aristocratic license.

Wholesome family life was the "natural" setting in which the potentially unruly, disorderly, and even threatening female body could be contained and controlled. Furthermore, such containment and control were assumed to be in conformity with nature. Diderot's own prescriptions for the education of women, including his daughter, echoed this understanding. It was "the organ proper to her sex" that predisposed women, in contrast to men, to excesses of emotion. In contrast to Cartesian thought, Diderot believed the brain could not be separated from the body. As a result, women could not be treated like men, and therefore "if a relatively poor intellectual education was necessitated by a girl's biological condition, so her biological condition demanded an advanced sexual education" (Jacobs, 1979: 94).

The happy domestic scenes of Chardin and others stressed conjugal love and, more importantly, maternal love. As Carol Duncan (1982) has demonstrated, the happy mother eulogized by Diderot, Rousseau, and a whole host of novelists and playwrights, was exhaustively illustrated in eighteenth-century art. The fecund nursing mother was a central figure in the numerous genre scenes, and this paralleled the philosophical and literary discussions of the importance of maternal breast-feeding. The solution to France's social problems was to be sought in the restoration of women, as mothers, to their natural function — nursing their children. As Rousseau pointed out:

> Let mothers deign to nurse their children, morals will reform themselves, nature's sentiments will be awakened in every heart, the state will be repeopled. . . . The attraction of domestic life is the best counterpoison for

bad morals . . . When the family is lively and animated, the domestic cares constitute the dearest occupation of the wife and the sweetest enjoyment of the husband. Thus from the correction of this single abuse would soon result a general reform; nature would soon have reclaimed all its rights. Let women once again be mothers, men will soon become fathers and husbands again. (*Emile*, 1, p. 46)

Greuze best illustrates the Rousseau dictum. His work, *The Beloved Mother*, a sketch of which was exhibited in the 1765 Salon, prompted the following assessment from Diderot:

this is excellent both from the point of view of talent and morality. It preaches population and paints most movingly the happiness and the inestimable worth of domestic peace. It says to every man who has a heart and soul, "Keep your family in comfort; give your wife children; give her as many as possible; don't give them to anyone else, and be assured of a happy life at home." (Quoted in Brookner, 1972: 110)

Although some fashionable, aristocratic women were depicted as mothers, it was most often young rustic or bourgeois women who were the subjects. The practice of wet-nursing seems to have gradually been superseded by maternal breast-feeding amongst the wealthier women as the century progresses, whereas the use of wet-nurses by working-class women seems to have increased (see Badinter, 1981). The threat to population increases that wet-nursing represented was seen to be compounded by the increased use of contraception on the part of aristocratic and wealthy bourgeois women. It was the general belief that the population of France was in decline; consequently the illustrations of fecund, breast-feeding mothers were a part of the political concern with reversing this demographic trend:

The idea that women might exercise choice in this area, that they might choose to limit or avoid childbirth, alarmed respectable men of letters, who produced a torrent of pamphlets extolling the joys of motherhood, proclaiming it the only natural state for women and condemning the immorality and selfishness of those who would deprive the state of its population. (Duncan, 1982: 215)

Dutiful mothers can obviously only be produced as a result of careful education and training.[10] Rousseau's discussion of the education of Emile and Sophie is the exemplar of education in terms of "natural" difference that would be the basis for the moral rejuvenation of society. The education of Emile is designed to preserve his natural inclinations for independence and free will; that recommended for Sophie is designed to "complement" that advised for Emile and to produce the dependent, loving wife and mother.

Rousseau's focus was on Emile as the political actor in the reformed State in which the natural inclinations of men would be respected; but in practical terms it was daughters, reared by dutiful mothers, who were more significant if the reformed State was to become reality. Depictions of chaste, virginal innocents, who nevertheless hinted at erotic charms for the "upright" husband and father, were another popular genre theme. Greuze was a past master of this genre. The depiction of women, and especially young girls, as "nature's children" who "titillate even while posing as virtuous" (Levy, 1966: 150) characterizes Greuze's paintings.

Greuze's work, whatever the particular subject matter, was seen to conform to the aesthetic dictum, advanced by the Abbé Du Bos and endorsed by Diderot, that a good work of art is one that arouses the emotions. As a result, the content, the subject matter of the work of art, is of vital importance in ensuring that positive emotions are generated in the viewer. The standards of appreciation which Diderot upheld — "Move me, astonish me, unnerve me, make me tremble, weep, shudder, rage, then delight my eyes afterwards, if you care to" — are merely a more explicit version of the requirements of the Abbé Du Bos and precisely the sort of standard "which assured the success of the pictures of Greuze" (Brookner, 1972: 50).

Greuze's work allowed the spectator the luxury of demonstrating *sensibilité*, the experience of intense but virtuous feelings that was the mark of individuals in tune with their "natural" being. For example, Mathon de la Cour, on observing Greuze's painting of a young girl crying over a dead bird (*Jeune fille qui pleure la mort de son oiseau*), stated: "On several occasions I have looked at it for hours on end, delighting in that sweet and tender sadness which is worth more than physical pleasure; and I have come away from it filled with a delicious melancholy" (Brookner, 1972: 108). Greuze's numerous *jeunes filles* were tender, virginal, but inviting innocents who were the precursors of loving wives and dutiful mothers.

Patriotic Female Figures

The dutiful wife and the virginal daughter were a staple of both pre-Revolutionary and post-Revolutionary art. In the later part of the eighteenth century, the cult of sensibility remained significant but the "feminine" emphasis upon the display of feeling was gradually displaced by the stoical "masculine" fortitude of the patriot. The male nude becomes a more significant metaphor for revolutionary virtue, and classical antiquity becomes the source of moral prescriptions for the rejuvenation of society.

The work of Jacques-Louis David (1748–1825) expresses the moral and political idealism embodied in classical forms. His *Oath of the Horatii*, exhibited in the 1785 Salon, which depicted the patriotic oath of the three brothers before their departure for battle, combined classical form and reference with an expression of patriotic enthusiasm. The revolutionary message was not lost on observers. Rosenblum (1967: 70) points out that "so emblematically clear is David's image of sworn loyalty that in 1794, at a vast Republican demonstration organized by David and Robespierre, the youth and the old men re-enacted these idealistic gestures." Included in the scene of the oath are the mother of the Horatii and her two daughters. They are depicted, in stark contrast to the male figures, as overcome by grief, almost cowering on the righthand side of the picture. As Walters (1978: 213) describes the work, "masculinity is a metaphor for everything public-minded, rational and revolutionary; energy and virtue are concentrated in the male. He divides the sexes rigidly. On the one side is the male world with its stern and even brutal idealism, its energetic commitment to action; on the other side is femininity, associated with family affection, intimacy, all the graces of life." Dutiful mothers and virginal daughters become the female exemplars of revolutionary and patriotic belief and practice. The subordination of women according to "nature" becomes a necessity for the construction of the revolutionary utopian State.

The idea of the maternal body as the basis for the nourishment of the revolutionary State continues and is given full expression in the use of heroic female images. Delacroix's *Liberty Leading the People* is one of the most striking representations of the maternal body as basic nourishment for the masculine construction of the orderly, harmonious State. In Delacroix's painting, the bare-breasted figure of Liberty stands above the figures of dying men, brandishing the tricolour. The maternal breast is fully recognized as a public site; it stands for the protection of liberty and justice:

> She is bare-breasted because Liberty has to be seen to be the mother of the people. She stands for the human rights of all those brave men fighting around her precisely because she wields this tremendous maternal authority. She nourishes their manhood, their courage, their ideals, supporting them in their cause. (Mullins, 1985: 170)

In the new revolutionary State, however, the real life maternal protector of liberty and justice is confined most firmly to her purely domestic functions. As Fox-Genovese (1984: 24) concludes, "the victory of male individualism had imposed the universality of female domesticity" in post-Revolutionary France.

Conclusion

Art is not a neutral exercise; it is infused with cultural and political meaning. By the same token, the body is not neutral; it also takes on meaning and significance in regard to the construction and organization of society. Most especially, the female body is a site for some of the most important cultural and social signs because of the presumption of its ever-present sexual danger for men. In turbulent eighteenth-century France, controlling and confining the female in the interest of a reformed patriarchal State became a central concern and generated a number of contradictory positions in regard to the female ideal, although these contradictions were united in the basic understanding of the incommensurability of biology. These contradictions are visible in representations of two Venuses: *Venus Coelestis* and *Venus Naturalis*. According to the former, women were arbitrators of romantic love or, as *Venus Naturalis*, sublime temptresses of male desire. In practice, however, both images were less than ideal for the majority of women, especially for women who took seriously the idea that they could contribute to public life or that they were equals to men. At all social levels, women led subordinate lives according to their "natural" role. This role emphasized women's subordination to male authority within family life as the foundation for the State. Wholesome family life was depicted as the setting where women cultivated the domestic virtues of piety, humility, and sobriety, so that the potentially unruly and threatening female body could be controlled. Graceful goddess, tempting mistress, dutiful mother, or virginal daughter — all were constrained in their public as opposed to private domestic lives. Thus the art of the period participated in the debates surrounding the problematic female body and the search for solutions to a social life lived in harmony with "nature" — that is, a search for a life that would ensure personal happiness as well as social stability and order in the patriarchal State.

Notes

1 For example, Levy, (1966: 121) quotes Madame du Châtelet, "We must begin by saying to ourselves that we have nothing else to do in the world but seek pleasant sensations and feelings."

2 Aristocratic women may have been celebrated and depicted (as in Watteau's work) as the arbiters of love, but in the social and political context in which such dominance is exercised, it is *only* as lovers that women might exert control. Such dominance was, however, as limited and ephemeral as their youth and beauty.

3 As Fox-Genovese (1984: 5) points out: "Few would dispute the influence of the galaxy of notable eighteenth-century women who have mesmerized historians and critics since their own day: Mme du Maine, Mme de Lecin, Mme de Pompadour, Mme d'Epinay, Mme Geoffrin, Mme du Deffane, Mme de Lespinasse, Mme du Châtelet, and so many more. But today we question the extent of that influence, the terms on which it was exercised, women's own perceptions of their roles, and the implications that the roles of some had for the fate of women as a group."

4 The women artists in pre-Revolutionary France were usually regarded as women first who happened to be artists. As Diderot commented on a painter he regarded as neglected: "she was talented but she lacked youth, beauty, modesty and coquetry and this accounted for her lack of popularity." Artists like Elizabeth Vigée-Lebrun were both artistically and socially successful as a result of their charm and beauty as much as for their artistic talent.

5 The shifting and uncertain borderline between fine art and pornography is obviously difficult to anchor and maintain as Levy's comments illustrate. For a comprehensive discussion of this issue, see Linda Nead, "The Female Nude: Pornography, Art and Sexuality" in *Signs: Journal of Women in Culture and Society*, Vol. 15, No. 2, Winter 1990.

6 Trans.: "Degradation of taste, colour, composition, figures, expression and drawing technique has followed step by step on moral depravity."

7 Trans.: "Such pleasant vice, with inimitable and rare extravagance! There is so much imagination, such telling effect, enchantment, ease."

8 It was the eighteenth-century conception of "nature" that undermined the abstract liberal argument for individual freedom and gender equality.

9 Trans.: "a great magician" . . . "the best in using colour at this Salon [exhibition] and one of the foremost in all painting."

10 Diderot, for example, designed his own daughter's education to fit her for marriage and motherhood. He "spoke to Angélique freely about the realities of sex and childbearing, and paid for her to attend lessons in sexual anatomy given by Mlle Biheron with the aid of realistic wax anatomical models" (Jacobs, 1979: 94).

Questions

1 Does greater depiction of female figures have anything to do with increased respect or consideration for women?

2 To what extent may the social message conveyed through representation in art be assumed to be consciously motivated?

3 What are the indicators that these paintings are addressed primarily to a male viewer?

4 How could the Revolutionary slogan of "liberty and equality" exclude women?

References

Badinter, Elizabeth. 1981. *Mother Love: Myth and Reality, Motherhood in Modern History*. New York: Macmillan.

Bukdahl, Else Marie. 1982. *Diderot, Critique d'art*. 2 vols. Copenhague: Rosenkilde and Baggeer.

Brookner, Anita. 1972. *Greuze: The Rise and Fall of an Eighteenth-Century Phenomenon*. London: Elek.

Clark, Kenneth. 1956. *The Nude*. New York: Doubleday Anchor Books.

Douglas, Mary. 1982. *Natural Symbols: Explorations in Cosmology*. New York: Pantheon.

Duncan, Carol. 1982. "Happy Mothers and Other New Ideas in Eighteenth-Century French Art." In Norma Broude and Mary D. Garrard (eds.), *Feminism and Art History*. New York: Harper and Row.

Fairchilds, Cissie. 1984. "Women and Family." In Samia I. Spencer (ed.), *French Women and the Age of Enlightenment*. Bloomington: Indiana University Press.

Fox-Genovese, Elizabeth. 1984. "Introduction." In Samia I. Spencer (ed.), *French Women and the Age of Enlightenment*. Bloomington: Indiana University Press.

Jacobs, Eva. 1979. "Diderot and the Education of Girls." In Eva Jacobs, W.H. Barber, Jean H. Bloch, F.W. Leakey, Eileen Le Breton (eds.), *Women and Society in Eighteenth-Century France: Essays in Honour of J.S. Spink*. London: Athlone Press.

Lerner, Gerda. 1982. *The Creation of Patriarchy*. London: Oxford University Press.

Levy, Michael. 1966. *Rococo to Revolution*. New York: Frederick A. Praeger.

Mullins, Edwin. 1985. *The Painted Witch*. London: Secker and Warburg.

Nead, Linda. 1990. "The Female Nude: Pornography, Art and Sexuality," *Signs: Journal of Women in Culture and Society*, Vol. 15, No. 2 (winter).

Pollock, Griselda. 1988. *Vision and Difference*. London: Routledge.

Rosenblum, Robert. 1967. *Transformations in Eighteenth-Century Art*. Princeton: Princeton University Press.

Rousseau, Jean-Jacques. 1979. *Emile, or On Education*. Trans. Alan Bloom. New York: Basic Books.

Schama, Simon. 1989. *Citizens: A Chronicle of the French Revolution*. New York: Alfred A. Knopf.

Schiebinger, Linda. 1987. "Skeletons in the Closet: The First Illustrations of the Female Skeleton in Eighteenth-Century Anatomy." In Catherine Gallagher and Thomas Laqueur (eds.), *The Making of the Modern Body*. Berkeley: University of California Press.

Stanton, Donna C. 1980. *The Aristocrat as Art*. New York: Columbia University Press.

Vigée LeBrun, Elizabeth. 1927. *The Memoirs of Elizabeth Louise Vigée LeBrun*. Trans. Gerard Shelley. New York: George H. Doran Co.

Walters, Margaret. 1978. *The Nude Male*. New York: Paddington Press.

Representation of Women in Chinese Fiction: The Female Body Subdued, Re(s)trained, (Dis)possessed

Rosemary Haddon
Asian Studies
University of British Columbia

Since the May Fourth movement (1919) Chinese literature has had a strong humanist tradition, exposing the oppression of women along with other forms of social injustice. Nevertheless, the Confucian ideal of womanhood, based on submission, lingered on and appeared in male fiction as late as the 1940s. In the 1960s, male "feminist" writers took up the cause of women in Taiwan, but often perpetuated old stereotypes. In the 1970s, the plight of women was related to western exploitation, and women in Taiwan became a "nationalized" commodity. Here the author provides evidence of how the "nativist élite" collaborated in this exploitation. Other contemporary women writers are beginning to treat formerly forbidden themes, such as sexuality and violence against women. Even so, their representations of women often conform to male paradigms.

Chinese Fiction and 'Women's Liberation'

In 1919, China experienced an enormous upheaval, the May Fourth movement, which the historian Chou Tse-tsung defines as a "combined intellectual and sociopolitical movement to achieve national independence, the emancipation of the individual, and a just society by the modernization of China" (Chou, 1960: 358–9). This movement had long-lasting consequences for all areas of Chinese social and economic life, including the status of women. The representation of women in fiction since May Fourth reflects the conceptual awareness of women's social position on the part of Chinese writers and intellectuals that was engendered by the liberation ideology of May Fourth, as well as women's attempts to realize full emancipation, which were also seeded at that time. Women's struggles for liberation are a common theme in Chinese fiction, appearing first in the works of male writers and, more recently, in those of contemporary women writers in both China and Taiwan. In part, May Fourth itself resulted from China's relations with the West, reflected in the themes of imperialism and colonialism which appear in the nativist literature (*xiangtu wenxue*) of Taiwan.[1] While women's liberation in China is still incomplete,[2] it remains a dominant theme in modern Chinese literature, and contemporary writers are beginning to broach the previously forbidden topic of female sexuality. This paper will discuss some aspects of women's liberation as projected through fictional representation since the tumultuous years of 1919.

While fiction is "just fiction" and not "real life," it is a signifying practice that reflects the social and ideological order (Belsey, 1980: 46). Excluding the socialist realism type of Chinese literature, which served as a vehicle for the Chinese Communist party during the Cultural Revolution, those discourses in Chinese fiction that are self-consciously linked to social praxis fall into at least four categories, each with a different focus: androcentrism, which is related to the Confucian ideal of women found in what I designate the "Confucian code of reference";[3] liberal humanism marked by May Fourth; women and colonialism (in Taiwan); and, most recently, feminism in relation to sexuality. These themes can all be found in a variety of fictional works. Other than the first, which is rooted in pre-revolutionary traditional thought, they belong to the modern era, so that we can assess the contemporary status of women from them. They not only provide insight into Chinese social life but serve to illustrate the evolution of women's consciousness, which in Taiwan occurred in post-colonial society and, in China, since Mao.

The majority of writers discussed in this paper are well known in Chinese literary circles: the first three belong to Taiwan's nativist school of literature, and one of them considers himself to be a feminist; the others are women writers working in contemporary China.

The Confucian Code of Reference: Incarceration and Submission

The emancipation of women was one of the major concerns of the 1919 Chinese revolution for national liberation. Accordingly, one would assume that Chinese women have made advances in throwing off the traditional constraints of pre-revolutionary China; at the very least, one might assume that women living in modern China are freer from these constraints than their pre-May Fourth counterparts. Yet Lü Heruo's "Cai zi shou" (Wealth, Sons, Longevity), written by a man in 1942, still points to a fictional ideal of female behaviour derived from the Confucian value system. While not commonly seen in recent fiction, the ideal in this story testifies to its lingering presence. Although the feminist consciousness in this story is difficult to ascertain, and although the theme of "Wealth, Sons, Longevity" is not liberation *per se*, this story points to the root cause of women's oppression and thus mirrors the themes of liberation found in May Fourth literature.[4] For the reader unfamiliar with Chinese topics of discourse, "Wealth, Sons, Longevity" provides a point of departure for a discussion of Chinese female subjugation.

Written during a period of traditionalism in Taiwan under Japanese colonial rule, this story presents a household scenario in which the female character, Yumei, falls victim to the ideal of the virtuous Chinese wife. Yumei's subjugation is a product of her almost total silencing, which accords with the strict Confucian female ideal, and this ideal — supposedly bankrupt after May Fourth — is, in turn, a reflection of Chinese androcentric discourse.[5] Within this discourse, representation of women consists of little more than an idealized female metaphor.

The opening of "Wealth, Sons, Longevity" establishes a utopian landscape, creating the illusion of human perfectibility and an ideal human society. Birdsong and bamboo, sparkling paddy fields, and the rural architecture of the Hall of Fortune and Longevity represent a sanctuary evoking enlightened coexistence. "A stony pathway runs through Niumianpu village at the place where the houses are clustered together. From there, it heads south and descends a slope" (Lü, 1942: 45). The first sign that the text is a dystopian and not a utopian narrative is conveyed through cultural signifiers whose referents belong to the Confucian cultural code. This code first appears in the master's fear of "contact between female members of the household and visitors giving rise to 'moral inconvenience,'" which leads him to discourage visitors from entering the home (*ibid.*, 47). The Confucian dictum of *nannü shoushou bu qin*,[6] proscribing close social intercourse between the sexes, compels Zhou Haiwen to close up and lock the many chambers of the Hall of Fortune and Longevity and to publicize a multitude of household rules forbidding outsiders to lay eyes on any family member. The physical design of the main hall and the parlour and the fact that "the countryseat was a distant throw from common folks' homes" (*ibid.*, 47) emphasize the separateness of the Hall, which is matched by the alienation of its inhabitants.

Inside the Hall, patriarchal symbolism is nowhere more evident than in the "spirit tablets,"[7] which serve symbolically as the hub of the domestic activity of the house. Zhou Haiwen takes a second wife in order to beget more sons and, at the same time, he thereby secures his many patriarchal interests. His new wife is modest, virtuous, and self-effacing.[8]

Yumei is a perfect complement to her husband, whose philosophy of *cai zi shou* — more money, more sons, and a long life — derives also from the Confucian dictum regarding the regulating of a household.[9] However, when a former concubine, Autumn Fragrance, re-enters the Hall of Fortune and Longevity a reversal ensues, as the mantle of mistress falls to her and the master descends into debauchery. This reversal culminates in the story's tragic outcome.

Unfortunately, Yumei gives birth to a girl shortly after her marriage to Zhou Haiwen. Punished by exclusion and the withdrawal of food, she contracts puerperal fever and goes insane. At this point in the text, the narrator fails to condemn Confucianism as the source of the household's misery and instead calls upon the irrational to explain the series of tragic events. "There's no doubt about it," someone said, "she must have become tainted at the time of Zhou She Niang [her mother-in-law]'s death. Women in labour and old people are most prone to *xiang chong*"[10] (*ibid.*, 80). By resorting to superstition instead of pointing to traditional society as the *prima facie* cause of suffering, the narrator has inadvertently undermined what could otherwise become a critique of Confucianism. "Wealth, Sons, Longevity" concludes with Yumei being led to the asylum. Like other fictional instances of female insanity,[11] Yumei exits in silence, a victim of the Confucian code which, it is said, was founded by "an eater of women." "Wealth, Sons, Longevity" throws light on the traditional Chinese social praxis which the May Fourth Chinese intellectuals laboured so hard to change.

The Liberal-Humanist Code of Reference: Male Views of Woman as Prostitute, Mother, Saint

Modern China is a culture in which the production of meaning originates largely with men. During the period of May Fourth, however, China's best-known modern writer, Lu Xun, had already turned away from the androcentric perspective still found in "Wealth, Sons, Longevity" in order to give expression in literature to what he saw as the causes of the social oppression of women. With his works, a tradition of liberal humanism began which dominated Chinese literature until 1949. Lu Xun's famous short story, "New Year's Sacrifice" (1924), for example, attributes the suffering of the female protagonist, Xianglin Sao, to feudalistic forces operating in the old society, primarily superstitions regarding widowhood. These attitudes are blamed for Xianglin Sao's social exclusion, her decline into beggary, and, eventually, her death. As an antitraditionalist, Lu Xun was the first thinker to articulate the adverse social effects of culture on women, as well as on others.

Mao Dun, a second May Fourth male writer, rejected Lu Xun's general critique of feudalism in favour of a more specific concept of patriarchy. In his "gallery of heroines" (Hsia, 1974: 165), women are presented as the second sex in a male-dominated society, and they sometimes succeed, although most fail, in their search for self-realization. These women are more than merely a symbol of all the oppressed, as in Lu Xun's short stories; rather, they constitute a gender category whose struggle to gain emancipation is drawn primarily in terms of women's struggle against men. As opposed to the old tradition of using women's predicament as a projection of social or political abuse, Mao Dun articulated a conception of difference and applied it to women in order to criticize current Chinese society.

To the credit of these two prominent male authors, writers after 1919 began to explore the question of women in many new ways. Issues such as marital bondage and female chastity, arranged marriages, divorce, women and education, female adultery, and prostitution began to be examined in literature for the first time. The range of topics examined by these writers is taken by one contemporary Chinese male critic as evidence of a feminist consciousness among some modern Chinese male writers, of whom Mao Dun is one outstanding example.[12] Nonetheless, one may question whether male writers, some of whom make feminist claims, can be wholly successful in dismantling androcentrism. In Huang Chunming's "A Flower in a Rainy Night," the male voice is sympathetic; nonetheless, the female character, Baimei, is betrayed by certain ideological and androcentric interests. What claims to feminism can we concede to this male writer, keeping in mind that he is writing in a patriarchal culture?

After a period in which Taiwan society looked toward the West for inspiration and solutions, the male nativist writer, Huang Chunming, together with a second male writer of Taiwan, is credited with "turning the focus of examination upon the sufferings of the villages and village folk who were dominated completely by foreign economics and culture" (Chen Yingzhen, 1977: 64). Because of the subject matter of his works — the sufferings, struggles and desires of the village folk — Huang Chunming has been variously described as a "writer with a conscience," a "humanist," and "the spokesperson for the little people," and as one who "grieves over the destiny of humankind" (Huang, 1978: 641). Huang's "A Flower in the Rainy Night" is one of this author's most humanistic works and illustrates his depiction of women.

"A Flower in the Rainy Night" was warmly received by the Taiwan public when it appeared in print during 1967. One critic claims that the heroine, Baimei, is "one of the most memorable and positive characters in modern Taiwan fiction" (Goldblatt, 1980: 121). Another, Wang Der-wei, states that the plot of "A Flower in the Rainy Night" — a veteran prostitute who dreams of the day when she can have a baby of her own, and later, when she is pregnant, brings good luck to her village — "is welcome, by readers, feminists [and] nonfeminists [alike]" (Wang, n.d.: 22). Wang claims that the story is a feminist victory: Baimei has "turned the tables around by using a male customer to carry out her fantasy" (*ibid.*).

"A Flower in the Rainy Night" opens with a scene in a low-class brothel in the fishing village of Nanfangao, where the prostitute Baimei has served the fishing fleet for fourteen years. Baimei was sold first as a child by her parents, then resold by her parents into prostitution. She dreams of a child of her own, because "only a child of her own would give her something in this world to call hers" (Huang, 1967: 209), and commences to select from her clientele the right person to father her child. Attracted to a kind young fisherman, Baimei leaves the brothel and returns home, hoping she has achieved her aim. Her dream is realized, and Baimei's pregnancy evolves in tandem with hagiographic descriptions of how she protects the village folk from a typhoon, got more money for the village potato crop, and so on. In her home town, Baimei has taken on the stature of small-time sainthood. Once ostracized because of her profession, which had erected "walls that kept her rigidly separated from the rest of society" (*ibid.*, 240), Baimei finds that motherhood has brought her reintegration into society.

Written by a male author, this poignant story presents a valuable achievement in its acknowledgement of female desire. I would suggest, however, that its warm reception in Taiwan was not entirely due to the (very genuine) sympathy it expresses, for overt female oppression or the minor victories of a prostitute. Rather, I believe that its popularity is more likely due to the recognition of the story's patriarchal message by a community in which literary merit is determined almost exclusively by men. The classic solution offered for the dilemma of the fallen woman is none other than a continuation of the myth surrounding motherhood, in which points are inadvertently scored for the patriarchal interests dominating reproduction. Baimei herself has won some minor victories; nonetheless the text's binary opposites (derided prostitute and venerated madonna) preclude her autonomy as a woman and make her less emancipated than the heroines of Mao Dun.

The Colonial Code of Reference:
The "Nationalized" Female Body

One of the most significant issues in nineteenth- and twentieth-century Asia has been the impact of the West, particularly of Western colonialism. While China was not a true colony, as was India, it was subjected to a semi-colonial status as a result of the Chinese Opium Wars (1839–42). In the twentieth century, patterns of colonization appeared in Manchuria and Taiwan under Japanese rule. During decolonization and the establishment of semi-colonialism in Taiwan by Japanese and American business interests after World War II, these two imperialist powers instituted a form of dependency that led left-wing critics in Taiwan to label the post-war decades in that country a "second colonial period."[13] During the 1960s and 1970s, collaboration with off-shore investors by the Nationalist (KMT) government of the Republic of China also brought benefits to the Nationalists. A major expression of this collaboration involved the sexual manipulation of Chinese women: Chinese women became "nationalized" or sexually exploited nation-wide for the purpose of obtaining foreign exchange. One form of this nationalization is the phenomenon of Japanese sex tours, which is explored by the writer Huang Chunming among others (see Huang, 1974).

A spinoff of the theme of nationalization is examined by the woman writer Zeng Xinyi, whose "I Love the Professor" (1977) levels the accusation that the national developmental policy was reinforced at home through the Taiwan nativist elite. The nationalized female population forms a class of "gendered subalterns," to use a term applied by Gayatri Spivak to women in India.[14]

In "I Love the Professor" the representative of the nativist elite is a Westernized scholar who returns to Taiwan after obtaining a doctorate from Harvard. The "subaltern" who speaks through the "I"–narrator is an office worker who, since childhood, has idolized learning and believed that, equipped with it, she would be "adept at understanding the world" (Zeng, 1977: 179–80). Attracted to Zhang as an "honest, upright scholar" and a "charming intellectual, hard-working and enthusiastic man," the narrator engages in a love affair (*ibid.*, 157, 158). "I Love the Professor" is largely devoted to descriptions of the tender interaction between the lovers, doubts as to Professor Zhang's sincerity on the part of the narrator (whose position as subaltern becomes increasingly clear), and the colonized woman's idolization of the world of academe.[15] She recognizes that Zhang is an elitist: "Zhang oozed with the easy fortunes of the affluent . . . and was sufficiently self-confident and authoritative to be classed as an elitist intellectual" (*ibid.*, 160–1). When he talks with her it is with "probity and honour" (*ibid.*, 161). The doctoral degree is for her a symbol of her quest for knowledge. In her words: "I had always pursued the truth — this was the ultimate belief and greatest meaning of my life" (*ibid.*, 174). While idolizing learning, however, her feelings are tinged with ambivalence: as an insider, Zhang has revealed information about the workings of the academic world which makes her feel that "post-secondary education is hypocritical and extravagant" (*ibid.*, 168).

Nonetheless, when Zhang abandons her for a Cantonese girl, the subaltern, overcome by a "grisly" sense of shame, throws herself into her studies. She prepares to take the joint entrance exam for university, and when she finds that she has been admitted to a department she likes, she is "delirious with joy" (*ibid.*, 180). Overshadowed by this happiness, the pain Zhang has brought her gradually subsides. Reconciled to the fact that her relationship is over, the narrator visits Hong Kong where Professor Zhang has taken up a teaching post, and this concludes the story. Her feminist awareness has increased, and her encounter with power has made her conscious of her dependence. Now more free of the patriarchal code than the prostitute Baimei, her feminist transformation is greater than the prostitute's. She speaks out very eloquently on this issue:

> Before contemplating [marriage] or anything else I would first steel myself to physical and mental health. I would want to be independent and not rely on others either emotionally or where my livelihood was concerned. More importantly, I could not afford to erect false illusions or hopes on another person. In order to attain to this level of independence and maturity, I felt that I still had a long way to go. (*ibid.*, 182)

This attitude is very different from the Confucian code and also from the male dominated liberal-humanist one.

Contemporary Women Writers: Feminism and Liberation

In the 1970s and 1980s, Chinese women made many social advances and this, in turn, has been a major factor in women finding their own voice, especially in literature. Zhang Jie, a Chinese woman and a member of the Chinese Writers' Association, writes about women in a society undergoing rapid social change. Her works cover a wide range of themes — youth and love, discrimination against women, male supremacy, corruption, bureaucracy, and nepotism. At the same time, however, she still defends socialism as the best system for China. As a writer who "highlighted women's problems before authorities fully recognized them or took official action" (Yang, 1986: xi), Zhang Jie confronts highly controversial issues in her stories. One of her stories, "Love Must not be

Forgotten," justifies love outside marriage, implying that a true marriage is one based on love alone. In a society in which marriages are still traditionally arranged and in which love is not counted as an important factor, "Love Must not be Forgotten" caused a furor when it appeared in 1979.

"The Ark" was also controversial. This novella describes three women who are separated or divorced and their difficulties, not only in finding suitable work but in retaining their self-respect in a society which puts male interests first. It sparked much criticism, both positive and negative. Some readers applauded Zhang's efforts and claimed this as China's first feminist novel, though Zhang Jie herself denies that she is a feminist. Zhang's detractors, on the other hand, denounced her for the bitterness of her female characters which made them behave in an "unwomanly way" (Yang, 1986: xi), while others claimed that her bleak picture of women's difficulties was a distortion of socialism. Whatever may be said about the technical merits of Zhang Jie's work, the psychological realism of a piece such as "The Ark" offers insight into the contemporary realities of Chinese women.

The three women in "The Ark," Liu Quan, an office worker, Liang Qian, a movie director, and Cao Jinghua, a writer, share an apartment nicknamed the "widows' club." While all three are fairly successful professionally, they doubt their femininity: "Their voices were so coarse and unfeminine, though they were so accustomed to each other that they hardly noticed it. But what must men have thought of them?" Still worse, they doubt the value of their present lives: "They were all like nameless old windmills standing out in the wilds, relentlessly, unhurriedly turning, turning . . . forever chasing after dreams they could never realize" (Zhang, 1982: 177, 135).

All three women share the burden of being born female. Liu Quan, oppressed by the sexual harassment of her boss, laments: "Why had she ever been born a woman, carrying around with her the burden of feminine beauty? . . . And on top of this, why did she have to be a divorcee who, because she belonged to no one in particular, could become the property of everyone?" (*ibid.*, 121). Liang Qian, on the other hand, carries a double burden: she regrets the passing of youth, which she has had barely a moment to enjoy, while, at the same time, she suffers the guilt of renouncing motherhood:

> In any case, if she chose to follow a career, then she had to be prepared to sacrifice womanly pleasures, that was an irreconcilable truth. Women, like Mrs. Thatcher, who manage to combine the job of prime minister with baking cakes for her children, must be few and far between. (*ibid.*, 126)

The third woman, Jinghua, is a writer. Her articles have met with praise and blame: "Cao Jinghua, your elaboration of Marxism is a superb contribution to our overall understanding"; Jinghua must "correct her attitudes and conscientiously remove the mistakes in her political thinking" (*ibid.*, 147). While Jinghua lacks the self-doubts of her roommates, her present life as a middle-aged woman who has suffered years of abuse from her husband, and who is now an intellectual struggling for recognition, resembles the "image of a nearly burned down candle" in dire need of "recharging" (*ibid.*, 158). The situation of these three women can be summed up in the inscription prefacing the story: "You are particularly unfortunate, because you were born a woman . . ." — an old saying (*ibid.*, 113).

"The Ark" combines a critique of society with insights into gender issues. Unlike Marxist-oriented Chinese literature, which focuses on class or combines class with gender as the determinants of literary production,[16] "The Ark" is concerned with gender alone, reinforced with insight into female psychology that further marks Zhang's work as feminist. Zhang Jie asserts through the fictional Liang Quan that "true liberation was more than gaining improvement of economic and political status; it was also necessary that women develop confidence and strength in order to realize their full value and potential" (*ibid.*, 156). Women's liberation includes the recognition that women are not merely "objects of sex, wives and mothers," that "we have our own value and significance" (Zhang, 1982: 191). To crown her point, Zhang Jie concludes "The Ark" with a toast to women and the hope that the younger generation will grow up to understand how difficult it is to be a woman.

More recently, women writers in Taiwan and China have expanded on the issue of gender to write about rape, domestic violence, and sexuality. Li Ang's "The Butcher's Wife" (1983), for example, is a story about a young peasant woman who is brutalized by her pig-butcher husband and is finally driven to madness and commits murder. In this work, the husband finds the same satisfaction in hearing a woman cry out in pain as in butchering a pig. Praised for the author's "explicit and metaphorical merging of sexual and physical brutality" (Li, 1983: cover jacket), this work was awarded the United Daily News annual fiction prize in 1983.

Wang Anyi's *Love in a Small Town*, on the other hand, is the first work to emerge by a woman writer which focuses exclusively on sex. Based on a real-life story the author witnessed in the Anhui performing arts troupe, this novel was condemned during the anti-bourgeois liberalization campaign of 1987 as an example of how even "female comrades had degenerated into writing about sex" (Hung, 1988: preface). Flying in the face of diehard attitudes in China that sex is taboo, Wang Anyi insists that the novel is about human nature, not sex. Nonetheless, it was some time before *Love in a Small Town* was published in book form in China as one in a set of three novellas.

The two characters in *Love in a Small Town* are a pair of grotesque young dancers in a dance troupe. The woman "has thick legs, thick arms, a thick waist and very broad hips. Her breasts are twice the normal size, protruding like small hills, hardly like a fourteen-year-old's" (Wang, 1986: 2). As for her male counterpart, the text informs us that "Something must have gone wrong with his body; he has just stopped growing, and though he is eighteen, he still looks very much a child" (*ibid.*). Though neither is a principle dancer, they practice day and night together. After forty pages of text, during which three years have passed, the narrative reveals a subtext. The "she" in the story suffers from a "nameless yearning" while "acne inflames his every pore"; and at one point, "his lips find hers, biting almost viciously" (*ibid.*, 37, 39). The sexual encounters of the pair deepen and, in tandem, the language of the text becomes increasingly coded: the words "need," "bliss," "a sin," and "fear" give clues about sexual adventurism, without, however, offering explicit description. The most explicit passage reads as follows:

> They exhaust their imagination trying to find new ways and positions, but familiarity has eroded the sense of mystery and fun. Yet they cannot stop either; neither can do without the other. Although they come back exhausted, annoyed and disappointed every time, they still look forward to each outing with fervent expectation. (*ibid.*, 44)

The notion of sexual pleasure as sinful is a very strong one in puritanical China. Consequently, the author's repeated self-censorship sends a clear caveat to her readership: "[T]hey have sinned, and remain sinners. They are unclean"; they experience a "filthy and sinful yearning gnawing at them"; and, they have fallen into a "dark, filthy abyss" (*ibid.*, 49, 63, 71). At one point, their shame and desperation lead them to hurt each other, hinting at an underlying sadomasochism: "It is as if they will not be satisfied until they feel the pain"; but the "horror in their screaming lies precisely in the strange sense of pleasure hidden in it" (*ibid.*, 70). *Love in a Small Town* is a narrative about desire. As an expression of female sexuality, however, it passes on little or no understanding. The phrase "the scorching flames of desire" says little about intimacy. Even less successful is the encoding of female sexuality in the obscure language of disease, for example: "the hunger of the body is difficult to endure . . . Every time the crisis comes it is as damaging as a serious illness" (*ibid.*, 95). Though written by a woman, *Love in a Small Town* claims no separate position for women, nor does it work on behalf of women in reclaiming their bodies and minds. It remains on the level of description of sexuality found in traditional Chinese literature.[17] Although she is situated in a modern sociopolitical context, the nameless "she" in the novel remains as dispossessed of her body as were her Chinese female forebears.

Conclusion

In China during the second and third decades of the twentieth century, the tumultuous social and intellectual upheaval of May Fourth profoundly altered the centuries-old status of women. For the first time, the concept of female emancipation was explored as a realizable social goal. In fiction, too, the question of women was also broached for the first time, and, since then, the examination of this question has appeared in a variety of forms through a number of different discourses or cultural codes, explored here as Confucianism, liberal-humanism, colonialism, and feminism. These themes are apparent in the work of writers who are unaware of the extent of their influence. Thus, the charge of sexism which was laid against Huang Chunming by American feminists in the late 1970s may have struck him totally by surprise, considering his professed sympathy for Chinese women and opposition to female oppression.

Although contradictory, these themes coexist in competition. The Confucian code, for example, which espoused many elements of traditional thought, coexisted side-by-side with post-May Fourth works whose writers at times exhibited a high degree of feminist consciousness or, at other times, perpetrated female stereotyping. Evolving ahistorically, they also signified little apparent chronological development in women's social position since 1919. In the first new ideology to appear after the events of 1919 — that of liberal-humanism, which was set in place by the writer Lu Xun — the oppression of women was examined alongside a number of other social abuses, while traditional attitudes towards single women, whether widowed or divorced, continue to haunt and torment women in many writings by women in China in the decade of the 1980s.

In the colonial discourse, the exploitation of women is of a different kind, arising in modern-day Taiwan from the collusion of national and international interests. The dynamics of this process are explored by a woman writer, and yet there is again little marked progression toward the betterment of women's situation. As in the liberal-humanist discourse, women in this code suffer from a double standard, signifying that as long as male interests rank higher on the scale of social priorities, women will be unable to rise above a social structure that continues to perpetuate their status as second-class citizens.

Traditionally in China, the male voice has tended to dominate in literature (as well as in other fields), and this is certainly true in the field of liberal humanism. As long as men continued to speak for women, the ongoing silence of women was guaranteed. With the emergence of a plethora of women writers in the 1980s, however, women have finally begun to speak; nonetheless, these women still have a long way to go toward developing a voice or ideology of their own. In China, the socialist regime continues to guarantee that all intellectuals, including writers, are constant prey to the charge of contamination by Western bourgeois ideology. Chinese women writers who openly or otherwise espouse a feminist cause are also vulnerable to accusations of cultural colonization. Whether or not Chinese feminism takes a form recognizable as such by Western feminists, women in both China and Taiwan are also potentially plagued by charges from society at large that they have lost their identity as "real Chinese women." The advent of REAL Women, which has appeared as a relatively recent phenomenon in North America, would be nothing new in the more conservative context of Chinese culture.

In sum, the revolt and struggle for liberation on the part of Chinese women has proceeded on several fronts, and it involves different aspects of the female body. This struggle aims at the physical freedom of unrestricted movement (against a history of incarceration and restriction); the rejection of the roles assigned to women as idealized male metaphor (prostitute, mother, saint); breaking the silence by finding a voice; and the search to express female notions of feminine sexuality. Chinese women are struggling to define themselves, rather than continuing to be defined by and in relation to men and to male-dominated cultural codes. The question is: can they undertake this process successfully, without embracing an alien Western cultural code?

Notes

1 Taiwan's nativist literature deals with the subject of the Chinese homeland, with the peasant and other figures from the lower orders of Chinese social life, and with the sanctity of Chinese rural life. In this literature, rural traditionalism symbolizes a refuge from the forces of modernization and industrialism.

2 The subordination of women's issues by the current developmental policy of the government in the People's Republic of China is the topic of Phyllis Andors's *The Unfinished Liberation of Chinese Women, 1949–1980*. (Bloomington: Indiana University Press, 1983).

3 The cultural or referential code is one of the five codes of meaning formulated by Roland Barthes in *S/Z*. The Confucian cultural code as I also refer to it alludes to the body of knowledge shared by the Chinese community, specifically the body of Confucian thought.

4 The feudalistic causes of women's subjugation in China are the theme of Lu Xun's 1924 "Zhufu" (New Year's Sacrifice). Parallels between this story and "Wealth, Sons, Longevity" are evident.

5 This ideal of female behaviour is laid out in the *Four Books for Women* (*Nü sishu*), a Ming dynasty (1368–1644) classic, which provided educational material for women in traditional China. According to this classic, women must "serve the husband," exercise "restraint and moderation," "yield in harmony," etc.

6 From *Mengzi* (Mencius), "Liloushang" (*zhang*).

7 The spirit tablet is the main implement of ancestor worship in traditional China. In Chinese patriarchal society, male heirs ensure that the incense smoke (*xianghuo*) burns continually from one generation to the next before the ancestral shrine.

8 Yumei's behaviour accords perfectly with the model of female behaviour as it is laid out in the woman's version of the *Confucian Analects* (*Nü lunyu*), one of the *Four Books for Women*.

9 The *Daxue* (*Great Learning*, trans. James Legge) states: "The ancients who wish to illustrate illustrious virtue throughout the kingdom, first ordered well their own states. Wishing to order well their states, they first regulated their families." The patriarch Zhou Haiwen is not only concerned with regulating his household but is obsessed with economizing as well.

10 *Xiang chong* is the Chinese belief that coming in contact with a dead person, passing by a cemetery, etc., at a time when a person is particularly vulnerable, may induce illness, insanity or even death.

11 The most famous instance is Lin Daiyu in *Hong lou meng* (*Dream of the Red Chamber*).

12 The contemporary Chinese critic Wang Der-wei, claims that there is strong evidence for a feminist consciousness among Chinese male writers. See Wang Der-wei, "Feminist Consciousness in Modern Chinese Male Fiction."

13 Taiwan's first modern period of colonialism took place under Japanese rule from 1895 to 1945.

14 Gayatri Spivak's keynote address, "Postcolonialism, Resistance and the Gendered Subaltern," delivered at the International Summer Institute for Semiotic and Structural Studies, August 10, 1988, University of British Columbia, Vancouver, presented an almost exact parallel of this phenomenon in postcolonial Indian society.

15 Her colonization is of two kinds: the first stems from the uneasy balance of power between her and the returned Western scholar; the second between her and the power-ridden institutes of academe.

16 The genre of Chinese revolutionary opera such as "Baimaonü" (The White-Haired Girl) combines class with gender as the main determinants of literary production. This literary genre monopolized mainstream literary production during China's Great Proletarian Cultural Revolution.

17 *Jin pingmei* (*The Golden Lotus*), China's notorious erotic novel of the Ming dynasty (1386–1644) and some examples of erotic literature of the early Republican period are works which offer instances of explicit sexual descriptions.

Questions

1 What distinguishes the situation of women in China from that of women in North America or Europe?

2 In what ways is the oppression of women in Chinese society inseparable from the perception and treatment of their bodies?

3 To what extent are the themes identified in Chinese literature similar to those identified by Sydie in French art during the eighteenth century?

4 How can Chinese women benefit from the experience of Western feminists, and the reverse?

References

Andors, Phyllis. 1983. *The Unfinished Liberation of Chinese Women, 1949–1980*. Bloomington: Indiana University Press.

Barthes, Roland. 1974. *S/Z*. New York: Hill and Wang.

Belsey, Catherine. 1980. *Critical Practice*. London and New York: Methuen.

Chen, Yingzhen. 1977. "Wenxue lai zi shehui fanying shehui." Pp. 53–68 in Yu Tianzong (ed.), *Xiangtu wenxue taolunji*. Taipei: Yuanjing, 1978.

Chou, Tse-tsung. 1960. *The May Fourth Movement: Intellectual Revolution in Modern China*. Harvard: Harvard University Press.

Goldblatt, Howard. 1980. "The Rural Stories of Hwang Chun-ming." Pp. 110–33 in Jeannette L. Faurot (ed.), *Chinese Fiction from Taiwan: Critical Perspectives*. Bloomington: Indiana University Press.

Hsia, C.T. 1974. *A History of Modern Chinese Fiction*. New Haven: Yale University Press.

Huang, Chunming (Hwang Chun-ming). 1967. "A Flower in the Rainy Night." Trans. Earl Wieman. Pp. 195–241 in Joseph S.M. Law and Timothy A. Ross (eds.), *Chinese Stories from Taiwan: 1960–1970*. New York: Columbia University Press, 1976.

Huang, Chunming (Hwang Chun-ming). 1974. "Sayonara zaijian." Pp. 217–70 in *The Drowning of an Old Cat and Other Stories*. Trans. Howard Goldblatt. Bloomington: Indiana University Press, 1980.

Huang, Chunming (Hwang Chun-ming). 1978. "Yi ge zuozhe de beibi xinling." Pp. 629–47 in Yu Tianzong (ed.), *Xiangtu wenxue taolunji*. Taipei: Yuanjing, 1978.

Hung, Eva. 1988. Preface. Wang Anyi, *Love in a Small Town*. Trans. Eva Hung. Hong Kong: Renditions Paperbacks.

Li, Ang. 1983. *The Butcher's Wife*. Trans. Howard Goldblatt and Ellen Yeung. San Francisco: North Point Press, 1986.

Lü, Heruo. 1942. "Cai zi shou." Pp. 45–85 in Zhong Zhaozheng and Ye Shitao (eds.), *Niuche*. Guangfuqian Taiwan wenxue quanji 5 Yuanjing congkan 130. Taipei: Yuanjing, 1979.

Moi, Toril. 1985. *Sexual/Textual Politics: Feminist Literary Theory*. Terence Hawkes (ed.), London and New York: Methuen.

Wang, Anyi. 1986. *Love in a Small Town*. Trans. Eva Hung. Hong Kong: Renditions Paperbacks, 1988.

Wang, Der-wei. No date. "Feminist Consciousness in Modern Chinese Male Fiction." An unpublished manuscript.

Yang, Gladys. 1986. Preface to Zhang Jie, *Love Must not be Forgotten*. Trans. Stephen Hallett. San Francisco: China Books and Periodicals, Inc.

Zeng, Xinyi. 1977. "Wo ai boshi." Pp. 157–82 in *Wo ai boshi*. Yuanjing Congkan 80 Taipei: Yuanjing.

Zhang, Jie. 1982. "The Ark." Pp. 113–201 in *idem.*, *Love Must not be Forgotten*. Trans. Stephen Hallett. San Francisco: China Books and Periodicals, 1986.

I-less and Gaga in the West Edmonton Mall: Towards a Pedestrian Feminist Reading[1]

Janice Williamson
English Department
University of Alberta

Women are classified in modern society as consumers or as consumed, rather than as producers/creators. Janice Williamson takes us on a pedestrian tour of the West Edmonton Mall which shows us multiple (deforming) reflections of the female body as merchandise, decoration, and bait. Appeals to women as buyers are based on the image of the female body as primarily desirable to men, and on the assumption that women's primary goal is to create/preserve that desire. The Fantasyland Hotel incorporates numerous stereotypes, which this deconstructive "reading" reveals in a new light.

FEMALE VOICEOVER: THERE ARE FIFTY-EIGHT
ENTRANCES TO THE MALL.
THIS IS ONE OF THEM.

Entrance Number 1

The West Edmonton Mall (WEM) and the adjoining Fantasyland Hotel are sites of capital desire and consuming pleasure; both work to address and transform those who venture through the corridors as shoppers. An important cultural site in Edmonton, WEM's construction has altered the face of the city, shifting tourist revenues and urban life from downtown to the western suburbs, a flat suburban sea of bungalows. At latitude 53, Edmonton is the largest of Canada's northernmost cities. As a result of its relation to the hinterland, WEM can draw on a population which extends as far north as the Arctic, offering a simulated urban experience to Inuit, Indian and non-Native northerners.

Public relations spokespersons for the Mall claim that it is the second biggest tourist attraction in the province, surpassed only by the

Rocky Mountains and gaining fast. Sixty-five percent of mall revenues come from tourists. Visitors come by road from Montana to the south, Saskatchewan to the east, and British Columbia to the west. In various cities, WEM advertises their special cut-rate air flights for a weekend of shopping. Recently direct flights between Edmonton and Tokyo began to accommodate the huge number of Japanese tourists who flock to the mall. As though in reply to Canadian free trade with the U.S., a one-week trip from Tokyo billed as a "Tour of America" boasts stopovers in Vancouver, Edmonton, New York, and Los Angeles.

Edmontonians have an ambivalent relation to the mall. In response to the presentation of my research at the University of Alberta, the audience was divided; some shoppers frequented the mall while others had never crossed any of WEM's many thresholds and denounced WEM as having "destroyed the city" by emptying the downtown core of the city during non-business hours. As though in response to this criticism and the urban planning problems they created with their suburban mall, the Ghermazian brothers who own WEM developed The Eaton Centre and Center Suite Hotel, a downtown mall/hotel complex that opened in 1987. Although the city and provincial governments provided WEM with initial and ongoing support, the Ghermazians received especially generous financial contributions from the city of Edmonton for their suburban and downtown development, contributions that have been questioned by critics.

Entrance Number 4

This is the beginning of *The Canadian Encyclopedia* entry on cultural life in Alberta:

> Cultural life in Alberta has had to combat 2 major negative forces: the persistence of a "frontier ethos" that emphasizes economic materialism and rugged individualism; and a cultural dependency on external metropolitan centres such as New York, London, Toronto, and Los Angeles. (Vol. I: 55)

Alberta was one of the last of the provinces to be settled, and the harsh climate and varied landscape bred a community of rugged individualists. Explanations for this are various. According to some, the Albertan ethos can be traced to white settlement patterns. Saskatchewan, the neighbouring prairie province to the east, was in part settled by socialist Brits and has a history of farming cooperatives and communitarian leftist politics. While Alberta also has an early history of farming cooperatives, it was settled by many Americans who came from the south with the promise of individual liberty on their minds. The landscape in the south is dominated by ranches that cultivate self-reliant individual property owners and contribute almost half of Alberta's agricultural economy.

How do I, a recently arrived feminist critic and writer from the east, avoid colonial attitudinizing in my response to this "frontier ethos"? Autobiographical narrative is part of this story:

> *I blew into town in the summer of 1987 one day before the tornado. The faithful Yellowhead led me past the long horizon of Saskatchewan. The Ukrainian Village welcomes me to Alberta: signs of cultural differences, of wilderness, of oppression. I hear again my Ukrainian stepfather's stories of discrimination and exclusion growing up on the rural prairie. Detouring through Elk Island Park, I note how carefully it is marked out for city dwellers in the reassuring continuities of growth and rebirth; as though history were rewritten, the residue of bison herds graze along the roadway; nature trails are blazed with comforting stories of larvae connected to the butterfly and the tadpole connected to the oil rigs. Driving west now again: the surreal lights and silhouettes of the oil rigs, my first glimmer of Edmonton urban living. I'm not quite tourist since I'm fixing to stay. Do I belong here in bungalow heaven? My temporary remedy for moving mourning and melancholia is the mall. I come here for almost everything: though the food store has closed down, the liquor store is just across the street. This is one advantage of late monopoly capitalism. Almost everything is readable: displacement suppressed by the familiar frenzy of images: I can find a 1" nail in Canadian Tire, or Eatons, or Sears, or the Bay. I can find my new radio, have my computer fixed. I'll save the beach for a February day when the temperature dips to 40° below.*

My initial explorations of the mall led me to visit the "non-denominational" Marketplace Chapel staffed by Pentecostals and located just opposite Fantasyland Hotel on the second level of the mall. A twenty-seven-year-old female chaplain there explained to me the difficulties of organizing mall workers into a community of noon-hour swimmers at "The Beach." I suggested that her work might be to construct a sense of "depth" of "soul" in an environment of shining reflective flat surfaces. (The mall's own repetitive allusions to "the deep" in watery architectural themes underscore this obsession.) When asked to identify the chapel's relation to the mall, the chaplain responded with this revisionary biblical allusion: "The chapel is *in* the mall but not *of* the mall." Echoing the chaplain's insight, I ask myself, what kind of prepositional logic organizes West Edmonton Mall: "Is it *in* but not *of* Alberta?"

Mark Abley writes about the West Edmonton Mall in a travel narrative which documents his return to the Canadian West:

> In the mall's terms, consumption and existence are synonymous: to be unable or unwilling to buy is to have no reason to live. Glazed with the joys of acquisition, buyers hand away their earnings with delight. They

spend; therefore they are . . . The mall is a giant stage-set for the dramas of the dollar bill. (1986: 238–9)

I can respond to Abley's cultural pessimism with a series of questions: At 40° below under a sunny sky, what about the sheer pleasure of living in a fish bowl? How do we read the non-market pleasures of West Edmonton Mall? As a feminist critic, how do I read the mall without constructing my fellow shoppers, browsers, swimmers, tourists, and city dwellers as merely manipulated victims of capital or captains of false consciousness? As a writer can I imaginatively transform what he takes to be an unredeemable commercial landscape? Are there signs of resistance in his "drama of the dollar bill"?

Entrance Number 9

These are a few of the facts about the Mall and the adjoining Fantasyland Hotel. West Edmonton Mall's value is estimated by WEM as approximately $1.2 billion. The largest shopping mall in the world has been described as follows:

> Occupying a 110-acre site about six miles west of the centre of Edmonton, Alberta, this two-storey 5,200,00-square-foot structure . . . employs approximately 18,000 people . . . , contains almost 23 per cent of Edmonton's total retail space, takes in 42 per cent of all consumer dollars spent in shopping centres in the Edmonton area . . . and accounts for more than 1 per cent of *all* retail sales in Canada. (Hopkins, 1990: 5)

It has been built in three stages: the first 220 stores opened in 1981; the second phase, two years later, opened 240 stores and services; and phase three in 1985 added 368 stores and services.

The mall includes a skating rink, a water park, a theme hotel, a miniature golf course, an amusement park, a life-size replica of Christopher Columbus' *Santa Maria*, and more submarines than dive in the Canadian Navy. Throughout the mall, there are "over 250 domestic and exotic birds, mountain lions, tigers, spider and squirrel monkeys, black bears, French leopards and jaguars." Four Atlantic bottlenose dolphins perform throughout the day, while in small tanks nearby sharks, alligators, penguins, and harbour seals circle aimlessly for our viewing pleasure. Sensitive to criticism from animal rights activists, all of these animals are, according to WEM publicists, sent to the WEM Game Farm outside of Edmonton "for rest and relaxation." In fact, many of the bird and animal exhibitions have disappeared over the past years, suggesting either that protests have been successful or that the cost of animal care is simply too burdensome.

Entrance Number 32

French critic Henri Lefebvre observes that:

> the concept of everydayness does not . . . designate a system but rather a
> denominator common to existing systems including judicial, contractual,
> pedagogical, fiscal, and police systems. Banality? Why should the study
> of the banal itself be banal? Are not the surreal, the extraordinary, the
> surprising, even the magical, also part of the real? Why wouldn't the
> concept of everydayness reveal the extraordinary in the ordinary? (1987:
> 9)

Feminist writers and critics have also located their politics in everyday
particulars as opposed to the universalist absolutes of patriarchal logic.
How does a feminist locate "the extraordinary in the ordinary" shopping
mall? How does she define her relation to it, her strategy of analysis,
her object of study? Who is this Alice in Text Land?

In an essay modestly titled "Things To Do With Shopping Centres,"
Meaghan Morris (1988) subtitles her text "Pedestrian Notes on Modernity." The notion of pedestrian feminism conveys a doubled critique.
First, it provides a countercultural alternative to the high modernist
excavations of feminist critics, a critique which asks "how do classical
theories of modernism fall short of women's modernity?" (1988: 202).
And second, the figure of the "pedestrian, or the woman walker," offers
a mobile position from which the feminist critic can move freely between
sensory, physical experience and detailed analysis. Ambivalently posi-
tioned, she is both inside and outside. While Lefebvre looks for the
"extraordinary in the ordinary," Morris's pedestrian feminist resists the
pose of "celebrant" by maintaining a critical distance:

> Ambivalence allows a thinking of relations between contradictory states
> . . . . Above all, it does not eliminate the moment of everyday discon-
> tent — of anger, frustration, sorrow, irritation, hatred, boredom, fatigue.
> Feminism is minimally a movement of discontent with "the everyday"
> and with wide-eyed definitions of the everyday as "the way things are."
> (Morris, 1988: 197)

Rachael Bowlby cautions the critic from homogenizing women into
the undifferentiated category of shopper. She begins her essay on modes
of modern shopping with the apparently self-evident statement: "women
shop." In questioning the notion that women are natural shoppers, she
reminds us of another ideological assumption, that women mother *naturally*:

> shopping and mothering are both, in a certain sense, part of women's
> "reproductive" roles, but the definitions of woman's nature implied by

the assignment of each as a "naturally" feminine task are in fact not the same. Motherhood is associated with self-denial and deferral to others' needs. Shopping, while in one way regarded as an indispensable task, is also regarded as a field for the exercise of self-indulgent pleasures which are nonetheless taken to be "feminine" in the same way as are different, responsible qualities attributed to the mother. (1987: 186–7)

For many women shoppers, the categories "shopping" and "mothering" overlap; there is a slippage between the two "reproductive" experiences of "natural" woman, her tasks and pleasures, especially in winter when the mall offers a warm and sheltered space to walk and entertain children. In my interviews with shoppers at the mall and in their responses to my WEM slide presentations, women provide varied perspectives on local shopping culture. For many, consuming is not considered a primary activity in the mall. In one interview, a woman shopper commented that she visited the mall "because of him," pointing to her four-year-old son who was entertained by the animals. A feminist therapist noted that for many of her female clients with small children, WEM's Beach, Fantasyland, and animal displays provided entertainment for the children and a meeting place for mothers isolated by winter.[2]

Most Edmontonians refer to West Edmonton Mall as "The Mall," giving it the status of an archetype. But some women resist its draw, commenting that prices at WEM are often higher than at other malls. One woman claimed defiantly that she traveled three hours to the south to shop in Edmonton's rival city Calgary. An extended study of women and the mall would need more in-depth interviews with not only these shoppers, but also the shop clerks and managers.[3]

Entrance Number 39

WEM appears to embody the progressive history of the arcade and mall in its own three-stage development. Hiking from the oldest section of the mall to the newest, the pedestrian encounters increasingly exotic terrain. First-phase WEM simply linked up large department stores creating an enclosed shop-filled "street." Aside from several animal enclosures, the only entertainment is provided by two large-scale perpetual motion machines. The creation of an artisan, these machines delight viewers and harass shopkeepers with their atonal beeps and bongs.

Second-phase additions included a series of fountains, the Ice Palace skating rink, Fantasyland Amusement Park, and Bourbon Street, a theme street of bars and restaurants — all entertainment features familiar to Albertans. Here the mall becomes a more comprehensive environment, more "city" than simply "street." However the theme street is Bourbon

Figure 1

Europa Boulevard

Street, an exotic locale that submerges any discussion of racial otherness and indigenous peoples in a fascination with the black culture of New Orleans, a topic that we will explore later. Some of the fountains in this section of the mall are designed to remind us of Versailles and were originally musically coordinated to spit fire and water to the tune of popular classics like Beethoven's Ninth Symphony.[4]

The final phase of WEM added more delirious entertainments, including a beach and water area with dolphins, submarines, and a ship, as well as the theme rooms of the Fantasyland Hotel. Here the mall becomes a "world" spilling over with faraway environments reminiscent of Disneyland fictions. It is appropriate that Europa Boulevard (Fig. 1), the interpretive replica of the Faubourg-St-Honoré and a reminder of the nineteenth-century Paris arcade, is part of this third-stage development, for here the mall encodes its own history which returns like the repressed.[5]

Walter Benjamin analyzed the nineteenth-century Paris arcades and noted than any object's authenticity "is determined in part by its testimony to the history which it has experienced" (Benjamin, 1969: 221). Our word "authentic" derives from the Greek word meaning "perpetrator or mastery."[6] Europa Boulevard encodes and masters its own history in an attempt to embody its own "authenticity." Architect Johann Friedrich Geist defines the arcade's seven characteristics as: "access to the interior of a block; public space on private property; a symmetrical street space; a skylit space; a system of access; a form of organizing retail trade; [and] a space of transition" (1983: 12). He traces the links between the arcade and the eastern bazaar, noting that after Napoleon waged his 1798–9 Egyptian campaign as a challenge to British monopoly on Mediterranean trade, the first Parisian arcade built in 1799 was called "Passage du Caire." Geist notes, however, that the bazaar is historically determined and a response to "a specific society and era" that required "a public space protected from traffic and weather and a new means of marketing the products of a blossoming luxury goods industry" (*ibid.*, 12). He describes how the arcade, as architectural space, became "a department store, a market hall, a bath house, or a prison." Which of these architectural uses is echoed in West Edmonton Mall depends on one's reading of the mall. Europe in WEM is no more than a fiction. Indeed this mall space is not called Europe but Europa, a character in Greek mythology who was kidnapped and raped by Zeus, who "calmed her fears by promising her that the whole continent should be called Europe after her, and her children should be kings" (MacPherson, 1971: 97).

What is the significance of this feminization of space? Judith Williamson (1986) points out that "one of the most important aspects of images of 'femininity' in mass culture is not what they reveal but what they conceal. If woman means home, love, and sex, what 'woman' *doesn't* mean, in general currency, is work, class, and politics" (1986: 103). And isn't it work, class, and politics that are suppressed in WEM's Europa which celebrates the pleasures of a well-ordered bourgeois public space? The suppression of the class and cultural history of the arcades includes the suppression of those who work in them. In front of the façade of European culture hangs a sign announcing "Corporate Meeting Rooms" upstairs.

According to WEM advertising, Europa Boulevard with "exclusive fashion boutiques" is "fashioned after various European city streets." European culture is framed here as fashion. Gail Faurschou (1990: 235) notes that "under the abstract sign of pure contemporaneity, fashion is able to recycle any and every object that was once endowed with cultural value." In WEM, historical space is emptied of particulars and becomes a sign indicating the "class" of exclusive fashion boutiques. But this is, of course, only an illusionary exclusivity. Expensive stores are located in other sections of the mall, and, while representatives of larger corporate chains like the American designer Ralph Lauren, Canadian Roots enterprises and avant-garde shops such as Parachute are located here, the rest of the mall, especially on the upper (class) level, also has a number of more expensive shops. As in other contemporary shopping centres, "the prevailing market philosophy for the 1980s . . . has been to develop spectacles of 'diversity and market segmentation,' that is, to produce images of class, ethnic, age, and gender *differentiation* in particular centres . . . because the display of difference will today increase a centre's 'tourist' appeal to everyone else from elsewhere" (Morris, 1988: 204–5). In the seemingly endless list of stores in the West Edmonton Mall, the corporate trick of double and triple naming creates the illusion of competition in place of monopoly, so that consumers comparison shop in different boutiques whose profits accrue to a singular corporate manager.

The set of Europa performs its own strip tease, giving herself away too easily. In gazing across the wrought iron fences, the greenery below could be parkland. However, closer observation reveals a miniature golf course complete with mobile mannequin golfers and a voyeuristic film crew. Illusion takes other, more concrete forms on the streets of Europa; just down the street from a stand selling fake sketches of European streets, a bronze sculpture of a woman stands beside a brass railing. The woman fingers a vanished string of beads, now broken off by vandals. Her high-heeled pumps, short skirt, and v-necked top reveal a full youthful body. Her face is lined with age. This woman represents "la femme de la rue," a street-smart female version of Benjamin's (1969) "flaneur." But Benjamin's flaneur was a bohemian intellectual, a scholar "on the road," whereas this mute figure shows woman as prostitute, and its leading characteristic is the commodification of her body and her sexuality. Indeed, in his essay "Paris, capital of the nineteenth century," Benjamin refers to the image of "the prostitute, who is saleswoman and wares in one" as representative of "the ambiguity attending the social relationships and products" of the nineteenth-century nude. Rachael Bowlby analyzes and expands Benjamin's metaphor:

> It was above all to women that the new commerce made its appeal, urging and inviting them to procure its luxurious benefits and purchase sexually attractive images for themselves. They were to become in a sense like prostitutes in their active, commodified self-display, and also to take on the one role almost never theirs in actual prostitution: that of consumer. (1985: 11)

Entrance Number 41

In this theoretical context, it is thus fitting that scantily clad prostitutes are the only depiction of working women in the mall. Woman as prostitute becomes *mise en scène* on Bourbon Street, a New Orleans theme street lined with restaurants and bars. At the entrance to this

Figure 2

The Arrest of Prostitutes on Bourbon Street

street, life-sized mannequins enact a street scene depicting the arrest of prostitutes (Fig. 2). Two female prostitutes are accosted by a white male police officer. A Harlequin figure left over from another dismantled display looks on. One female figure's arm is tattooed with an Oedipal "papa"; metal handcuffs dangle from her wrist. Another woman, eyes white with rage, shakes a clenched fist towards a white policeman whose power is inscribed on the woman's body through his uniform and very real handcuffs.[7]

Bowlby (1985) notes that "the commodity can be anything at all, since it is defined not by any substance or given utility, but simply by virtue of the fact that it 'goes to market,' in Marx's phrase, with a price, a social value: it can as easily take the form of a person or a person's times as that of a physical object (1985: 26). Women as primary consumers develop "a reciprocal relation with commodities" in this tableau of the prostitute; woman on this second street is bought and sold. Consumed by consumption, shopping is both women's work and identity. Bowlby writes that in a consumer culture "what is by definition one's own, one's very identity or individuality, is at the same time something which has to be put on, acted or worn as an external appendage, *owned* as a property nominally apart from the bodily self" (*ibid.*, 27–8). In WEM's representations of the prostitute, sexuality becomes property to be bought and sold, and the female body, a fetishized commodity form.

Transplanted from New Orleans, Bourbon Street encodes fantasies of the carnival through theatrical tableaux. Bahktin's notion of the "carnavalesque" signals that there is "no formal distinction between actor and spectator . . . [which] creates an authorized transgression of the usual norms and a second, inverted world, parallel to that of the official culture" (Hutcheon, 1988: 30). The carnival in Bourbon Street is, however, a perverse simulation, since the relation between spectator and actor is fixed. The actors are indeed dummies and the street only *appears* to be public since buskers and pamphleteers are regularly evicted for trespassing on the mall's private property. Thus spectators rarely, if ever, enter into a participatory role in the street theatre. Although the mall won't tell, and youth agencies are reticent about going public in order to preserve the mall's cooperation, WEM, like other malls, is a second street where child prostitution and drug rings pose a serious problem, particularly in the case of young runaways.[8] Ironically, the blurring of public and private property that the street-like simulations of the mall seem to signal is *actually* erased by the mall in response to problems with crime. A four-man publicly funded police force patrols the streets alongside WEM's private security guards and security system.

Near the entrance to Bourbon Street, a band of black minstrels beckon tos shoppers with their silent paralytic song. Dominant culture's knowledge suggests that people of colour have particular stereotypic qualities; in this case, blacks have rhythm. On a balcony above the minstrels, woman *is* the city. A woman of colour and a white woman beckon from above the Bourbon Street Saloon. "A Steak Sandwich only $3.95," they announce. Further down the street, another woman in 40s dress stands with her hand on her hip smoking a cigarette behind a wrought-iron fence. A sign points the way up the stairs to the cleaners, the tailors, the rooms above. And what's hidden upstairs? When I first began my research I was shocked to discover at the end of the street that a female mannequin's legs, one with a red garter tucked around the thigh, hung suspended just inside a window frame. When WEM first opened, a scream accompanied the mechanical thrust of her body through the window. Local feminists protested and the scream was removed, but the legs remained — a sign of unreflective violence toward women. A few days after I presented my research in Edmonton, the windows were closed, hiding the woman's legs from view.

Mardi Gras, the traditional New Orleans Carnival, disguises performers' identities through masquerade. In one WEM tableau at the end of the street we are shown signs of 'identities' marked by gender, class, culture, and racial differences. A thick-hipped woman in gold stiletto heels is painted into a mermaid's wet suit. A serpent, sign of Medusa as mystery and castration, slithers across her forehead. Behind her, a masked man in full Mardi Gras costume signals to the radical "other" of the black man. Between these figures, a black field hand plays the saxophone on a crate stencilled "Dixie." This is the south and these are the reductive signs of "blackness": rhythm and the plantation overall blues. In the mall, history is informed by advertising's lack of interest in historical particulars. John Berger (1972: 140) describes the effects of publicity's mythologizing of history: "The fact that [historical references] are imprecise and ultimately meaningless is an advantage: they should not be understandable, they should merely be reminiscent of cultural lessons half-learnt." What's missing in WEM's sculptural representations of southern blacks is their history as enslaved labour power. This absence is underscored in a New Orleans artifact which sits in regal splendour on Bourbon Street: the wrought-iron shoeshine bench. The workers are absent; the shoes, the clients are missing. This is a sign of class difference and of work, but there are no embodied subjects here, just an elegant trace of some nostalgic past.

Entrance Number 46

Standing above "WEM's Beach," a simulation of a tropical locale, I think of Annette Funicello, beach blanket bingo, all that sand. The beach in February; in Edmonton, it's probably Hawaii. Under the fake turquoise ocean, machines can whip up six-foot waves, cranked out in six different wave patterns of non-saline water. The waves can travel so high and far that they're thinking of holding a surfing championship. This must be Hawaii — the palm trees, the tropical temperatures, the moist air, the "sun" (lamps). Waves lap onto the beach and shoppers peer out towards an imagined warmth; the mechanical horizon lies obscured in the distance.

With all of this watery promise, is the mall then an island, like woman, "mysterious, distant, a place to take a holiday?" Judith Williamson (1986: 107) notes that in advertising, woman can be "turned into an island, . . . reeking of exoticism." As a sign of the other, of difference, she offers "a package tour of the natural." If space is feminized through a variety of means in the mall, what difference *within* is suppressed as a result of this gender coding? Novelist Rudy Wiebe notes that the colonization of the Canadian imagination extends to our disavowal of our northern character. According to Wiebe (1989: 30), we "whore" after the iconography of palm trees and beaches and fetishize signs of tropical elsewhere. Leaving aside the binary structure of race and gender in his figuration of white virginal Arctic versus dark, sexualized, exotic other, this notion of the suppression of the northern is reinforced in my interview with Jon Sutherland, the architect of WEM's Fantasyland Hotel, which opened in 1986 and features 356 rooms; 212 are theme rooms, which provide another set of entrances to the imaginary of WEM.

While specialized lobbies, transitional spaces, organize the theme floors,[9] it is important to note that the hotel itself has virtually no lobby. The hotel entrance from the outside is marked solely by hotel personnel arranged behind a counter on one side of a corridor. Nearby a bar called the Fantasy Lounge spills out into the mall across from the Marketplace Chapel. The lobby of the Fantasyland Hotel is but another corridor in the mall. This spatial non-differentiation between mall and hotel is part of the strategy of the developers. According to Sutherland in a personal interview, the goal was to "get the shoppers out of their rooms" and into the mall as quickly as possible. Providing no social space means that the leisurely congregating of hotel guests will not divert them from locations where they can purchase drinks or food. In Fantasyland, identity and agency are restricted to consumption.

Sutherland described how hotel management marketed prospective theme concepts before the hotel was built. In fact, several of the architect's favourite theme room designs were scrapped when they were deemed unpopular with shoppers. Abandoned thematic concepts included a "Russian Room" modeled after the Kremlin and an "Eskimo Room." In this latter room, guests would have slept in a half-igloo, reclined on dog-sled couches and relaxed in a chilling reconstruction of an ice-fishing scene encircling the jacuzzi. Unsurprisingly, perhaps, public polls suggested that the most popular room was the Polynesian Room. Twice as many of these rooms were constructed in order to address this fascination.[10] In the Polynesian Room, stylized motifs tell a story of liquid theatre. In bed, a bricolage of sailing ship and fish tails, the body, fluid, drifts between the sailed surface and watery depths in the belly of the turquoise deep. In case this atmosphere proves too soporific, the pale red glow of a volcanic peak "smoking" in a corner of the room reminds occupants that their passion is both explosive and uncontrollable.

When sex and desire are prepackaged around a market research scheme, how is the erotic theatre of the Fantasyland Hotel organized? According to Gail Rubin (1984: 280), the highest order of good sex sanctioned by our culture is "heterosexual, marital, monogamous, reproductive . . . and occur(s) at home." Erotic discourse and practice in our culture is ordered by "sexual essentialism — the idea that sex is a natural force that exists prior to social life," and by "sex negativity [which defines sex as] . . . a dangerous, destructive, negative force" (*ibid.*, 275, 278). Fantasyland Hotel room decor appears to have thematized these ideological convictions in spatial spectacles of narcissistic self-regard, both in the fractured multiple "I"s spilling out of the jacuzzi's mirrored walls and in the voyeuristic gaze modelled in three-dimensional sculptures installed in most of the rooms.

Nowhere is this more evident than in the "Hollywood Room." Mary Ann Doane (1987: 24) writes that the film frame is "a kind of display window and spectatorship a form of window shopping." The Hollywood Room sets both these terms in motion, the name evoking the ideal female object of consumption, the fetishized Hollywood star. Both Fantasyland Hotel as a self-directing theatrical space and WEM itself reinforce the interrelatedness of spectacle and commodity form. In The Hollywood Room, the guest is made into a spectacle, with stars at her head and feet (the carpet is wired with tiny lights). This twinkling vertiginous space is fractured again in the mirrors which surround the bed and enclose the jacuzzi.

In other rooms, the occupant's gaze is returned by sculpted human figures. The Roman Room provides us with a bust of Julius Caesar, as well as a Roman girl in a diaphanous gown who pours the water in the "authentic Roman bath." A variation of this architectural and sculpted "look" is found in the Victorian Room; the human sculpture refuses to look. This room features a bed in the back of an elegant Victorian coach; the mannequin driver, his back to the sleeper, guides the coach and dreaming passengers straight through the wall. The backside of a horse in bas relief from the wall is joined by leather reins to the driver's hands.[11] This cold-shoulder coachman reminds travelers of both class relations and the possibility of an illicit gaze at the mere turn of a head. The propriety in the detailed Victoriana of the room helps to construct guilty pleasures as tantalizingly sinful.

The Pick-Up Truck Room recalls the street-life of prairie towns and tells a most dramatic story of desire, organized around the stop-and-go, off-and-on, up-and-down rhythms of traffic lights, cops, and illicit pick-ups. Each half-ton truck was installed before the upper floors were constructed above. The trucks' flat beds provide sleeping quarters, which are further transformed into asphalt roadways with black bedspreads and a yellow line separating sleepers into right and left lanes. Antique gas bars, oversized stop signs, and the red/stop, yellow/yield and green/go blinking lights provide atmospheric order day and night.

The rear window/screen of the truck gives the voyeuristic look another twist. This room is advertised as including a bed for a child under twelve. The child's bed is located in the cab of the truck; the rear window of the cab allows for surveillance of the bed. Once again the theatre calls for a spectatorial role in the theme room's erotic drama. Nowhere is this gaze more obvious than in the figure of the policeman in the Pick-

Up Truck Room. A full-sized blue-eyed uniformed figure, whistle raised to his lips, looms large over the mirrored jacuzzi, multiplied into troops of censorious police. WEM publicists note that this figure was the most controversial in the hotel on nights when awakening sleepers screamed in fright on glancing up at this authoritarian figure.

This lesson was taken to heart when another floor of conventionally decorated "Executive" rooms were remade into VIA Rail Rooms and Arabian Night Rooms. The latter rooms recall the Persian origins of the Ghermazian brothers who own WEM. The VIA Rail Rooms are one of the sole reminders in WEM of its location north of the forty-ninth parallel. Telling features include a sign which alerts bathroom visitors to train rules at station stops and a nostalgic framed museum portrait of a caboose and conductor, both recently banished from most Canadian VIA rail lines as a cost-cutting measure. The colour and textures in this room are pink and grey, their blandness almost identical to the nondescript decor of the Fantasyland Hotel's lower-priced "Executive" rooms. When Sutherland described the Via Rail Room to me, he reminded me of the three-dimensional representation of a train steward who helped 'establish' the specificity of the train theme. A bald portly "Frank," the steward, stands with an empty tray extended on one hand. Curiously, he has no pupils in his eyes. Sutherland assured me that the maker of the mannequins, Vancouver's Ray Tanner, had intentionally closed Frank's eyes in order to fittingly convey the figure's subservience. Other mythologies about the steward's eyes have created alternative explanations. The hotel publicist explained that guests had complained of being frightened by the Pick-Up Truck Room's policemen whose penetrating gaze followed them everywhere. If one were to extend the mythologies into representations of Canada, two interpretations arise: Canada is represented in the hotel as either subservient or a zombie.

Entrance Number 53

The Ghermazian brothers are seeking to establish malls elsewhere in Europe and North America. They have been unsuccessful in Canada, but Leeds, England, took seriously their proposal for a $6.5-billion project, including retail and hotel space as well as housing and possibly offices, warehouses, and a marina. Leeds hired Dr. Clifton Young, a marketing professor at the University of Alberta, to investigate the feasibility of the proposed gigantic mall. A headline in *The Edmonton Journal* outlined Dr. Young's critical assessment: "Mall mecca for fun, cheap labour." According to Young, the mall works in Edmonton because its hinterland location makes it a tantalizing sign of the urban and thus attracts isolated communities. In addition, the city's University of Alberta, the second largest university in Canada, and several other post-secondary institutions, provide thousands of students who, along with part-time women, form a labour pool that, in Young's words, "is reasonably intelligent, has a relatively good work ethic, and will work nonstandard hours, part-time and for relatively low wages."[12]

While women workers are depicted only as prostitutes in the mall, at the entrance to Fantasyland is a social-realist monumental bronze sculpture of the male worker as cultural hero. Three men drill right through the marble floor for oil, providing one of WEM's only reminders of local economic history and "one of the few hints that the mall spreads across the Canadian west" (Abley, 1986: 242). The depiction of white masculinity as the policeman in the case of Bourbon Street is, I've suggested, the sign of the law. However, these bronze workers drilling for oil are mediators between things "natural," the invisible oil, and things "cultural," Alberta's economy and the visible excess of corporate capital exhibited in WEM. With the boom/bust oil economy, this bronze acts as a kind of nostalgic recorder; the bucks in the mall require different workers. On Saturday nights, the women who live on WEM's part-time wages without benefits line up outside the mall, awaiting husbands and friends who have cars. These workers, the repressed subjects which disappear in WEM's theatre, remind us of the fantasy behind "Fantasyland."

Notes

1 This paper is part of a longer study which developed from a presentation during a 1988–89 lecture series at the University of Alberta. My thanks to engaged listeners and colleagues at various conferences at the universities of British Columbia, York, Calgary and at The Banff Centre. My thanks to Robert Wilson who first initiated me into the unsolved mysteries of WEM. For several years I became the unofficial tour guide of the mall for visiting cultural critics; W.J.T. Mitchell, Dorothy Smith, Kathleen Martinade, Terry Goldie, Constance Penley and Brian Rusted offered insightful conversations. Special thanks to Cynthia Wright for sharing her expertise on arcades and counter-culture. An eighteen-minute video, "A Pedestrian Feminist Reading of West Edmonton Mall," based on this paper is available through Video Pool Inc., 300–100 Arthur Street, Winnipeg, Manitoba, R3B 1H3.

2 Gail Faurschou (1990: 242) notes that the activity of shopping offers compensatory pleasures in many communities: "The power and seduction of consumption lies in the degree to which it establishes itself as the only form of collective activity in which the atomized individual of bourgeois society can participate."

3 This latter route could draw on Susan Porter Benson's historical analysis of "the clerking sisterhood," which concludes that saleswomen in the early part of this century had a contradictory identity and relation to consumption:

> The work culture of saleswomen suggests that the society of mass consumption was not, and is not, a seamless whole. Consumer capitalism had created and defined saleswomen's roles as workers along with their female roles as consumers, but their patterns of independence and resistance made them less than paragons of either role . . . Perhaps the position of the saleswoman was not in fact unique after all, but rather an extreme case of the dilemma of all workers under consumer capitalism — driven by the social relations of the workplace to see themselves as members of the working class, cajoled by the rewards of mass consumption to see themselves as middle-class. (1986: 271)

4 Throughout the mall there are "Art" referents. Antique Chinese vases in plexiglass cases are located in the first phase of the mall as well as at the entrance to Europa Boulevard. The viewer is reminded of W.F. Haug's economic analysis:

> Capital, with art at its disposal, not only shows off as a connoisseur and admirer of Fine Art but also, in its esoteric interests, adopts the lofty illusion that it is the highest creation of the human spirit, and not profit, which is its determining aim. Thus everything good, noble, beautiful and great seems to speak for capital. Art is used to dazzle, as a tool to create the illusion that the domination of capital is legitimate, and just as valid as the domination of the good, the true, and the beautiful, and so forth. In this way works of art can become a means, among others, of stupefying the public. They are deployed as one of many techniques of creating an illusory solution to the contradiction between capitalist private interest and the vital concerns of society as a whole. (1971/1986: 129)

5 Nader Ghermezian announced at the opening ceremonies of this third stage of the mall: "Here history is in the making . . . What we have done means you don't have to go to New York or Paris or Disneyland or Hawaii any more. We have it all here for you in one place in Edmonton, Alberta, Canada!" (Wiebe and Wiebe, 1989: 81–2).

6 Incidentally, "perpetrator" derives from "to accomplish," as in "to bring about or carry out (as a crime)" (Webster's Ninth New Collegiate Dictionary).

7 One day while passing by this installation I encountered one of the few signs of shoppers' resistance to the representation of women in the mall. Someone had stretched a woolen glove over the woman's fist, taping the fingers into a defiant gesture directed against the officer of the law.

8 For an exploratory analysis of the social issues in the mall, see an unpublished paper by Phil McManus entitled "Social Issues Pertaining to West

Edmonton Mall." McManus claims that prostitution and drugs in the mall require significant intervention by youth and social service organizations.

9 Each theme floor has an elevator lobby decorated with corresponding elements: Hollywood lights, a Pick-Up Truck police mannequin, a Victorian settee, a Canadian Via Rail poster of a train, and a Polynesian volcano.

10 Polynesian rooms with waterbeds are known as "Polywater" rooms, a concept which has thus far escaped deconstruction.

11 The association in Victorian pornography of horses and leather with sado-masochistic fantasies has been documented by a number of writers.

12 Clifton Young generously provided me with a copy of his unpublished paper, "Thoughts on West Edmonton Mall and the Evaluation of Mega-Land Use Proposals."

Questions

1 What more could be said about the role assigned to the women who work in the West Edmonton Mall?

2 Do women need to feel guilty for enjoying shopping? Do they benefit in any way from the 'escape' afforded by shopping centres?

3 Since women are likely to be the majority of shoppers, why is the mall built on the premise of the male viewer? Can one envisage an equivalent space built on the premise of woman as viewer?

4 How does the feminization of space through gender encoding have the effect of contributing to the invisibility of women rather than to their social visibility?

References

Abley, Mark. 1986. *Beyond Forget: Rediscovering the Prairies.* Vancouver and Toronto: Douglas and McIntyre.

Benjamin, Walter. 1969. "The Work of Art in the Age of Mechanical Reproduction." In Hannah Arendt (ed.), *Illuminations.* New York: Schocken Books.

Benson, Susan Porter. 1986. *Counter Cultures: Saleswomen, Managers, and Customers in American Department Stores, 1890–1940.* Chicago: University of Illinois Press.

Berger, John. 1972. *Ways of Seeing.* London: British Broadcasting Corporation.

Bowlby, Rachael. 1985. *Just Looking: Consumer Culture in Dreiser, Gissing and Zola.* New York: Methuen.

Bowlby, Rachel. 1987. "Modes of Shopping: Mallarmé at the Bon Marché." In Nancy Armstrong and Leonard Tennenhouse (eds.), *The Ideology of Conduct: Essays in Literature and the History of Sexuality*. New York: Methuen.

Chalmers, Ron. 1989. "Mall Mecca for Fun, Cheap Labor," *The Edmonton Journal*, May 2 E1.

Doane, Mary Ann. 1987. *The Desire to Desire: The Woman's Film of the 1940s*. Bloomington: Indiana University Press.

Faurschou, Gail. 1990. "Obsolescence and Desire: Fashion and the Commodity." In Hugh Silverman (ed.), *Postmodernism in Philosophy and Art*. London: Routledge.

Geist, Johann Friedrich. 1983. *Arcades: The History of a Building Type*. Trans. Jane O. Newman and John H. Smith. Cambridge, Mass.: MIT Press.

Haug, W.F. 1971/1986. *Critique of Commodity Aesthetics: Appearance, Sexuality, and Advertising in Capitalist Society*. Trans. Robert Bock. Minneapolis: University of Minnesota Press.

Hopkins, Jeffrey S.P. 1990. "West Edmonton Mall: Landscape of Myths and Elsewhereness," *The Canadian Geographer*, Vol. 34, No. 1.

Hutcheon, Linda. 1988. *The Canadian Postmodern: A Study of Contemporary English-Canadian Fiction*. Toronto: Oxford.

Lefebvre, Henri. 1987. "The Everyday and Everydayness," *Yale French Studies*, Vol. 73.

MacPherson, Jay. 1971. *Four Ages of Man: The Classical Myths*. Toronto: Macmillan.

McManus, Phil. 1989. "Social Issues Pertaining to the West Edmonton Mall." Unpublished paper written for the City of Edmonton, Community and Family Services Housing and Planning Branch, June.

Morris, Meaghan. 1988. "Things to Do With Shopping Centres." In Susan Sheridan (ed.), *Grafts: Feminist Cultural Criticism*. London: Verso.

Rubin, Gail. 1984. "Thinking Sex: Notes for a Radical Theory of the Politics of Sexuality." In Carole S. Vance (ed.), *Pleasure and Danger: Exploring Female Sexuality*. Boston: Routledge and Kegan Paul.

Shields, R. 1989. "Social Spatialization and the Built Environment: The West Edmonton Mall," *Environment and Planning D: Society and Space*, Vol. 7: 147–64.

Wiebe, Rudy and Christopher Wiebe. 1989. "Mall." *Alberta*, Vol. 2, No. 1.

Wiebe, Rudy. 1989. *Playing Dead: A Contemplation Concerning the Arctic*. Edmonton: NeWest Press.

Williamson, Judith. 1986. "Woman Is An Island: Femininity and Colonization." In Tania Modleski (ed.), *Studies in Entertainment: Critical Approaches to Mass Culture*. Bloomington: Indiana University Press.

Young, Clifton. No date. "Thoughts on West Edmonton Mall and the Evaluation of Mega-Land Use Proposals." Unpublished paper.

Section Two

Repression of the Female Body

A Suitable Case for Treatment? Premenstrual Syndrome and the Medicalization of Women's Bodies

Janet M. Stoppard
Department of Psychology
University of New Brunswick

Many women recognize the description of PMS symptoms as part of their experience and welcome a physical explanation for their mood changes. Nevertheless, clinical research is inconclusive regarding the nature of this 'disorder,' and the acceptance of the menstrual cycle as implicitly problematic tends to reinforce archaic prejudice against women. By examining the evidence and the situations in which PMS is diagnosed, this paper raises central issues concerning the relationship between female physiology and mental health.

PMS — Progress or Prejudice?

The heavy pain beforehand makes the woman feel bloated, weighted down with the engorged pelvic mass. The griping pains at the onset may severely incapacitate her. Almost worse than all this is the preceding week's depression, seemingly miraculously lifted with the onset of the flow. Women vary in how they view these ordeals . . . (Ashurst and Hall, 1989: 25)

I expect that most women will readily recognize the "ordeal" described in the quotation above as referring to the days in the menstrual cycle just before bleeding begins. For some women, this premenstrual phase of the cycle is indeed an ordeal, with a week or more in each cycle spent in extreme discomfort and distress.

In recent years, the term *premenstrual syndrome* or PMS has gained prominence as a way of referring to certain kinds of menstruation-related complaints that women experience. For some women, being able to name their menstruation-related problems as PMS has provided a welcomed medical validation of their concerns. Too often in the past, complaints that by their nature can be experienced only by women tended to be neglected by the medical profession. Problems such as menstrual discomfort, postpartum depression, and the hot flashes of menopause were viewed, at best, as a necessary consequence of the ability to bear children. At worst, these specifically female problems were dismissed as being either imaginary (it's just in your head) or a form of malingering. Now, women can seek help for premenstrual complaints with the expectation that their concerns will be taken seriously and symptomatic treatment offered. Although the cause of these female problems may not yet be fully known, this understanding is presumed to be only a matter of time as scientific knowledge accumulates.

While not denying the reality of the unpleasant, unwanted changes experienced by some women during the menstrual cycle, conceptualizing such experiences as PMS may have consequences that are less than positive for women as a whole. On closer examination, the idea of PMS, while seeming to replace the "raging hormones" stereotype as an account of women's behaviour, may simply offer a more sophisticated version of this old prejudice. For example, if PMS is viewed as a medical disorder, should women who experience severe premenstrual problems be considered as having a disease? If so, is this disease present only during the premenstrual phase of the cycle, or is the entire menstrual cycle to be characterized as diseased? Since most, if not all, women experience some degree of cyclical changes in association with menstruation, how is "real PMS" to be distinguished from normal menstrual experiences? Are all menstruating women to be considered slightly ill for part of the monthly cycle? The PMS concept validates women's experiences of premenstrual distress, while at the same time legitimizing medical authority on the meaning of this experience. (Who decides if a woman's symptoms should be called PMS?) Moreover, by promising medical treatment for premenstrual symptoms, women are encouraged to blame their problems on their bodies rather than considering alternatives.

There are other warning signs that the PMS concept and its accompanying medical assumptions may represent a mixed blessing for women. PMS has been used with limited success as a legal defence in two cases in England in which women were charged with murder (see Hey, 1985; Kendall, this volume). In each case, medical witnesses attested to the fact that the woman suffered from severe PMS and that, as a result, during the premenstrual phase of the cycle her responsibility for her actions would be diminished. Based on this variant of an "insanity plea," one woman was acquitted and the other placed on probation. These legal decisions give credence to the idea that women are likely to become irrational and unable to control aggressive impulses just before menstruation. In North America, the lack of an official diagnosis for PMS is no longer an impediment to attempts to use a PMS defence for women charged with violent and other crimes. The diagnosis Late Luteal Phase Dysphoric Disorder (LLPDD), essentially equivalent to PMS, is included in the most recent version of the catalog of diagnoses for mental disorders — the DSM–III–Revised (American Psychiatric Association, 1987) — which is the key authority on diagnostic decisions in North America. LLPDD is included as a tentative diagnosis and is proposed for official adoption in the 1994 revision of the DSM, which is currently underway. Although its status is still unofficial, the LLPDD diagnosis already is being used in clinical research.

Along with this medical legitimization of PMS as a disorder have come increased development and promotion of drug treatments aimed at the population of PMS sufferers. The widespread appearance of advertisements on TV and in women's magazines for preparations that claim to offer relief for menstruation-related complaints implies that drug manufacturers see a large untapped market for their products. Given the dubious record of women's experiences with drugs designed to relieve symptoms associated with the female reproductive biological processes (e.g., DES, estrogen replacement, Thalidomide) or to prevent conception (the Pill), the promise of yet another pharmacological cure for women's health problems needs close scrutiny (Eagan, 1985).

In the remainder of this paper, I want to explore the implications for women generally, and more particularly for women's struggles to control their bodies, of the PMS concept and the recent developments around the presumed existence of this disorder. As a first step in this exploration process, the next section provides a brief overview and evaluation of current knowledge about PMS and women's experiences of cyclical changes in relation to menstruation.

Questions of Evidence:
What Do We Know about PMS?

According to recent reviews, many women (estimates range from 5% to 95%) report that, just before menstruation, they experience increased feelings of depression, anxiety, and irritability, accompanied by physical discomfort (bloating, breast tenderness, etc.) (Ussher, 1989: 47). In some unknown proportion of women, these cyclical patterns are particularly pronounced and the premenstrual changes are so severe that they interfere with the woman's usual activities and social relationships. It is important to note that the cyclical pattern called PMS not only involves physical discomfort (painful periods or dysmenorrhea), which is common and for which various pain-relieving treatments are available, but also involves a marked increase in unpleasant mood states (dysphoria). The presence of psychological distress is the hallmark of PMS (and LLPDD).

Given that these changes occur regularly in relation to the premenstrual phase of the female hormonal cycle, a plausible hypothesis is that they are the result of a hormonal imbalance or deficiency. Reports that PMS sufferers gain a measure of relief when prescribed the hormone progesterone have been interpreted as support for the role of a hormonal disturbance underlying the disorder (Dalton, 1984).

It is unclear from available information about PMS, however, whether the characteristic symptom pattern (or syndrome — a cluster of symptoms which tend to occur together) represents an exacerbation of the normal cyclical changes associated with menstruation or is a distinct condition. This raises the question of what we know about changes associated with normal menstruation. Without some baseline of what is a normal or usual experience of menstruation, the possibility of differentiating PMS from other kinds of menstruation-related experiences is unlikely to be attained. A common belief held by women (and men) is that an increase in negative moods premenstrually is an inevitable feature of women's experience in relation to the menstrual cycle. As in the case of PMS, these mood fluctuations are assumed to be related in some way to the changes in hormonal levels during the cycle.

Although many studies have explored the question of mood fluctuations in relation to the menstrual cycle, findings have been inconsistent and contradictory. Part of the reason for these conflicting findings lies in the fact that investigators often have not designed their studies so that alternative explanations can be ruled out. For example, women are more likely to report experiencing negative moods premenstrually than at other times in the cycle if they are aware of the purpose of the study and if their reports are given retrospectively rather than being recorded concurrently on a daily basis (McFarland, Ross, and DeCourville, 1989). Even when these methodological problems are overcome, another obstacle is the lack of appropriate control conditions, so that the findings can appear to show an increase in negative mood premenstrually, although other interpretations are possible. For instance, in most studies no comparison is made with other cycles (e.g., days of the week) or with non-menstruating groups (e.g., men). Any changes in women's mood correlated with the phases of the menstrual cycle are then assumed to be due to hormonal changes across the cycle and no alternative interpretations are considered. [See McFarlane and Williams (1990) for a more detailed discussion of the methodological problems in research on menstruation-related changes in mood.]

A recent Canadian study, in which these methodological problems were satisfactorily addressed, yielded findings that are inconsistent with the assumption that negative moods increase before menstruation. Mc-Farlane, Martin and Williams (1988) compared daily ratings of mood pleasantness-unpleasantness in three groups: normally cycling women, women taking oral contraceptives, and men (pseudo-cycle). The only significant differences in mood between the groups occurred for the menstrual phase (the week beginning with the onset of bleeding) and the follicular phase (the week after the menstrual phase) of the cycle: normally cycling women reported more pleasant moods than did either of the other two groups. When mood ratings over the menstrual cycle were compared with those over the days of the week (Sunday through Saturday), McFarlane *et al.* found that mood fluctuated more during the week than during the menstrual cycle. Thus, this study found no evidence for the presumed premenstrual increase in negative mood. At the same time, however, it did report an increase in physical symptoms (bloating, cramping, etc.) during the premenstrual and menstrual phases of the cycle.

If the pattern of premenstrual changes labeled as PMS is to be accurately diagnosed, there needs to be a shared definition to which professionals can refer in deciding whether the symptoms that a particular woman reports are PMS, some other problem, or simply a variant of normal menstrual experience. Compilations of the range of unwanted, unpleasant premenstrual changes reported by women have revealed more than 150 potential symptoms (Laws, 1985: 37). The DSM diagnosis of Late Luteal Phase Dysphoric Disorder (LLPDD), mentioned already, lists ten symptoms, at least five of which (including at least one of the first four) should have been present for most of the time during the premenstrual (late luteal) phase of most menstrual cycles in the previous year. The symptoms are as follows: 1) marked mood lability; 2) persistent and marked anger or irritability; 3) marked anxiety or tension; 4) marked depressed mood or thoughts; 5) decreased interest in usual activities, work, friends, hobbies; 6) fatigability or marked lack of energy; 7) difficulty concentrating; 8) marked change in appetite; 9) hypersomnia or insomnia; 10) other physical symptoms such as breast tenderness, bloating, headaches, etc.

Although these DSM criteria for diagnosing LLPDD are presented in a way that suggests scientific objectivity, it should be emphasized that their validation awaits further research (Gallant and Hamilton, 1988: 271). A brief reflection on how many combinations of five symptoms (with at least one of the first four) can be created from the list above (there are 186) indicates the wide range of experiences that could fit the diagnosis. Moreover, the qualifier "marked," which precedes several of the symptoms, gives little help to physicians in deciding whether a woman's premenstrual complaints should be considered symptomatic of the disorder. The DSM criteria for LLPDD have been formulated in an effort to resolve the definitional uncertainty. However, with the ambiguity surrounding the specific DSM criteria and the lack of agreement among professionals in the field regarding the symptoms of the disorder, a consensus on the definition of PMS remains elusive.

Nevertheless, it has been argued that despite the lack of agreement on how PMS should be diagnosed, women with severe premenstrual symptoms do report relief with treatments such as progesterone, and this should be interpreted as support (albeit indirect) for the existence of a premenstrual disorder. Currently, however, except for uncontrolled case studies and the testimony of women who have undergone treatment (see Cassara, 1987), there is no compelling evidence that any of the proposed treatments are responsible for the reported improvements. No treatment (psychotropic drugs, hormonal preparations, vitamins, etc.) has been found to be more effective than a placebo in controlled studies (McFarlane and Williams, 1990: 99). One interpretation of these findings is that an important factor in the relief of premenstrual symptoms is having women's experiences taken seriously and receiving social support (Lander, 1988: 92).

Based on available research, current knowledge about PMS (or LLPDD) can be summarized as follows: there is no consensus on how PMS should be defined or identified for diagnostic purposes, nor on what causes it and what is effective treatment. Despite this somewhat pessimistic summation, medical professionals and PMS sufferers concur in the belief that it would be premature to reject the PMS concept as having little utility for clinical and research purposes. For those women who suffer severe premenstrual distress and discomfort, the PMS concept, even with its shortcomings, provides an important validation of their experiences. Without having PMS as a way of naming premenstrual complaints, some women fear a return to the past neglect of women's health problems. How reasonable is such a position? Do the advantages of retaining the PMS label (or a similar diagnostic term) outweigh the disadvantages of working to develop a formulation of women's menstruation-related experiences that avoids the disease-laden connotations of PMS? To address these questions requires a closer examination of the assumptions implicit in the PMS concept.

What's in a Name?
PMS and the Politics of Labeling

The diagnostic label of PMS (or LLPDD) is gender-specific in that it can apply only to women. As Gallant and Hamilton (1988: 271) have pointed out, this gender-specificity immediately raises concerns about the potential for stigmatizing of women, who continue to be socially disadvantaged in relation to men. Furthermore, the PMS label is not neutral. By naming the disorder in terms of the menstrual cycle, women's reproductive biology is clearly seen as central to the problem. The label directs attention to internal bodily processes and in so doing encourages a downplaying of nonbiological, situational aspects of women's lives (Gallant and Hamilton, 1988: 274). Use of the PMS construct has the effect of taking women's problems out of context and isolating them from social reality, so that alternative nonbiological approaches to understanding women's experiences are less likely to be considered.

Availability of the PMS label as a way of accounting for some aspects of women's experience also encourages others (e.g., spouses, employers) to explain women's behaviour in biological terms. For instance, if a woman's behaviour is inconvenient to others, it can be explained away by PMS, thereby minimizing or ignoring the contributing role of others in interpersonal conflicts. Harrison, for example, cites the case of a husband who maintained that his wife was "fine for two weeks out of the month. She's friendly and a good wife. The house is clean. Then she ovulates and suddenly she's not happy about her life. She wants a job. She wants to go back to school. Then her period comes and she is all right again" (1984: 50). As this example clearly illustrates, use of the label PMS can further disempower women who already lack power in their everyday lives. According to Harrison (1984), the husband quoted above wanted his wife to receive medication so that she would be a "good wife" throughout her cycle.

If negative moods, irritability, and anger during the premenstrual and menstrual phases of a woman's cycle (up to two weeks of every month) can be construed as PMS symptoms, then any behaviour shown by a woman that is inconsistent with traditional views of femininity may be attributed to PMS. Thus, aspects of a woman's behaviour that conflict with stereotyped notions of passive, compliant, accommodating womanhood can be bracketed off from the rest of her behaviour and interpreted as symptoms of an illness. When such behaviour is perceived as irrational and out of control, the woman is denied responsibility for her actions. At the same time, the role of hormones in men's negative moods is never considered. In the operation of this double standard, women's moods require explanation while men's moods are given legitimacy as an authentic response to the situation.

The PMS construct also serves to separate women from each other. If premenstrual symptoms are seen as linked to female biology, there is little reason or inclination for women to share and compare experiences as a source of collective knowledge. When PMS is understood as an individual problem with biological origins, women are likely to believe that the most appropriate people with whom to share their experiences are doctors, not other women. In this way, the use of the PMS label to describe and explain some aspects of women's behaviour has the effect of dividing women from each other and from themselves. While viewed by some as a sign of progress in improving the quality of women's lives, on closer inspection the PMS label also functions to maintain, rather than challenge, women's disadvantaged position in society. To understand why the PMS label has so readily gained acceptance among women requires us to consider the more general phenomenon of the way women's bodies have become medicalized.

The Medicalization of Women's Bodies

The concept of medicalization "refers to the process and product of defining and treating human experiences as medical problems" (Bell, 1987: 153). Like pregnancy, childbirth, and menopause, menstruation — a normal biological process — has become part of the domain of biomedical science, to be managed by medical means. Although not an inevitable consequence of medicalization, one outcome of this medical control is that normal human processes are defined within a disease framework. Thus, in the medical conception of PMS, menstruation is not only seen as the cause of pathology (premenstrual symptoms) but itself becomes pathologized. The medical view of women's bodies implicitly takes male biology as the norm for human health. Against this male-biased standard, female reproductive biology, with its inherent cyclicity, is seen as deviant. Women's biological differences from men are recast in terms of illness or disease. In effect, the medical model reproduces women as deficient or dysfunctional men.

One consequence of this medicalization process is that women learn to blame their bodies for unwanted, unpleasant experiences. Since women are encouraged to understand their negative experiences as somehow originating in their bodily processes, it is hardly surprising that so many women have ambivalent feelings about their bodies and more particularly about menstruation. In the absence of alternatives to the dominant medical view of menstruation, women who experience severe premenstrual changes are likely to seek help for their complaints from the medical experts who claim special knowledge in understanding and treating such problems. Since resistance to the medicalized view of the female body can be achieved only by denying the reality of some women's experiences of menstruation-related changes, a woman's wish to have her experiences validated by a medical expert becomes understandable.

The central dilemma posed by PMS is this: how can we validate women's experiences and at the same time challenge the medicalized view of menstruation-related changes as symptoms of an underlying biological pathology? How can women reclaim their bodies from the grip of medicalizations, while avoiding the pitfalls of privileging either biological or social explanations for women's experiences in relation to menstruation (Ussher, 1989: 70)?

Reclaiming the Body

Much of our knowledge of women's menstruation-related experiences is secondhand. Women's accounts are first put through the lens of the medical perspective before emerging in refocused form in the professional literature as descriptions of "premenstrual symptoms." While this literature may provide some insight into premenstrual problems, it tells us little about how women in general experience menstruation. Only when women have a shared knowledge of what a normal woman, complete with normal menstrual cycles, is like will there be a basis for determining when there is deviation from a normal pattern (Laws, 1985: 49). Such woman-centred knowledge, properly disseminated would make possible the validation of women's experiences in their own right without deferring to a male-defined standard of normal human function. Also needed are new ways of naming women's experiences in relation to menstruation that are free of the negative connotations of PMS. According to Laws 1985: 45), an important part of this process of "collective self-discovery" is that all women, not just those for whom cyclical changes are problematic, need to discuss PMS as a political construct. Women need to understand how PMS functions ideologically to justify sexist beliefs (and the practices that stem from them) which masquerade as scientific knowledge about women.

Rejection of the PMS concept does not mean denying women help for their menstruation-related complaints. As Gallant and Hamilton (1988: 275) point out, clinicians can be sensitive to women's concerns without pathologizing their experiences as a mental disorder. In fact, the opportunity for personal growth and the development of coping skills is likely to be enhanced when a woman's experiences are not attributed solely to biological forces over which she has no control.

In conclusion, the struggle to reclaim the female body involves the development of more positive self-images in which female experiences of cyclicity are integrated as part of women's understanding of themselves as women. Affirmation of women's wholeness as both biological and social beings will be truly possible only when PMS is no longer a plausible answer to the question: What is wrong with women's lives?

Questions

1 Can PMS be compared to hysteria as a medical catchword designating women's "unreliability"?
2 Are there ways in which women's menstrual cycle might be construed or experienced as something positive?
3 Does the medicalization of women's normal reproductive functions result in more problems than it solves? Do female physicians make a difference?
4 In what ways might a feminist definition and analysis of PMS differ from a strictly medical approach?

References

American Psychiatric Association. 1987. *Diagnostic and Statistical Manual of Mental Disorders*. (3d ed., rev.). Washington, D.C.: American Psychiatric Press.

Ashurst, Pamela and Zaida Hall. 1989. *Understanding Women in Distress*. London: Tavistock/Routledge.

Bell, Susan. 1987. "Premenstrual Syndrome and the Medicalization of Menopause: A Sociological Perspective." Pp. 151–73 in Ginsburg and Carter (eds.), *Premenstrual Syndrome: Ethical and Legal Implications in a Biomedical Perspective*. New York: Plenum.

Cassara, Virginia. 1987. "A View From the Top of a Consumer Organization." Pp. 207–12 in Ginsburg and Carter (eds.), *Premenstrual Syndrome: Ethical and Legal Implications in a Biomedical Perspective*. New York: Plenum.

Dalton, Katherina. 1984. *Premenstrual Syndrome and Progesterone Therapy*. (2d ed.). London: Heinemann.

Delaney, Janice, Mary Jane Lupton, and Emily Toth. 1988. *The Curse: A Cultural History of Menstruation*. Urbana and Chicago: University of Illinois Press.

Eagan, Andrea. 1985. "The Selling of Premenstrual Syndrome: Who Profits from Making PMS 'the Disease of the 1980s'?" Pp. 80–9 in Laws, Hey, and Eagan (eds.), *Seeing Red: The Politics of Pre-Menstrual Tension.* London: Hutchinson.

Gallant, Sheryle and Jean Hamilton. 1988. "On a Premenstrual Psychiatric Diagnosis: What's in a Name?" *Professional Psychology: Research and Practice*, Vol. 19, No. 3: 271–8.

Golub, Sharon. 1983. *Lifting the Curse of Menstruation.* Binghamton, N.Y.: Haworth Press.

Harrison, Michelle. 1984. *Self-Help for Premenstrual Syndrome.* (Rev. ed.) Cambridge, Mass.: Matrix Press.

Hey, Valerie. 1985. "Getting Away with Murder: PMT and the Press." Pp. 65–79 in Laws, Hey, and Eagan (eds.), *Seeing Red: The Politics of Pre-Menstrual Tension.* London: Hutchinson.

Lander, Louise. 1988. *Images of Bleeding: Menstruation as Ideology.* New York: Orlando Press.

Laws, Sophie. 1985. "Who Needs PMT? A Feminist Approach to the Politics of Premenstrual Tension." Pp. 16–64 in Laws, Hey, and Eagan (eds.), *Seeing Red: The Politics of Pre-Menstrual Tension.* London: Hutchinson.

McFarland, Cathy, Michael Ross, and Nancy DeCourville. 1989. "Women's Theories of Menstruation and Biases in Recall of Menstrual Symptoms," *Journal of Personality and Social Psychology*, Vol. 57: 522–31.

McFarlane, Jessica, Carol Martin, and Tannis MacBeth Williams. 1988. "Mood Fluctuations: Women Versus Men and Menstrual Versus Other Cycles," *Psychology of Women Quarterly*, Vol. 12, No. 2: 201–23.

McFarlane, Jessica and Tannis MacBeth Williams. 1990. "The Enigma of Premenstrual Syndrome," *Canadian Psychology*, Vol. 31, No. 2: 95–108.

Ussher, Jane. 1989. *The Psychology of the Female Body.* London: Routledge.

Weideger, Paula. 1976. *Menstruation and Menopause: The Physiology and Psychology, the Myth and the Reality.* New York: Knopf.

Sexual Difference and the Law: Premenstrual Syndrome as Legal Defense

Kathy Kendall
Neuropsychiatric Research Unit
University of Saskatchewan

Building on the arguments presented by Stoppard, this paper places the medicalization of PMS in the larger context of the construction of women's bodily difference as defective or deficient. Through feminist deconstruction, the author links the problems associated with the legal practice of using PMS as criminal defense to the medical regulation of women. By revealing the political and economic motivations that govern the dominant view of PMS, the author makes us aware of the ways in which apparent attempts to help women overcome a specifically feminine problem may actually perpetuate broader structures of women's oppression.

"Equal" versus "Special" Treatment

In 1980, 1981, and 1988, much controversy surrounded three sensational British murder cases. Three women charged with murder had their charges reduced to manslaughter because the courts found that Premenstrual Syndrome (PMS) had diminished these women's responsibility for their actions. Despite the fact that the women were not simply acquitted, and that their releases were contingent upon receiving treatment, there was public uproar that these women had literally "gotten away with murder" (Sommer, 1984; Edwards, 1988). It is within this context that PMS has become a controversial issue within feminist discussions of justice for women. On one hand, acknowledgment of PMS as a factor in the commission of a crime may help to provide the defendant with a lighter sentence. On the other hand, legal recognition of PMS may contribute to sexist notions about women being at the "mercy of their raging hormones." Feminists are faced with the difficult question of whether to lobby the courts to recognize PMS as a defense to crime or as a mitigating factor in sentencing — a strategy which would give special treatment to women based upon their unique female functions — or whether feminist goals of justice would be better served by keeping PMS out of the courts. Thus, PMS is situated within broader debates concerning equal versus special treatment of women.

This paper explores current controversies surrounding PMS in feminist studies of justice. Beginning with an overview of cases that have been brought forward in the Canadian courts, we will examine the problems that arise when justice for women is posed in terms of biology: should women should be seen and treated as identical to, or as different from, men? What I shall suggest instead is that as feminists we should challenge, not reinforce, the ways in which women are currently categorized in and before the law. I shall deconstruct PMS as a "natural" category, linking its emergence to social and political rather than biological processes. In this way, I argue that feminist discourses on justice for women can transcend the narrow confines of patriarchal law designed to protect male control over women's bodies.

Premenstrual Syndrome in the Courts

The most sensational of the Canadian cases in which PMS has been entered by the defense occurred during 1987 and involved a woman who seriously assaulted her husband with a weapon. PMS evidence was a significant factor in determining her sentence; the defendant received three years' probation rather than imprisonment because the judge felt that the woman would not receive proper treatment for her PMS if incarcerated (Osborne, 1989; Sheehy, 1987). As unusual as this case may appear, it reflects determinations in earlier cases. In 1984, two Alberta provincial court judges considered PMS evidence in sentencing shoplifters. One woman found guilty of stealing $24 in food items was put on three years' probation, conditional on her receiving psychiatric care. The second defendant was acquitted, not because the judge accepted PMS as a disease but because evidence demonstrated that the woman was irrational and did not intend to shoplift. The judge did, however, note that the woman's state of mind may or may not have been caused by PMS (Fennell, 1984; Osborne, 1989). Gray (1981) briefly notes three 1981 eastern Canadian cases in which PMS was cited as the primary mitigating factor in sentencing two defendants charged with shoplifting and one defendant charged with assault, while a Victoria judge rejected PMS as a defense for failing to give a breath sample (*Vancouver Sun*, June 23, 1988).

Since PMS is by its very nature a defense which is only available to menstruating women, the feminist response to the use of PMS within the courts has been mixed. Those who advocate the use of PMS as a defense maintain that PMS should be treated as any other organic illness, and to deny this as a defense to a woman would be unjust (Chait, 1986; D'Emilio, 1985; Wallach and Rubin, 1971). Arguing from liberal premises, these feminists maintain that fears of misuse are unfounded because, with the erosion of sexism and the availability of treatment, the syndrome's most serious symptoms will fade. They believe that by limiting the use of the term PMS to only those women most severely affected by the syndrome, people will recognize that chronic PMS affects only a small number of women rather than women as a class. Feminists following this approach accept PMS as a "natural" category. Rather than challenging the existing legal framework, they choose to work within it. Feminists who do not support the use of PMS in the courts are more critical of the legal system and of PMS as a category. They argue that PMS could reinforce notions of women as being inferior to men, thus giving substance to and legitimating discriminatory practices both within the law and beyond it (Allen, 1984; Edwards, 1984, 1988; Laws, 1983). For example, Fausto-Sterling (1985: 5) notes that an American judge acquitted a dentist accused of rape and sodomy after the defendant held that the plaintiff had reported the incident during a period of premenstrual irrationality. In the unreported case of *In re H*, a British woman was denied custody of her child because it was claimed that she had PMS (D'Emilio, 1985). Likewise, a British Columbia Supreme Court judge considered a woman's PMS condition to be an important factor in denying her custody [*Babcock* v. *Babcock* (5 December 1986) New Westminister E001084 (B.C.S.C.)]. Those against the use of arguments based on PMS in the courts further regard it as a way to exert social control over women. The legal recognition of PMS as a disease may deflect attention from other social and economic causes of crime and could, more generally, invalidate women's actual and legitimate feelings of anger. For instance, both Christine English and Marsali Edwards suffered habitual abuse from the men they killed (Edwards, 1984; Laws, Hey and Eagan, 1985; Riessman, 1983). Finally, based upon their scrutiny of PMS research, these feminists point out that there is not enough empirical evidence to support a relationship between PMS and antisocial behaviour, including the commission of crime (Horney, 1978; Parlee, 1973, 1974), or to prove the existence of PMS at all (Holtzman, 1986).

Justice for Women: Sameness versus Difference

Feminist debate over PMS is part of a larger question about whether or not sexual difference should be legally acknowledged. Feminists conditioned by the classical liberal assumption that the only legitimate basis

for ascribing rights to persons is their ability to reason have historically argued that women's capacity to reason is at least equal to that of
men. This assertion has tended to downplay the significance of physiological differences between the sexes because the rationalist framework
sees such differences as irrelevant to the attainment of political rights
(Jaggar, 1990: 240). The downplay of sex differences has also been a
strategic move: feminists are well aware of a tradition of using biologically reductionist arguments to justify women's unequal status. As a
consequence, many have felt that more will be achieved for women if
biological differences between the sexes are de-emphasized or ignored.
In short, they believe that sex-blindness, or identical treatment between
men and women, is necessary to achieve sex equality (Williams, 1984).

The "sameness" approach toward equality has been challenged on a
number of points. Sheehy notes:

> that the model assumes the continued existence of the current social and
> political structure and necessarily measures "equal treatment" by pre-
> vailing norms and values. These norms have been shaped by a society
> that has historically oppressed women, and the norms are therefore male-
> defined. Thus women can advance and attain equal treatment and rewards
> only to the extent that they can mimic male career patterns and values.
> Women risk losing further ground under this model because when they
> fail to achieve "success" under the rule of identical treatment, it may be
> concluded that women really are inferior! (1987: 4)

Another problem with the sameness framework is that it does not recognize experiences that are specific to females. For example, women can
be denied rights and protections relating to pregnancy, such as maternity leave (Williams, 1984; Eisenstein, 1988). A third problem Sheehy
(1987) notes, is that the judiciary in Canada has applied the equality
model in such a way as to benefit male but not female litigants. Finally,
the rhetoric of gender neutrality obscures the real social and economic
inequalities facing women and tends to conceal the fact that men and
women have had very different histories, different assigned social roles
and "natures," and different degrees of access to power (Okin, 1989: 10).

Acknowledgement of the limitations and problems inherent in the
equality-sameness model has led a number of feminists to advocate recognition of women's difference within law. As Jaggar (1990: 241) notes,
these feminists have recalled the other side of the Aristotelian dictum:
"justice consists not only in treating like cases alike but in treating different cases differently." Sheehy (1987) identifies three models that accept
women's unique differences to varying degrees. The first approach advocates identical treatment with biological exceptions. This model is
closely aligned with the sameness approach, recognizing only women's

immutable biological differences — pregnancy and lactation — while ignoring all other social and economic differences between males and females. The second model holds that all policies and laws must be fashioned to take into account all variance between men and women, including physical, social, psychological, economic, and political differences. Finally, the subordination principle model identifies women's inequality in terms of their subordination to men rather than differences between them. Accordingly, laws and policies are assessed to see whether they contribute toward the subordination of women.

Each of these models has its own weaknesses and limitations. Taken together, however, the main concern is that legal recognition of female difference could be "as much a sword to be used against women as a shield to protect them" (Holtzman, 1986: 715). Many feminists have documented the ways in which women's reproductive capacities have been used against them to perpetuate and justify their subordinate status (Fausto-Sterling, 1985; Hubbard, Henifin, and Fried, 1979; Ehrenreich and English, 1978; Sayers, 1982). While feminists invoke difference to liberate women, support for the acknowledgement of difference could come from antifeminist factions such as sociobiologists who would use legislated sex differences against women. For example, Goldberg (1973: 93) writes that "men and women differ in their hormonal systems . . . every society demonstrates patriarchy, male dominance and male attainment. The thesis put forward here is that the hormonal renders the social inevitable." Further, there is the danger that legal policies derived from the acceptance of sex differences, purportedly designed for women's special protection, will have negative consequences for women. For instance, Williams notes:

> The protective labor legislation that limited the hours that women could work and barred them from certain dangerous occupations such as mining may have promoted their health and safety and guaranteed them more time with their families. But it also precluded them from others where the entry point was the night shift, and may have contributed to downward pressure on woman's wages by creating a surplus of women in the jobs they were permitted to hold. (1982: 196, n. 114)

A further difficulty with the difference approach is that it encourages us to think about women's bodies as all differing in the same way from the male body, seen as the patriarchal norm (see Eisenstein, 1988). It encourages us to regard all women as alike and to ignore differences between women, such as those attributable to race, class and sexual identity. The female body thus constructed as *the* feminist norm is white and heterosexual. Harding describes the double-bind of the "sameness versus difference" debate:

> Contemporary feminism does not embrace the goal of treating women "just like men" in public policy. So we need to articulate what these differences are. However, we fear that doing so feeds into sexual biological determinism . . . The problem is compounded when it is racial differences between women we want to articulate. How can we choose between maintaining that our biological differences ought to be recognized by public policy and insisting that biology is not destiny for either women or men? (1989: 32)

Rhode (1990: 197) maintains that in practice sexual differences have been both overvalued and overlooked by the courts. In some circumstances, the courts have turned biological difference into cultural imperatives. Either way, women's special situation has been completely ignored, difference is perceived as natural, and wider questions surrounding the social construction and consequences of difference are left unaddressed. For these reasons Smart (1989: 82) advocates that we escape the "sameness versus difference" debate. She argues that neither strategy can guarantee that it will not be harmful to women. Further, Smart criticizes both views as presuming men to be the norm against which women-as-equal or women-as-different are measured. Neither approach challenges the patriarchal power of law; instead, each attempts to find the most advantageous way of "squeezing the interests of women past the legislators and judiciary." Rather than limiting ourselves to the confines of debate, Smart advocates that feminists move to decentre law by deconstructing it and providing alternative discourses.

Beyond the Impasse of Equal or Different Treatment

Smart's interest in deconstruction is influenced by post-structuralist claims that there is no essential identity or "natural" core within the human subject (Alcoff, 1988: 415). Instead, post-structuralism asks how particular statements unite to construct what becomes understood as "human nature." Thus post-structuralism focuses on discourses as "systems of language, objects and practices." It implies a practice both of speech and action; who, it asks, speaks on a particular object or event, and when, where, and how? (Haug, 1987: 191). Post-structuralism directs us to an examination of practices that arise when the status of "truth" becomes affixed to the dominant discourse. Further, post-structuralists recognize that varying discourses are constantly competing for status and power, and that alternative discourses can become important foci of resistance.

Feminists have found much promise in this method of inquiry, which allows us to challenge patriarchal "truths" about women, including the inevitability of women's subordinate status. As a method, deconstruction allows us to question previously taken-for-granted assumptions and to recognize the political interests involved in them. It reminds us that just as discourse can be constructed, so can it be deconstructed, challenged and changed; as we become aware of the different ways in which meaning and practice are constructed, we can advance subversive alternatives. Thus feminists can engage in resistance by offering "discursive space from which the individual can resist dominant subject positions" (Weedon, 1987: 111).

Increasingly, feminist legal scholars are looking toward deconstruction as a useful method enabling them to move beyond grappling with the content of law toward focusing on the construction of meanings (Smart, 1989; Eisenstein, 1988). Smart (1989: 162) regards law as a "discourse which is able to refute and disregard alternative discourses and to claim a special place in the definition of events." Following this, she argues that feminists should first challenge the power of law by making visible the ways in which law operates to define meaning and practice, and second redefine these meanings and practices by providing alternatives. This implies that rather than accepting categories that currently frame legal practice, feminists must reveal the ways in which these categories, as claims to "truth" about women and sexual difference, are historical and cultural, not natural, constructs. In doing so, we will be able to link apparently natural — hence neutral — legal categories to the patriarchal control of women, of women's bodies. Debates concerning PMS provide feminists with the opportunity to examine processes whereby the patriarchal regulation of women is affected through law. Through this exercise in deconstruction, as feminists we can challenge law.

Deconstructing PMS

The term "premenstrual tension" was first used in 1929 by gynecologist Robert T. Frank in *The Female Sex Hormone*. In a subsequent paper, Frank (1931: 1054) described case studies of female patients experiencing a premenstrual feeling of "indescribable tension," "irritability," and "a desire to find relief by foolish and ill considered actions." PMS did not gain wide recognition, however, until Dr. Katherina Dalton became involved in its promotion. Recognized as the world's leading expert on PMS, Dalton has enthusiastically supported progesterone therapy as treatment for PMS and has served as witness for the defense in the three British murder cases previously mentioned. Dalton uses the term premenstrual syndrome to define "symptoms or complaints which regularly come just before or during menstruation but are absent at other times of the cycle" (Dalton, 1978: 26).

Since Dalton's coinage of the term, there has been a great deal of PMS research, most of which has been carried out within the medical model. Yet, as a recent review of the scientific literature on PMS concludes, despite large investments of time and money, there has been little progress made toward finding the cause of PMS or in developing successful treatment (McFarlane and Williams, 1990; see also Stoppard, this volume). This focus on methodological shortcomings, however, only further legitimates, rather than challenges, current approaches. By engaging in the debate on these terms, feminists are implicitly conceding that the guilt, legal responsibility, and punishment of female offenders can be decided simply by careful scrutiny of the scientific evidence (Allen, 1984: 31). Recognizing this, a number of feminist scholars not only question the methods employed by medical researchers but question PMS itself by putting it in its historical and political context. They have asked why "investigators feel compelled to seek evidence of menstrual debilitation" (Sommer, 1982: 110).

Recognizing that PMS was originally constructed as a medical disease and that physicians claim responsibility for its treatment, these feminists see PMS as part of the medicalization of women's bodies. A number of well-documented studies note that women's experiences have been medicalized more often than those of men and that medicine has concentrated upon women's reproductive processes as the center of female pathology (Ehrenreich and English, 1978; Penfold and Walker, 1983). Riessman (1983) outlines several reasons why women have been more susceptible than men to medicalization. First, women's biology matches closely with medicine's biomedical orientation. That is, visible markers of biological processes exist in women (such as menstruation, birth, and lactation) whereas they are more hidden in men. Second, women's social roles put them in contact with medicine more often than men. For example, many women have more contact with the family doctor because they function as the family health monitor, taking children to the doctor and often arranging their husbands' appointments. Since women frequent health services more often than men, they have more opportunity to report various symptoms of ill health. Further, women are more likely than men to report feelings of ill health because it is more culturally acceptable for them to do so. Finally, women's structural subordination to men has made them vulnerable to medicine's expansion. Patriarchal relations are then further replicated in the doctor-patient relationship.

Given women's biological, social, and psychological suitability to the biomedical model, medicine has been a powerful force in defining women's experiences. For this reason, it is important to dislodge medicine from its privileged position. This process can begin by exposing the historical conditions and political processes through which apparently "natural" categories — such as PMS — have been produced. The remainder of this chapter will deconstruct PMS, drawing upon the work of Conrad and Schneider (1980), who describe medicalization as occurring in five stages that take place in various arenas of contest. Both the stages and arenas of contest are interconnected in a dynamic process. Bell summarizes these stages:

> First, the prior designation of deviance to the behaviour in question; second, medical discovery of etiology and/or treatment; third, claimsmaking and counter-claimsmaking by professionals and nonprofessionals about the proposed medical definitions of the behaviour; fourth, a struggle for "ownership" of the problem; and fifth the institutionalization of the problem. The arenas of contest in which medicalization comes about include intraprofessional and interprofessional disputes, lay and public challenge to or support of medical definitions of the problem, and legislative politicking and court cases. (1987:154)

The first stage involves "the prior designation of deviance" to the condition in question. Both now and in the past, in Western society behaviour linked to the menstrual cycle has often been regarded as deviant (Weidger, 1976; Delaney, Lupton and Toth, 1976; Ussher, 1989). Edwards (1988) cites a number of nineteenth-century British trials involving women appearing on charges of violent assault, arson, and theft, in which the matter of menstruation was introduced by the defense. In her historical study of gynaecological operations on the insane in the Asylum for the Insane in London, Ont., Mitchinson (1980) notes that medical theories and practice linked women's reproductive systems to insanity. Negative beliefs surrounding the menstrual cycle continue to persist. Parlee (1974) found that male and female college students share stereotypes that associate menstruation with debilitation and negative moods, and Clarke and Ruble (1978) found similar assumptions among girls who have not yet menstruated and young adolescent boys. An American nationwide survey found that 35% of the 1,000 men and women interviewed felt that menstruation affects a woman's ability to think (Research and Forecasts, 1981: 8).

The second stage of medicalization, the discovery of a medical etiology, can be attributed to Frank (1931), who claimed that premenstrual tension was caused by an excess of estrogen. Norris (1987) points out that Frank's theoretical discovery coincided with the first advances made in medical research toward isolating estrogen.

There has a been a great deal of claimsmaking and counter-claims-making over the definition of the behaviour, the third stage of the process. As noted previously, there are a number of competing etiologies accounting for PMS. McFarlane and Williams (1990: 96) provide an extensive listing of the biomedical theories, some of which are: progesterone deficiency, excess aldosterone, deficiency of vitamin B_6, excess prostaglandins, and hypoglycemia. Psychological hypotheses have focused upon cognitive factors such as expectation and attribution (Koeske, 1987; Koeske and Koeske, 1975; Ruble, 1977; Bains and Slade, 1988) and various psychiatric disorders (Halbreich and Endicott, 1987; Hurt *et al.*, 1982; Kashiwagi, McClure, and Wetzel, 1976). Sociobiologists have forwarded their own theory, claiming that PMS is an evolutionary survival mechanism (Rosseinsky and Hall, 1974).

The fourth stage of medicalization, a struggle for "ownership" of the problem, is currently underway, with both intraprofessional and interprofessional contention over PMS. Professionals in gynaecology, endocrinology, psychiatry, psychology and law are competing over the etiology, treatment, and definition of PMS. Bell (1987: 155) states that at this stage "one is likely to find appeals to the ultimate arbiter of power and legitimacy, the state, to recognize and officially endorse the medical designation." It is here that medicine meets law. Law and medicine often have a symbiotic relationship, each deploying power from the other. Smart (1989: 96) purports that "legal and medical discourses have tended to make women no more than their bodily functions and processes, or bits of bodies." Taken together, these two institutions create powerful discourses which often reduce women to their reproductive processes.

The final stage of the medicalization process, the institutionalization of PMS, is presently occurring. The medical and legal hold over PMS is being strengthened by the encroachment of PMS into other institutions and realms of everyday experience. Currently, PMS is recognized by the Canadian justice system and, after much debate, was included in the *Diagnostic and Statistical Manual of Mental Disorders III-R* (see Stoppard, this volume). Presently it is being considered for inclusion in *DSM-IV*, which is expected to be released in 1994 (Adler, 1990). As Caplan (1987) notes, the *DSM* is a very important book, as its diagnoses are recognized by hospitals, insurance companies, and the courts.

The above overview allows us to see that PMS has been historically and socially constructed and that there has been considerable struggle over its meaning. An examination of the possible motives encouraging physicians to medicalize PMS reveals its political nature even further. Riessman (1983) contends that the coexistence of various market conditions may account for the motivation of medicine actively to create and gain control over new disease categories. To begin with, there is a declining birth rate. This means that there are fewer babies for gynaecologists to deliver, and new areas must be opened up in order to secure a successful and profitable practice. Further, there is a greater number of gynaecologists per capita today than ever before. And finally, as a result of the postwar baby boom, there are more women in their thirties and forties today than ever before: a large pool of women of appropriate age. Taken together, these three conditions — lower demand, increased supply, and clients of the appropriate age — could encourage gynaecologists to extend their domain by actively seeking out new disease entities.

Sayers (1982) and Martin (1987) believe that PMS research may have served historically to displace women from the labour force. They note that research showing the debilitating effects of menstruation proliferated after World Wars I and II and during the 1970s. These were all times when women made incursions into the labour force and when they appeared to pose an obstacle to the full employment of men. Given this pattern, it is not surprising that after the start of World War II, when women were needed in the paid work force, a great many studies concluded that menstruation was not an occupational liability. Laws (1983) suggests that the current preoccupation with PMS may be an antifeminist response to the contemporary women's movement, which has allowed women to make some advances both in and outside the labour force. In her analysis of the media, Parlee (1987: 199) found a number of 1970 and 1980 scientific and newspaper articles carrying the message that women are unfit for top occupations because of the "raging hormonal influences of the menstrual cycle."

At the same time, women are claiming the label of PMS and are seeking treatment for it. As one commentator stated: "women are now going public with their stories and demanding treatment — including the controversial natural progesterone therapy" (Gonzalez, 1981: 1393). It is important that we understand why women are adopting the PMS label. First, women are regularly told that their complaints are "all in their heads." The fact that physicians are recognizing PMS means that women's cyclical experiences will be acknowledged and opens up the possibility that attention will be paid to other aspects of women's lives (Riessman, 1983: 10). Second, the women's health movement may have encouraged women to be more assertive in demanding health care and treatment. Inspired by feminists urging women to take control over their bodies, a woman experiencing menstrual discomfort may seek help for the discomfort (*ibid.*). Further, women confront many stressors which lead to anger and other feelings typically associated with PMS. But women are typically socialized to believe that they should neither experience nor express these emotions. One of the few exceptions to this is during the PMS phase, when negative mood and behaviour are expected. Women may internalize cultural attitudes towards menstruation and express unpleasant moods and behaviour at a "legitimate" time — during the PMS phase — while attributing such expressions solely to biology. Pirie (1988: 642), for example, found that many of the women she interviewed "could only legitimate feelings of anger and frustration (largely arising out of dual career obligations) when they were understood to be biological rather than social relational responses."

Although individual women may find short-term benefit by claiming PMS, as a strategy to improve the social status of all women it may cause more harm in the long run. This is because even though the label of PMS permits women to be angry and express themselves at specific times during the month, it simultaneously "invalidates the content of their protest" (Riessman, 1983: 11). The earlier discussion on medicalization has shown us that medicine, based upon the biomedical model, will account for PMS simply in terms of an individual pathology. Individual women, rather than the fundamental structures of existing institutions that produce frustration, loneliness, and powerlessness, become the focus of inquiry. The prescribed treatment is individual change rather than social change. In a broader sense, women's oppression can become medically managed. "If women's reactions to oppression can be explained in terms of individual pathology, or as a function of feminine psychology, the objective facts of her oppression are obscured and need not be changed" (Penfold and Walker, 1983: vi).

Conclusion

Embedded in the larger debate over "sameness versus difference," the question of whether or not to use PMS as a defense in the courts has feminists at a standstill. One strategy to escape this double bind has been to challenge the power of law through deconstruction which reveals PMS to be a medical construct. Establishing PMS as a medical problem may benefit individual women, who may then use PMS in a legal defense, but the long term effect is to maintain and perpetuate women's oppression. By exposing the medical and legal discourses on PMS, we may be able to provide an alternative discourse. One alternative is to relocate women and their symptoms within their social environment. Our bodies must be understood as grounded in our physical existence but immersed in a wider social, political and economic system which mediates our experience of the body (Zita, 1989: 205). Any examination of women's bodies must therefore also consider women's social being, class, race, sexual orientation, and other factors. Within this framework, PMS cannot be regarded simply as a disease requiring chemical intervention but as an area of interplaying biological, social, and cognitive factors. Future feminist analyses should closely examine the relationship between race, class, sexual orientation, and PMS. Putting PMS into this context leads us to address the various dimensions of women's oppression and to see that remedies require extensive social transformation. Such an understanding would also radically transform the criminal justice system. If crime stems from social, political, and economic problems, then justice should be pursued through social transformation.

An immediate place to begin is to make alternative views of PMS accessible to women. For example, many feminist writers and organizations advocate dealing with PMS outside of mainstream medicine through self-help approaches. The Vancouver Women's Health Collective (1985) has produced a pamphlet which includes a section on the medicalization of PMS. The National Film Board's *What People Are Calling PMS* critically looks at medicine's approach to PMS. Resources such as these can encourage women to think more critically about PMS and can provide them with alternative ways of thinking about it.

Questions

1 What types of medical conditions should be acceptable as legal defense, for both men and women?
2 How can a special case be made for women on reproductive (anatomical) grounds without defining reproduction as women's primary social role? Can the arguments which might be used apply to men?
3 Should women's primary responsibility for childcare be taken into consideration when female offenders are sentenced?

References

Adler, Tina. 1990. "Causes, Cure of PMS Still Eludes Researchers," *American Psychological Association Monitor*, January: 10–2.

Alcoff, Linda. 1988. "Cultural Feminism Versus Post-Structuralism: The Identity Crisis in Feminist Theory," *Signs*, Vol. 13, No. 3: 405–36.

Allen, Hilary. 1984. "At the Mercy of Their Hormones," *M/F*, Vol. 9: 19–26.

Bains, G.K. and P. Slade. 1988. "Attributional Patterns, Moods, and the Menstrual Cycle," *Psychosomatic Medicine*, Vol. 47: 35–45.

Bell, Susan E. 1987. "Premenstrual Syndrome and the Medicalization of Menopause: A Sociological Perspective." Pp. 151–73 in Benson E. Ginsburg and Bonnie Frank Carter (eds.), *Premenstrual Syndrome. Ethical and Legal Implications in a Biomedical Perspective*. New York: Plenum Press.

Caplan, Paula. 1987. *The Myth of Women's Masochism*. Scarborough, Ontario: Signet.

Chait, Linda. 1986. "Premenstrual Syndrome and Our Sisters in Crime: Feminist Dilemma," *Women's Rights Law Reporter*, Vol. 9, Nos. 3/4: 267–93.

Clarke, A.E. and D.N. Ruble. 1978. "Young Adolescents' Beliefs Concerning Menstruation," *Child Development*, Vol. 29: 231–4.

Conrad, Peter and Joseph Schneider. 1980. *Deviance and Medicalization: From Badness to Sickness*. St. Louis: C.V. Mosby.

Dalton, Katherina. 1978. *Once A Month*. Great Britain: Fontana.

Delaney, Janice, Mary Jane Lupton, and Emily Toth. 1976. *The Curse: A Cultural History of Menstruation*. New York: E.P. Dutton.

D'Emilio, Joann. 1985. "Battered Woman's Syndrome and Premenstrual Syndrome: A Comparison of Their Possible Use As Defenses to Criminal Liability," *St. John's Law Review*, Vol. 59: 558–87.

Edwards, Susan. 1984. *Women on Trial*. Manchester: Manchester University Press.

Edwards, Susan. 1988. "Mad, Bad or Pre-Menstrual?" *New Law Journal*, July 1: 4568.

Ehrenreich, Barbara and Deidre English. 1978. *For Her Own Good — 150 Years of the Experts' Advice To Women*. Garden City, N.Y.: Anchor-Doubleday.

Eisenstein, Zillah. 1988. *The Female Body and the Law*. Berkeley: University of California Press.

Fausto-Sterling, Anne. 1985. *Myths of Gender: Biological Theories About Women and Men*. New York: Basic Books.

Fennell, T. 1984. "Premenstrual Shoplifting: Two PMS Illness Pleas Bring Justice With Mercy," *Alberta Report*, May: 30.

Frank, Robert T. 1931. "The Hormonal Causes of Premenstrual Tension," *Archives of Neurology and Psychiatry*, Vol. 26: 1053–7.

Frank, Robert T. 1929. *The Female Sex Hormone*. Baltimore, Md.: Charles C. Thomas.

Goldberg, Steve. 1973. *The Inevitability of Patriarchy*. New York: William Morrow.

Gonzalez, Elizabeth Rasche. 1981. "Premenstrual Syndrome: An Ancient Woe Deserving of Modern Scrutiny," *Journal of the American Medical Association*, Vol. 245, No. 14: 1393–6.

Gray, Charlotte. 1981. "Raging Female Hormones in the Courts," *Macleans*, 94, June 15: 46–8.

Halbreich, Uriel and Jean Endicott. 1987. "Dysphoric Premenstrual Changes: Are They Related to Affective Disorders?" In Benson E. Ginsburg and Bonnie Frank Carter (eds.), *Premenstrual Syndrome. Ethical and Legal Implications in a Biomedical Perspective*. New York: Plenum Press: 351–67.

Haug, Frigga. 1987. *Female Sexualization*. London: Verso.

Holtzman, Elizabeth. 1986. "Premenstrual Symptoms: No Legal Defense," *St. John's Law Review*, Vol. 60: 712–5.

Horney, Julie. 1978. "Menstrual Cycles and Criminal Responsibility," *Law and Human Behavior*, Vol. 2, No. 1: 25–35.

Hubbard, Ruth, Mary Sue Henifin and Barbara Fried (eds.). 1979. *Women Look at Biology Looking at Women*. Cambridge, Mass.: Schenkman.

Hurt, Stephen et al. 1982. "Psychopathology and the Menstrual Cycle." In Richard C. Friedman (ed.), *Behavior and the Menstrual Cycle*. New York: Marcel Dekker.

Jaggar, Alison. 1990. "Sexual Difference and Sexual Equality." In Deborah L. Rhode (ed.), *Theoretical Perspectives on Sexual Difference*. New Haven: Yale University Press.

Kashiwagi, T., J.N. McClure and R.D. Wetzel. 1976. "Premenstrual Affective Syndrome and Psychiatric Disorder," *Disorders of the Nervous System*, Vol. 37: 116–9.

Koeske, Randi Daimon. 1987. "Premenstrual Emotionality: Is Biology Destiny?" In Mary Roth Walsh (ed.), *The Psychology of Women*. New Haven: Yale University Press: 137–46.

Koeske, R.D. and G.F. Koeske. 1975. "An Attributional Approach to Moods and the Menstrual Cycle," *Journal of Personality and Social Psychology*, Vol. 31: 473–8.

Laws, Sophie. 1983. "The Sexual Politics of Pre-Menstrual Tension," *Women's Studies International Forum*, Vol. 6, No. 1: 19–31.

Laws, Sophie, Valerie Hey, and Andrea Eagan. 1985. *Seeing Red: The Politics of Pre-Menstrual Tension*. London: Hutchinson.

Martin, Emily. 1987. *The Woman in the Body*. Great Britain: Open University Press.

McFarlane, Jessica, Carol Lynn Martin, and Tannis MacBeth Williams. 1988. "Mood Fluctuations: Women Versus Men and Menstrual Versus Other Cycles," *Psychology of Women Quarterly*, Vol. 12: 201–23.

Mitchinson, Wendy. 1980. "Gynecological Operation on the Insane," *Archivaria*, Vol. 10: 125–44.

Norris, Ronald V. 1987. "Historical Development of Progesterone Therapy." In Benson E. Ginsburg and Bonnie Frank Carter (eds.), *Premenstrual Syndrome. Implications in a Biomedical Perspective*. New York: Plenum Press.

Okin, Susan Moller. 1989. *Justice, Gender and the Family*. New York: Basic Books.

Osborne, Judith. 1989. "Perspectives on Premenstrual Syndrome: Women, Law and Medicine," *Canadian Journal of Family Law*, Vol. 8: 165–84.

Parlee, Mary Brown. 1987. "Media Treatment of Premenstrual Syndrome." In Benson E. Ginsburg and Bonnie Frank Carter (eds.), *Premenstrual Syndrome. Ethical and Legal Implications in a Biomedical Perspective.* New York: Plenum Press: 189–205.

Parlee, Mary Brown. 1974. "Stereotypic Beliefs About Menstruation: A Methodological Note on the Moos Menstrual Distress Questionnaire and Some New Data," *Psychosomatic Medicine*, Vol. 36, No. 3 (May-June): 229–40.

Parlee, Mary Brown. 1973. "The Premenstrual Syndrome," *Psychological Bulletin*, Vol. 80, No. 6: 454–65.

Penfold, Susan and Gillian Walker. 1983. *Women and the Psychiatric Paradox.* Montreal: Eden Press.

Pirie, Marion. 1988. "Women and the Illness Role: Rethinking Feminist Theory," *Canadian Review of Sociology and Anthropology*, Vol. 25, No. 4: 628–48.

Research and Forecasts Inc. 1981. *The Tampax Report. Summary of Survey Results On a Study of Attitudes Towards Menstruation.* New York: Research and Forecasts, Inc.

Rhode, Deborah. 1990. *Theoretical Perspectives on Sexual Difference.* New Haven: Yale University Press.

Riessman, Catherine Kohler. 1983. "Women and Medicalization," *Social Policy*, Vol. 14: 3–18.

Rosseinsky, D.R. and P.G. Hall. 1974. "An Evolutionary Theory of Premenstrual Tension," *The Lancet*, October 26: 1024.

Ruble, Diane. 1977. "Premenstrual Symptoms: A Reinterpretation," *Science*, Vol. 197: 291–2.

Sayers, Janet. 1982. *Biological Politics.* London: Tavistock Publications.

Sheehy, Elizabeth A. 1987. *Personal Autonomy and the Criminal Law: Emerging Issues for Women.* Ottawa: Canadian Advisory Council on the Status of Women.

Smart, Carol. 1989. *Feminism and the Power of Law.* London: Routledge.

Sommer, Barbara. 1984. "PMS in the Courts: Are All Women on Trial?" *Psychology Today*, August: 36–8.

Sommer, Barabara. 1982. "Cognitive Behavior and the Menstrual Cycle" In Richard C. Friedman (ed.), *Behavior and the Menstrual Cycle.* New York: Marcel Dekker.

Ussher, Jane. 1989. *The Psychology of the Female Body.* New York: Routledge.

Vancouver Women's Health Collective. 1985. *Premenstrual Syndrome: A Self Help Approach.* Vancouver.

Wallach, Aleta and Larry Rubin. 1971. "The Premenstrual Syndrome and Criminal Responsibility," *UCLA Law Review*, Vol. 19: 209–312.

Weedon, Chris. 1987. *Feminist Practice and Poststructuralist Theory.* New York: Basil Blackwell.

Weidger, Paula. 1976. *Menstruation and Menopause.* New York: Knopf.

Williams, Wendy. 1982. "The Equality Crisis: Some Reflections on Culture, Courts, and Feminism," *Women's Rights Law Reporter*, Vol. 7, No. 3.

Williams, Wendy. 1984–85. "Equality's Riddle: Pregnancy and the Equal Treatment/Special Treatment Debate," *New York University Review of Law and Social Change*, Vol. 13: 325–80.

Zita, Jacquelyn. 1989. "The 'Premenstrual Syndrome': Diseasing the Female Cycle." In N. Tuana (ed.), *Feminism and Science*. Bloomington: Indiana University Press.

Assessing Reproductive Wrongs:
A Feminist Social Work Perspective

Kelly E. Maier
Women's Studies
Simon Fraser University

From a social work perspective, new reproductive technologies raise difficult questions concerning the conditions that justify intervention by the State when women's rights are presented as being in opposition to those of the unborn child. While the notion of fetal rights has been discussed primarily during debates on abortion, it also surfaces during medical intervention into childbirth. Maier examines two recent cases in which decision-making by the mother was overridden by medical authorities and social work practitioners acting "on behalf of the unborn child." Although the principle of the primacy of women's rights was eventually upheld by the relevant Supreme Courts, these cases dramatize the tenuous nature of women's control over their bodies. Taking a feminist perspective, Maier critically assesses the role which social workers should play in upholding the rights of women against patriarchal interests in reproduction.

Reproductive Rights — and Wrongs

The purpose of this chapter is to analyze what I call "reproductive wrongs" from a feminist social work perspective. In the title I use the term "assessing" for several reasons. First, assessment accurately describes what a social work practitioner does. Second, what follows from assessment in social work practice is a plan of action, or intervention strategy. My hope is that a critical assessment of reproductive wrongs will lead to practical action. Feminist social workers *should* and hopefully *will* engage in the urgent task and ongoing process of assessing reproductive wrongs and taking action to stop them. In a profession in which females predominate as both workers and clients, few issues have more potential to illuminate both what women have in common and the diversities of oppression which women experience on the basis of race and socio-economic class (see Hanmer and Statham, 1989: 7–21). Undoubtedly, reproductive issues will become increasingly complex in the next decade as reproductive technologies make possible social arrangements previously unthought of and, quite literally, inconceivable (see CRIAW, 1989; Overall, 1989). Unravelling these complex issues and developing strategies for change from a feminist perspective is a major challenge for women in the 1990s.

What do I mean by reproductive wrongs? Simply, I am referring to violations against women because of their assumed or actual ability to become pregnant — the fact of their having wombs. Thus defined, reproductive violation is a form of violence against women and of female-gendered injustice, that is, discrimination on the basis of being female. As women we are still defined socially, medically, and legally by our assigned sex-role status derived from our biology — in this case, our having wombs. Most at risk for reproductive violations will be women who are marginalized or disenfranchised because of their race, class, ethnicity, sexual orientation, or marital status. Reproductive violation can be understood as a continuum which includes, at one end, overt reproductive violence, and, at the other, reproductive harassment.[1] Reproductive violation is more specific than, yet clearly a part of, the spectrum of violence against women.[2] In this paper I shall discuss two cases of reproductive wrongs which illustrate reproductive violence against women: the Baby R case in British Columbia and the Angela Carder case in Washington, D.C. Both highlight the patriarchal control of pregnant women, and both represent forms of reproductive violation.[3] These cases bring into sharp focus the exercise of patriarchal control of women's bodies and the wrongs done to individual women because of their reproductive capacity and pregnant condition.

The Case of Baby R

On May 20, 1987, a pregnant woman, "Rose," arrived at the Grace Hospital in Vancouver, B.C., in premature labour. She was told by the attending obstetrician that her fetus was in a footling breech position and advised that "the best course of action was the standard management option of a caesarean section" (Brighouse, 1987: 1). Rose disagreed, stating that she had given birth vaginally on four previous occasions. This disagreement with the attending obstetrician led to the eventual apprehension of Rose's fetus. Understanding that Rose "would have to be committed before surgery could be performed without her consent" (Brighouse, 1987: 13), the physician attempted to obtain a psychiatric assessment to determine if the provision of "diminished responsibility" under the Mental Health Act could be applied. Clearly, psychiatric commitment for this purpose would have been a misuse of the Mental Health Act which, by law, may be invoked to impose only psychiatric, not medical, treatment.

When this line of action failed the obstetrician declared the fetus to be a "child" who, he claimed, was in need of protection; the social worker was then legally mandated to investigate. After reviewing Rose's past social history, and under the direction of the Superintendent of Family and Child Services and legal advisors to the Ministry of Social Services, the social worker apprehended Rose's unborn fetus — an unprecedented event in this province. This action required a finding that the fetus was "a child in need of protection" under the Family and Child Services Act. Through it, the social worker gave the obstetrician verbal consent for medical care of the fetus but not for any medical procedures to be performed on the pregnant woman (Brighouse, 1987: 1; Davis, 1987: 1). After viewing the ultrasound showing her fetus in a footling breech position, Rose verbally agreed to the caesarean section. She was six hours into labour and "consented" while being wheeled to the operating room (MacDonell, 1988:3–4).

As in the case of all apprehensions by Family and Child Services, the case of Baby R was heard by the Provincial Court of British Columbia, from July 13 to 16, 1987. The focus at this hearing was on Rose's social welfare history in the child welfare records. These records noted the apprehensions of Rose's four other children, her past mental health problems, her limited parenting skills, unpredictable and inappropriate behaviour, and inability to keep appointments. The doctor declared Rose's fetus to be a child "in the process of being born." The judge accepted the doctor's definition, declaring that "This is not a case of Women's rights . . . . This is simply a case to determine what is best for the safety and well being of this child" (Davis 1987: 6). In the court's view, Rose's negative social welfare history legitimated the apprehension. The preoccupation by the Court and attendant media coverage with Rose's background obscured the critical question: did her refusal to undergo a caesarean section constitute child abuse under the Family and Child Services Act? The reasons for judgement of the lower court did not at any point attempt to answer this question.[4]

I am not arguing that the "best interest of the child" principle, which child protection social workers are bound by, should be set aside, nor am I arguing that Baby R ought to have remained in Rose's care after birth. To focus on either of these issues is to ignore the central issue: Rose's right to bodily integrity, that is, her security of the person, and the coercive violation of her basic human rights under the guise of child protection. Caregivers have an obligation to obtain patients' informed consent for *any* medical treatment: "to be legally adequate, a patient's informed consent must be competent, knowing and voluntary" (Raines, 1984: 598; see also Englehardt, 1985; Jurow and Paul, 1984). A person's fundamental right to refuse medical treatment is well established in law; yet Rose's initial refusal of the caesarean section resulted in the case becoming one of child protection, which it clearly was not.

It is patently clear from the circumstances of this case that Rose's consent was far from free, as it was demanded with the threat of apprehending her fetus. Nor was her consent full, as she offered verbal agreement to the procedure only while being wheeled into the operating room. The question of how informed her consent was remains unclear; how adequately patients are given information is an issue unresolved in other cases of disagreement between physician and patient.[5] In Rose's case the legality of her consent was completely overlooked, as were the ethics of the doctor's actions. Rose's past history of poor parenting was used to justify the violation of her human rights. Rose was a pregnant female patient who disagreed with a prestigious obstetrician. She was non-compliant and for this she paid a heavy price. The social rationale used to justify the apprehension of Baby R shows how the most marginalized, powerless groups in society are most at risk and most vulnerable to enforced medical procedures — reproductive violations by another name.

The Case of Angela Carder

Reproductive wrongs are not confined to Canada. In the United States, reproductive violations are shocking in both their frequency and severity. A recent example is Angela Carder in Washington, D.C. Angela Carder's 14-year struggle with leukemia abruptly ended in June 1987, "two days after George Washington University Hospital performed a court-ordered Caesarean section over the objections of her family, her doctors and the lawyer appointed to represent her" (Gellman 1990: A1, A2). Angela was 27 years old when she died; the 26-and-a-half-week old fetus, given primacy of patient rights by the hospital administration, died two and a half hours after being forcibly extracted from its mother. Not only was Angela Carder denied treatment for her cancer, she was operated on against her will in "the best interests of the fetus." The caesarean section was considered to be a significant factor in her death two days later (Gellman, 1990). Control over Angela Carder's life was in the hands of the legal and medical professionals who were driven by the hospital administration to decide that her life could be sacrificed for that of her fetus. She was denied her most fundamental right to refuse medical treatment at the same time that she was denied the medical treatment she required to combat active cancer (NAWL, 1989: 13; see Sherman, 1989). When her fetus was attributed "personhood" rights in order to deny her own rights, Carder was subjected to reproductive violence. Angela's parents are suing the doctor and the hospital for medical malpractice and the case, in addition to being appealed, raises the question of the constitutionality of court-ordered caesarean sections in the United States.

On April 26, 1990 the Carder case was heard by the District of Columbia's highest court. Overturning the lower court decision, the D.C. Court of Appeals ruled "that a pregnant woman has a virtually unlimited right to decide the course of medical treatment for herself and her fetus" (*Vancouver Sun*, April 27, 1990; *Globe and Mail*, April 27, 1990; Gellman, 1990). Writing for the majority (which had a surprising seven-to-one margin) Judge John A. Terry stated that "the right of bodily integrity is not extinguished simply because someone is ill, or even at death's door" (Gellman, 1990: A1). The Carder decision is described as the leading precedent in American law on the question of whether a woman's right to care can be balanced against the interests of her fetus.

While the finding in this case — that pregnant women's constitutional rights to life, liberty and security of the person are being violated by court-ordered caesarean sections — gives some hope for the campaign for women's reproductive autonomy, it does not mitigate the fact that Angela Carder is dead and that the taking of her life should be called murder. Moreover, the hospital administration responsible for initiating this action — the self-appointed guardians of the fetus — should be held accountable. And finally, the question remains as to why such a significant case for women's reproductive and human rights has been so notably unreported in the media.

The Issue of Obstetrical Intervention

Many people, including social workers, hold the belief that physicians are experts and thus know best. In fact, the notion of a "good" patient is a compliant patient[6] in the paternalistic and patriarchal practice of medicine. Contrary to this conventional wisdom, however, a great deal of medical evidence, as well as a considerable body of feminist literature,[7] indicate that placing unquestioned faith in physicians is both unwise and unwarranted: physicians not only often disagree about the appropriateness of obstetric interventions, but they are often wrong. For this reason, blind trust in doctors may not only be misplaced but dangerous. For example, not so long ago physicians prescribed thalidomide and diethylstylbestrol (DES) for pregnant women. The consequences of both have been tragic; thalidomide was found to cause skeletal defects in fetuses, and DES was linked to vaginal and cervical cancer in the daughters and infertility in both the daughters and sons of women who took it (Greer, 1987). DES was prescribed to pregnant women for "normal" pregnancies, to prevent miscarriage and for what the pharmaceutical companies promised would be "bigger and better" babies (Greer, 1987:8).

A caesarean section is a major operation that poses significant medical risks of morbidity and mortality to a pregnant woman. Nonetheless, an increasing number of caesarean sections are being performed in Canada and the United States for a variety of non-medical reasons. What is more, in eleven American states over a six-year period from 1981 to 1987, the courts have forced women to undergo surgery — either caesarean operations or surgery on the fetus in utero (Furman-Seaborg, 1987: 9). In the first five cases in which caesarean sections were sought, the women subsequently delivered vaginally and uneventfully (Annas, 1987: 1213). In Canada, courts in two provinces have sought court injunctions — in British Columbia to force a pregnant women to undergo surgery, and in Ontario to detain a pregnant woman in hospital. In both cases the fetuses were apprehended using child welfare legislation. The trend for doctors increasingly to treat fetuses as their primary patients and for the legal system to treat pregnant women as criminals (NAWL, 1989; Rodgers, 1989) is frightening and becoming all too common (Sherman, 1989). Pregnant women are being forced to have caesarean sections; they are being detained in hospitals (Kolder *et al.*, 1987); they are even being prosecuted for "contributing to the delinquency of minors" when using drugs (*Times-Colonist*, May 10, 1989; *Times-Colonist*, Aug. 6, 1989; *Vernon Daily News*, Oct. 12, 1989). These types of actions and the underlying logic which make them possible graphically illustrate the "disembodiment" of pregnant women; they both admit and deny pregnant women's unique physical state vis-à-vis the fetuses they carry.[8] Furthermore, they highlight the impossibility of balancing women's rights and fetal rights (see Maier, 1988, 1989; NAWL, 1989). In essence, the state's interest in fetal well-being is rapidly undermining the rights of individual pregnant women.

In patriarchal medicine, pregnancy has been transformed from a condition that once carried an almost mystical status to one fraught with perils (see Greer, 1984). The risks of pregnancy for women have broadened beyond known medical risks to include risks associated with social class. Women with the least power and who are the most oppressed by virtue of their socioeconomic or racial status are the most vulnerable to having their fetuses apprehended or their pregnancies policed. In the United States, almost all the pregnant women involved in the reported physician-initiated court actions have been black, Asian, or Hispanic; almost half were unmarried; a quarter did not speak English as their first language; and all were poor (Kolder *et al.*, 1987: 1195). In Canada, both cases of fetal apprehensions involved socioeconomically marginalized women who were uncompliant patients. Overall, pregnant women are being forced to be "splendid Samaritans" (Zimmerman, 1987) at the same time as they are being denied access to abortions and basic material resources, such as an adequate guaranteed annual income necessary to maintain a minimal standard of living. These cases of reproductive violence reflect a profound distrust of and hostility toward women and are part of the patriarchal regulation of women's reproductive lives (see Ontario Coalition for Abortion Clinics, 1988; Rodgers, 1989).

Implications for a Feminist Social Work Practice

> No less than welfare or public housing, child protection plays a critical role in "regulating the poor." The poor are to be inspected, exhorted and disciplined when they fail to measure up to middle-class norms. The apprehension of their children is but one more coercive tool to keep them quiet, submissive and insecure. (Thompson, 1986: 58–9)

In the Baby R case, a social worker was used as an instrument of the state to infringe on a pregnant woman's human rights under the auspices of child protection. Child protection legislation was misused and the mandate of the social worker was seriously distorted. Much of the mainstream media discussion of the Baby R case further obscured the underlying issues, making it difficult to see who was abusing whom. While the stated reason for apprehending Baby R was to ensure that the caesarean section could be performed — purportedly necessary for the fetus's survival — this was clearly not the *bona fide* reason. If it were, the child would not have remained in custody after Rose consented to the surgery. In 1988 the Supreme Court of British Columbia found the apprehension of Baby R to be illegal (MacDonell, 1988), yet the child was never returned to his mother, on the grounds that Rose had no contact with the child while in care. This reasoning, I would argue, is a thinly disguised form of state entrapment.

In the future, social workers may increasingly be directed by policy or legislation to take similar actions (see NAWL, 1989).[9] If the state is permitted to use social workers as officers responsible for policing the health of the unborn, who — and from what gender, race, and class — will decide what constitutes fetal abuse or neglect? In the case of fetuses, what will "minimal standards" mean? Clearly, the best way to protect and care for the well-being of fetuses is to ensure that pregnant women have adequate material resources and supports before, during, and after pregnancy; access to education about pregnancy; and above all else, true choice about life options, which should include but not be limited to mothering (see Levine and Estable, 1981). An absolute prerequisite for this is a society in which all women have socioeconomic security and reproductive choices. Protection of the fetus is, however, unlikely to take this form. Therefore it is important to ask ourselves as social workers who, or what, is really being protected in these cases?

As I argue above, the real issue is not fetal well-being but rather control of women's bodies. Since we are told that this is not only justifiable, but *necessary*, pregnant women are increasingly being treated as a "suspicious/risk" group (see Terry, 1989). Moreover, by attributing rights to fetuses that can then be used to violate pregnant women's fundamental human rights, the white, male-dominated fetal-protection racket threatens the integrity of every woman. When we, as social workers, become part of that racket, we violate our ethical principals and our professional integrity, and, what is worse, we potentially alienate ourselves from women. From a feminist perspective, we are faced with a dilemma: do we act as agents of social change and advocate the rights and dignity of all persons, or do we limit our roles to being agents of the state and simply enforce these new restrictions imposed on women? If we participate or are silenced, we comply in the reproductive violation of women as a social group.

The above cases raise certain questions for me as a feminist social worker. I want to ask: What role, if any, did the social workers play? Perhaps more importantly, how did the social work departments in each case view the actions of the hospitals and medical professionals? If the social work departments *agreed* with the declaration of the fetus as primary patient, how would this be reconciled with the central mandate of social workers in medical settings, which is to act as a patient and family advocate? From an ethical standpoint, how does the social work profession view this case and other related cases? And finally, why are social workers nowhere to be found in the commentary on such cases, which have profound implications for women's health and welfare and human rights (see Dale and Foster, 1986)? I also want to understand more clearly how the reasons given by the lower court were used to justify these abuses, as this rationale will undoubtedly have enormous implications for the issue of consent, central to women's reproductive rights issues and the assessment of reproductive wrongs. The lower court reasoned that it was "unclear what the heavily sedated Ms Carder wanted done with the fetus" (*Globe and Mail*, April 27, 1990) in spite of the fact that the patient, her family and her doctors did not consent to the operation (see Sherman, 1989; NAWL, 1989: 13). As one legal reporter aptly put it: the lower court finding in the Angela Carder case is a pyrrhic victory for the hospital and courts (Sherman, 1989). The question that remains unexamined is whether these actions against Rose and Angela Carder are anything other than blatant examples of legislated and legitimated reproductive violence against women.[10] It is my hope that discussion and critical analysis of these cases will come from the ranks of the social work profession.

Conclusion

In British Columbia, the case of Baby R was a frightening example of the state flexing its muscles against a pregnant woman's prerogative to say "no" to a physician. Angela Carder's accelerated death in Washington D.C. was the direct result of medical-legal intervention to save the fetus she carried, a decision taken without consideration for her life. Both cases illustrate the patriarchal control of women's bodies and are reproductive violations. As a society, we are at a crisis; we are seeing the state's interest in the well-being of fetuses supersede concern for the well-being of women, and male interest in fetuses as their property create a social and political climate in which a carefully orchestrated battle between the rights of fetuses and the rights of women is being staged. Yet the debate is really not about the well-being of fetuses at all: it is about male control over women. It is about denying women reproductive choice. It is about enforced motherhood. My concern is that the present construction of reproductive issues as "women's rights versus fetal rights" distorts the reality of the condition of pregnancy, literally and ideologically disembodying pregnant women as people in their own right.

The ongoing debate about when a fetus is viable and entitled to the rights of a person has pitted ethical and moral arguments in favour of the rights of fetuses against those that advocate women's rights to equality of medical treatment. As a social historian, Linda Gordon, noted:

> The attribution of human rights to the fetus . . . repeats nineteenth-century anti-birth control views which, . . . confounded abortion with contraception. This is not to deny the existence of moral issues about embryonic life. But right-to-life advocates do not usually fight for "life" in any systematic way. (1979: 30)

The notion of maternal culpability and the practice of reproductive violation is part of the current "social production" of woman-specific ills (see Walters, 1990). If women do not willingly go along with this idealized, sacrificial model of femaleness, the state's actions force them to;

these policies and practices go unnoticed and unexamined in the social work literature, perhaps because as a profession our relationship to the state is both too close and too uncritical.

Social workers have a significant role to play in the debates about reproductive wrongs, as well as the actions necessary to end them. This requires that we shed the cloak of conservativism and reassert our role as advocates for human rights, client self-determination and social justice for all people. We must challenge the notion that it is "unprofessional" to name, confront and challenge the existing social and political arrangements that ultimately oppress women as a social group (see Marchant, 1986). Given that health and welfare are the domain of social work, and that the majority of Canadian social work practitioners are employed in health-care settings (Erickson and Erickson, 1989) where many of the worst incidents of reproductive violation occur, social workers are particularly well situated to intervene on behalf of women whose voices are being silenced and whose rights and bodies are being violated. Without a feminist perspective in social work, problems will continue to be assessed from a male-centered, or worse, misogynist point of view. If social work interventions are to go beyond reinforcing existing forms of discrimination, definitions of client problems must be reconsidered and social work interventions recast within a model of feminist praxis. Not only do social workers need to examine the politics of reproduction and motherhood, we must also be watchdogs and critically reframe the construction of cases and issues with the purpose of examining or reassessing the reproductive wrongs and violations against women — whether they occur in the form of harassment or outright violence — in order to take concerted action to end them.

Notes

An earlier version of this work, "Pregnant Women: Fetal Containers or People With Rights?" was published in *Affilia: Journal of Women and Social Work*, Vol. 4, No. 2 (May): 8–20.

1 The term "reproductive harassment" is one which I use to specify a type of violation women experience because of their female sex in the context of a society stratified by sex, class, and race. An example is the necessity for women to ceaselessly fight for abortion rights, as evidenced by Bill C-43 (proposing to recriminalize abortion).

2 I am thinking of all the acts, attitudes and images of violence against females as we experience and name them, from rape and murder to misogyny and pornography.

3 Other recent cases challenging women's reproductive autonomy such as the well-publicized Chantal Daigle and Barbara Dodd cases, though not discussed in this work (see Hardy, 1989), are significant to note because they can easily be situated at the harassment end of the spectrum of reproductive violation.

4 The mother of Baby R petitioned the Supreme Court of British Columbia to review the lower court decision. The feminist organization LEAF was granted intervenor status at the hearing which took place during June 1988. At this time, the main issue under consideration was whether an unborn child is a child within the meaning of the Family and Child Services Act, which would then grant the Superintendent of Social Services and Housing authority to apprehend. On August 5, 1988, the B.C. Supreme Court set the apprehension order aside, finding the apprehension unlawful and without jurisdiction. The court held that a fetus is not a child/person and that the apprehension was a specific interference with the rights of the pregnant woman.

5 For example see Bonavoglia (1987). In this case charges of murder were laid against Pamela Rae Stewart for failing to follow her doctor's orders.

6 See Rosser (1988) for a discussion of enforced patient compliance and of the general resistance to feminism in health care settings.

7 For a critical medical commentary on the fallibility of doctors' judgements in the context of the increasing incidents of court-ordered obstetrical interventions, see Kolder *et al.* (1987) and Annas (1987). For an especially rich source of historical documentation see Ehrenreich and English (1978), a classic feminist critique of patriarchal medical practice.

8 See Canadian Research Institute for the Advancement of Women (1989) for a comprehensive overview of the issues and questions embedded in debates about reproductive technologies: also Overall (1989).

9 If this seems far-fetched, consider that while the Baby R case was under appeal in the courts the Ministry of Social Services issued a directive, which could be called an *ad hoc* fetal protection policy, instructing social workers to consider a fetus a child under the Family and Child Services Act if a doctor declared it to be so.

10 Angela Carder's mother, Ms. Stoner, is proceeding with two lawsuits against the hospital and judge who, she believes, murdered her daughter for the sake of a fetus (see Sherman, 1989).

Questions

1 Would the media coverage of the Baby R case have been substantially different if the mother had been a well-educated, middle-class woman with a record of "good" parenting?

2 Would the discussion of the case of Baby R be different if the baby had died?

3 What is the relevance of the above questions? Are there any conditions when the State should override women's decision-making? What role should social workers take in decisions about reproduction?

4 How does the issue of reproductive wrongs illustrate the claim by McCannell, McCarthy and Herringer that most social policy aimed at women has been designed explicitly to benefit them in their capacity as wives and mothers and those who depend upon them in these roles?

References

Affilia (eds.). 1990. "On the Bias," *Affilia: Journal of Women and Social Work*, Vol. 5, No. 1: 97–102.

Annas, George J. 1987. "Protecting the Liberty of Pregnant Patients," *The New England Journal of Medicine*, Vol. 316, No. 19 (May): 1213–4.

Bonavoglia, Angela. 1987. "Reproductive Rights: The Ordeal of Pamela Rae Stewart," *Ms Magazine*, Vol. 16, Nos. 1/2 (July/August): 92–204.

Brighouse, Pat. 1987. "The Taking of Baby R," *Out of Line*, Vol. 2, No. 6 (August): 1, 4.

Canadian Research Institute for the Advancement of Women (eds.). 1989. *Reproductive Technologies and Women: A Research Tool*. Ottawa: CRIAW/ ICREF.

Dale, Jennifer and Peggy Foster. 1986. *Feminists and State Welfare*. London: Routledge and Kegan Paul.

Davis, B.K. 1987. "Reasons for Judgement in the Provincial Court of British Columbia," *Vancouver Registry*, No. 876215 (Sept.): 1–6.

Englehardt, H. Jr. 1985. "Current Controversies in Obstetrics: Wrongful Life and Forced Fetal Surgical Procedures," *American Journal of Obstetrics and Gynecology*, February: 313–7.

Ehrenreich, Barbara and Deirdre English. 1978. *For Her Own Good: 150 Years of the Experts' Advice to Women*. New York: Anchor Press.

Erickson, Rebecca and Gerald Erickson. 1989. "An Overview of Social Work Practice in Health Care Settings." In Holosko and Taylor (eds.), *Social Work Practice in Health Care Settings*. Toronto: Canadian Scholars Press.

Furman-Seaborg, Joan. 1987. "The Fetus as Patient, the Woman as Incubator." Unpublished paper presented to the Third International Interdisciplinary Congress on Women (June), Trinity College, University of Dublin, Ireland.

Gellman, Barton. 1990. "D.C. Court: Mother's Rights Outrank Fetus'," *The Virginian Pilots*, April 27: A1, A2.

Gordon, Linda. 1979. "The Struggle for Reproductive Freedom: Three Stages in Feminism." In Z. Eisenstein (ed.), *Capitalist Patriarchy and the Case For Socialist Feminism*. New York: Monthly Review Press.

Greer, Germaine. 1984. *Sex and Destiny: The Politics of Human Fertility*. London: Picador.

Hanmer, Jalna and Daphne Statham. 1989. *Women and Social Work: Towards a Woman-Centered Practice*. Chicago: Lyceum Books.

Hardy, Leslie. 1989. "A Matter of Control," *Leaflines: Women's Legal Education and Action Fund*, Vol. 3, No. 1: 1–5.

Jurow, Ronna and Richard Paul. 1984. "Cesarean Delivery for Fetal Distress Without Maternal Consent," *Obstetrics and Gynecology*, Vol. 63, No. 4 (April): 596–8.

Kolder, Veronika, Janet Gallagher, and Michael Parsons. 1987. "Court-Ordered Obstetrical Interventions," *New England Journal of Medicine*, Vol. 316, No. 19 (May): 1192–6.

Levine, Helen and Alma Estable. 1981. *The Power Politics of Motherhood: A Feminist Critique of Theory and Practice*. Ottawa: Centre for Social Welfare Studies, Carleton University.

MacDonell, J. 1988. "Reasons for Judgement in the Supreme Court of British Columbia," *Vancouver Registry*, No. A872532, (Aug.): 1–14.

Maier, Kelly E. 1988. "Do Fetal Containers Have Human Rights: A Feminist Social Work Perspective on the 'Baby R' Case," *Resources for Feminist Research*, Vol. 17, No. 3 (Nov.): 119–23.

Maier, Kelly E. 1989. "Pregnant Women: Fetal Containers or People with Rights?" *Affilia: Journal of Women and Social Work*, Vol. 4, No. 2 (May): 8–20.

Maier, Kelly E. 1990. "Assessing Reproductive Wrongs: A Feminist Social Work Perspective," Paper presented to the Canadian Women's Studies Association at the Learned Societies Meetings, (May) University of Victoria, B.C.; also part of a panel presentation to the conference "Moving Forward: Creating a Feminist Agenda for the Future," Trent University, Peterborough, Ont.

Marchant, Helen. 1986. "Gender, Systems Thinking and Radical Social Work." Pp. 14–32 in Marchant and Wearing (eds.), *Gender Reclaimed: Women in Social Work*. Sydney, Aust.: Hale and Iremonger.

Marchant, Helen and Betsy Wearing (eds.). 1986. *Gender Reclaimed: Women in Social Work*. Sydney, Aust.: Hale and Iremonger.

National Association of Women and the Law, Working Group on Health and Reproductive Issues. 1989. *A Response to Crimes Against the Foetus*. The Law Reform Commission of Canada, Working Paper #58. Ottawa: NAWL.

Ontario Coalition for Abortion Clinics. 1988. "State Power and the Struggle for Reproductive Freedom: The Campaign for Free-Standing Abortion Clinics in Ontario," *Resources for Feminist Research*, Vol. 17, No. 3: 109–14.

Overall, Christine (ed.). 1989. *The Future of Human Reproduction*. Toronto: Women's Press.

Rodgers, Sandra. 1989. "Pregnancy as Justification for Loss of Judicial Autonomy." Pp. 174–81 in C. Overall (ed.), *The Future of Human Reproduction.* Toronto: Women's Press.

Sherman, Rorie. 1989. "Forced Caesarean: A Pyrrhic Victory, a Court Battle," *The National Law Journal,* Jan. 16: 3, 22.

St. Peter, Christine. 1989. "Hopes and Dangers: Women Look at the Future of Reproduction." Pp. 1–11 in *Reproductive Technologies and Women: A Research Tool.* Ottawa: Canadian Research Institute for the Advancement of Women (CRIAW/ICREF).

Terry, Jennifer. 1989. "The Body Invaded: Medical Surveillance of Woman as Reproducers," *The Socialist Review,* Vol. 3: 12–43.

Walters, Vivienne. 1990. "Beyond Medical and Academic Agendas: Lay Perspectives and Priorities." Unpublished paper presented to the Canadian Sociology and Anthropology Association Conference at the Annual Learned Societies' Meetings (May) University of Victoria, B.C.

Women's Legal Education and Action Fund. 1988. "Memorandum of Argument in the Supreme Court of British Columbia," *Vancouver Registry,* No. A872582: 1–36.

Zimmerman, David. 1987. "Forcing Women to be Splendid Samaritans: Moral Doubts About Court-Ordered Obstetrical Intervention." *In a Word: Essays in Honour of Steven Davis.* Burnaby: Philosophy Department Special Publication, Simon Fraser University.

Newspapers

Globe and Mail. April 27, 1990. "Court backs pregnant women."

Times-Colonist. Aug. 6, 1989. "Infant dies causing epidemic of prosecutions."

Times-Colonist. May 10, 1989. "Mother charged as cocaine-full baby dies."

Vancouver Sun. April 27, 1990. "Course of medical treatment ruled up to pregnant woman."

Vernon Daily News. Oct. 12, 1989. "Police jail pregnant women for giving cocaine to minors."

Risky Business:
Medical Definitions of Pregnancy

Anne Quéniart
Département de sociologie
Université du Québec à Montréal

New reproductive technologies have transformed the perception of pregnancy by pregnant women themselves, as demonstrated in a study conducted by the author with pregnant women in Montreal. The focus here is on change in the definition of risk in pregnancy. This definition has shifted from an emphasis on risk to the mother to a preoccupation by both medical professionals and pregnant women with the potential risks to the fetus. We see an increasing tendency to hold the woman responsible for the quality of the "product" of pregnancy, while neglecting other influencing factors and issues related to women's own well-being.

Studying Maternity

Although most areas of women's lives have been neglected by traditional research, one thoroughly investigated aspect of women's lives in western societies is that supposedly privileged time of maternity. Although subject to medical authority, maternity is also the object of social and economic policies — budgetary projections, for example — as well as being central to many contemporary discourses (theological, scientific, and feminist). Quite surprisingly, though, we know very little about the way women live and feel pregnancy. Indeed, despite an abundant literature (sociological,[1] biomedical, popular) on maternity, there is little concerning what pregnant women experience. This lack prompted my study that attempts to understand maternity (the phenomenon) from within; that is, from the point of view of pregnant women. How do they experience their pregnancies? How do they perceive the various changes in their bodies? How much do they know about the new technologies of prenatal diagnosis? What meanings do they give to this event? These were among the basic questions addressed in a qualitative study that I carried out in Montreal among forty-eight women undergoing their first pregnancy.

Beyond the necessity of understanding maternity from within was the need to consider pregnancy in its multiple dimensions: social, affective, physical. Therefore, I borrowed an "integrating perspective" from ethnologists and anthropologists that would not split the lived experiences of pregnancy and delivery from the societal factors on which they rely, the norms and values to which they are related, and the institutional structures surrounding these events. Moreover, and again to avoid reducing maternity to its organic and biological components, I considered it as a social fact, as the intersection of a particular relationship of a woman to her body, with science, medical technology and other people. This would allow me to comprehend how the social can interact with the physical body, and how affective factors are related to social ones.[2]

The methodology used for the study was suitable for the development of "grounded theory" (Glaser and Strauss, 1967). It therefore required a qualitative approach, both flexible and adaptable, that could capture the inner dimension of the very complex experience we label as pregnancy. A series of in-depth interviews were carried out with forty-eight primiparous white women from Montreal who had given birth in hospital.[3] The women ranged in age from 19 to 40 years, and all were married or living with the father of the child. Their mean education level was 15.1 years of schooling. About half were currently working outside the home in white collar, semi-professional, or professional occupations. The remaining women mostly defined themselves as homemakers, although some were currently unemployed or students. To supplement the interviews, I also made systematic observations of four groups of women attending prenatal classes for a period of four months. The fifty women in these classes (also from Montreal) had sociodemographic characteristics similar to those of the women interviewed.[4]

This chapter examines the women's retrospective perceptions and experiences of the first few months of pregnancy. I will describe the increasing prevalence of a newly emerging concept of 'prevention' held by these pregnant women. This concept centres around the idea of risk which creates an obsession with 'normality' and which seems to drive women to extremes in order to obtain reassurance about their pregnancies. More generally, we will see how the medicalization of maternity, which has led to the hospitalization of birthing mothers and the increasing use of obstetrical technology, has now taken a new direction. Thus, a new process has begun to shape the experiences of women to such a degree that it reaches into their very physical being, as well as that of the child to be. This new medical intrusion in the life of women may be diffuse, but it is certainly insidious, legitimating its interventions and its discourse not only in the name of science, as it has up to now, but in the name of the fetus itself (Renaud *et al.*, 1987; De Koninck, 1988).

Pregnancy: A 'Risky Business'?

Pregnancy is a time of paradox. We claim that it is a natural female function — that it is women's normal role to bear and raise children. But we are also quick to see pregnancy as a risky experience and, through a subtle and revealing semantic slippage, give the entire responsibility for the risk status of a pregnancy to the woman herself. This process labels some pregnant women as being in a "high-risk" category; or more precisely, a high-risk pregnancy category.

In order to understand fully this shift in perception of pregnancy from a natural to a risky process, we must go back to the 18th and 19th centuries in France, when a wave of "populationism" (a phenomenon fostered by a slight birthrate decrease) drove physicians to undertake initiatives in reproduction, an area traditionally reserved to women[5] (Gélis, 1984; Laget, 1977, Ehrenreich and English, 1982). To assert their legitimacy, physicians defined pregnancy and childbirth as potentially pathological events, establishing the strange equation: "normal = unusual." Given the purported threat that pregnancy and childbirth represented to both mother and the newborn, physicians thus declared themselves essential. Thanks to their imposing array of scientific knowledge and, even more importantly, the range of technological instruments such as forceps, crochets, and levers that midwives were forbidden to use, only the physician was deemed able to "save" birthing women and their babies (Gélis, 1984). It is the perception of childbirth as a "potentially pathological phenomenon" that continues to legitimate the role of physicians in women's lives today (Arms, 1978; Scully, 1980).

With the increasing medicalization of life in the 20th century, especially with respect to reproduction, two shifts in emphasis have taken place. Firstly, we have moved from focusing on existing pathology to looking for potential problems through the notion of risk factors. Secondly, and more recently, the intrinsic risk of pregnancy has been transferred from the mother to the fetus (Renaud, 1987; De Koninck, 1987). It is no longer the mother or the pregnancy that is considered at risk, but rather the baby is perceived as encountering various risks during pregnancy (Autrement, 1985).

This preoccupation with the fetus is by no means new: it emerged gradually throughout the first quarter of the century. Some see it as a consequence of the shift from home birth to hospital birth, and with increased intervention during the process of childbirth, for example episiotomies and Caesarian sections (Shorter, 1984; Scully, 1980). What is relatively new, however, is how this preoccupation is now being applied to the very first moments of conception, if not earlier. This is true, not only for physicians but also for the public at large, especially following publicity surrounding the new reproductive technologies.

The Prevalence of the Risk Factor Ideology

Now more than ever, the growing interest in the fetus has come to be expressed in what I have labelled the "risk factor ideology." This can be defined as the set of doctrines that legitimate new social behaviours, constructing objective conditions of danger in order to justify new modes of intervention (Castel, 1983: 123). In other words, the risk factor ideology is based upon a substantial logic which aims, through various discourses and practices, both to legitimate insecurity (by giving specific meaning to it) and to prevent it. Present in all areas of social life, the ideology is part of new preventive strategies that have developed over the last few years (not without certain links to the state's economic divestment in the area of social policies). These strategies, while reinforcing individual responsibility, also, quite paradoxically, emphasize statistical correlations between heterogeneous elements, rather than give consideration to the individuals involved (Castel, 1983: 125). Moreover, the notion of risk factors is developing apart from that of danger: a risk does not result from the presence of a danger but is "caused by the relationship between abstract data or factors that render the undesirable events more or less prone to happen" (Castel, 1983: 122). As adopted by the health-care system, this perspective leads to the labelling of "high risk populations," in the same way that we speak of risky sectors of the economy or high-risk children in education.

It is in this way that one begins to estimate the level of risk to a fetus during pregnancy. More precisely, it is not just the mother's genetic background, but other variables such as age, weight, blood pressure, overall health, etc., as well as data related to personal habits and lifestyle, that are used to create multiple categories among pregnant women: namely, those at risk (read "those whose *fetus* is at risk") — be it high or low — and those who aren't. Moreover — and this is the insidious side effect of preventative strategies developed to deal with these risks — although the overall risk to the fetus depends on many different factors, only one of these — maternal behaviour — is mentioned in the literature and the written press. Women are being warned only against the evils of tobacco, alcohol, or "bad nutritional habits," not about broader environmental factors that may be risky.

In other words, discourses on "risk factors" tend to give all responsibility for the baby's proper development to the woman, focusing only on the impact her lifestyle can have on her future newborn's health. Forgotten — or at least receiving less emphasis — are the other factors which may also have consequences on the fetus, such as second-hand tobacco smoke.[6] We also tend to omit any potentially harmful effects that the environment (work schedule, type of work, stress, pollution) can have on fetal development, directly or indirectly, by affecting the mother's health.[7] In other words, and without debating the relevance of any of the scientific claims, I want to underline the fact that, too often, other factors (physical, social, genetic) that may have genuine consequences on the pregnancy but that cannot be controlled by women are simply put aside.

The Obsession with Normality

Throughout all the interviews with women in their first months of pregnancy, most displayed acute insecurity. This feeling can be mostly attributed to the increasing importance of the "risk factor" discourse. All of my subjects had been extremely receptive to it, to such a degree that certain women, for example, felt guilty about smoking or drinking alcohol in the first stages of their pregnancy, even though they were not aware at the time of being pregnant:

> During my whole pregnancy I kept worrying for my baby because before I knew I was pregnant, I went to a party and had quite a lot to drink. You tend to become very paranoid with all that's being said about what will happen to the baby if you drink and smoke during the first three months of pregnancy. They say your kid can be simple-minded. You get very scared about that. (Micheline, 32 years)

Moreover, while the initial insecurity of these women is quite understandable, given that this is their first pregnancy, it grows into a genuine obsession with normality under the pressure of the "risk factor ideology":

> I felt a lot of anxiety. First of all, will my kid be OK, normal? Will it be handicapped? Will it have everything? Then, will it be intelligent enough? What if it isn't a normal baby? What if it's missing something? (Delphine, age 24)

If there are any questions about the "normality" of the "product" — meaning the end result of the pregnancy, the baby — there must also be a great deal of questioning about the normality of the pregnancy process itself. Everything that we experience can be medically evaluated, and some women turned to "popular" medical literature as a point of reference. Today written information tends to replace the earlier oral tradition of knowledge passed from mothers to daughters (Morin, 1982). Women consult this literature not only for information, however, but for a point of reference, to compare their experiences with the medical 'ideal type' of pregnancy. This comparison, in turn, allows the pregnant woman who experiences symptoms similar to those described in the medical literature to reduce their importance, simply dismissing them as "normal" even though they may in fact indicate a real problem:

> I can say I had quite a normal beginning of pregnancy. I experienced some bleeding but apparently it's normal, well, I read somewhere it's caused by blood vessels. I was a bit worried about having a miscarriage but everything went well. If doctors say it's normal for some women then I suppose it's OK . . . That's what I kept telling myself. (Catherine, age 26)

The prevailing notion of normality can reach a point where it obscures, perhaps inappropriately, alarming symptoms of the body. Ultimately, the women's physical experience is subordinated to a medical ideology. Moreover, when women experience symptoms other than those depicted in the medical literature, or when they fail to find information concerning their specific case, they come to perceive their symptoms as problematic:

> In the beginning, I had problems. I lost blood and panicked because when you're pregnant you're not supposed to have your period, right? . . . and nothing about that was ever mentioned in the book. On the contrary, it was written that when you're pregnant, you stop having your period. (Dominique, age 32)

What we notice in these women is that their concerns arise from the lack of a normative definition. In other words, abnormality no longer stays within the boundaries of the clearly stated but glides over to the area of the un-said, the undefined. Everything happens as though uncertainty is no longer tolerable. That is what I consider to be a side-effect of the process of the medicalization of maternity: a process that focuses women's imagination on the distinction between "normal" and "abnormal"; a process presenting "normality" as being the only valid parameter of women's experiences.

Fear that something might happen to the baby or that it might be abnormal, a recurring concern throughout the interview, is emphasized by the women's lack of knowledge about where danger starts and where it stops: the normative area surrounding pregnancy continues to expand. Furthermore, the fear seems to be linked to, or at least increased by, the very mode of transmission of the risk factor ideology: a "suggestion/dissuasion" basis rather than a formal interdiction (Baudrillard,

1983). Consequently, women develop a sense of personal responsibility and self-blame instead of collective responsibility and social sanction. For example, pregnant women are not *forbidden* to smoke cigarettes or drink alcohol; rather, they are shown the potentially harmful consequences of those behaviours. The interiorization of social constraints ends up being supported and reinforced by that very process of psychological assimilation.

Moreover, research about normality has invaded the personal experience of pregnant women to such an extent that they are ultimately considered to be *the* responsible agent. Indeed, some of the women surveyed (those who are age 35 and older) were particularly insecure. According to my analysis, this stems from the unveiled association the medical profession has created between maternal age and the risk of genetic disorders, especially Down's Syndrome:

> Because of my age I was really scared about having a mongoloid baby. You can tell yourself that as soon as you reach 35 the risk increases exponentially. I used to visualize where the curve would bring me at age 40 and tell myself "God, at that age we're not talking about 'chance' anymore but about 'risk,' a genuine risk of one out of every 200, or something like that!" (Marie, age 40)

Although the relationship between a woman's age and Down's Syndrome is well established, we must remember that until recently the medical establishment largely ignored the possibility of a relationship to father's age: "the correlations linked to the mother's age too often neglect the fact that the father is very often older" (Postel-Vinay, 1985: 20–2). The earlier omission of men from statistical research demonstrates eloquently the dominant medical perception that the pregnant woman alone is responsible for the future child from the very first moments of conception, as does the continuing omission of "socioenvironmental" variables from much of the current literature. Such reductionism inheres in the risk-factor ideology, and thus strongly reinforces it.

A Need for Certainty at Any Price

It is not surprising that women feel the need for reassurance at all costs even if it means — and herein is another paradox — taking risks. The medical logic here is quite insidious: putting the emphasis on risks for the fetus in the first three months plays on the delicate feeling of fear and especially the sense of responsibility women can feel toward another being. In presenting obstetrical techniques as a means to remedy or correct risks, doctors are almost guaranteed the woman's favourable response. This is what filters through several of the interviews, with some subjects expressing the desire to get a test at the very beginning in order to know whether the baby is normal:[8]

> I'm all in favour of the tests to know if your baby is going to be normal. If it can reassure some women, then why reject it? There are quite enough worries in the first months. A friend of mine had an amniocentesis test and I think she had a better experience than I did. With that test you already know if everything is normal. It looks like pretty soon we're even going to be able to know the size of the baby, the colour of its eyes. Just by taking a test similar to the pap test. . . . amazing. (Myriam, age 22)

Moreover, many women are ready to undergo some risks in order to avoid others that seem to be more threatening. Their testimony concerning the amniocentesis test is revealing. Those who underwent it feel privileged to be informed very early that their baby is probably normal (even though only certain abnormalities can be detected). Even knowing the miscarriage risk that the test creates, they claim that "it is worth taking a chance in order to be sure the baby is normal." The others perceive the test as a privilege they have not been granted. They claim that given the choice, they would gladly take it because they want to be reassured.

Several testimonies show a gradual shift from one technique to another (Vandelac, 1985), minimizing the danger of tests that were considered very risky in the past (such as amniocentesis) or giving everyone some test that was once reserved for only very special cases (such as ultrasound). Among my subjects, only a few had an ultrasound scan because of pregnancy-related complications; the vast majority had a "routine" ultrasound just to be on the "safe side." For example, one woman claimed that "my doctor told me [that] we do it to see if the placenta is well located and to see whether there are any malformations with the fetus," while another respondent indicated that her doctor preferred her to have the ultrasound test "just to be sure everything was OK and also to reassure me." It would be most difficult for a woman imbued with the risk factor-ideology to refuse an ultrasound, when it is presented as a way to detect any deformities. Without questioning the medical (technical) efficiency of ultrasound, we should nevertheless wonder about the lack of adequate information given to women regarding the actual rate of fetal deformities or about the potential risks related to ultrasound exposure for fetal development (Braun and Valentini, 1984).[9] How can one choose when all of the parameters are not available? The use of ultrasound clearly shows the insidious way in which the medical profession suggests and channels choice (Barel, 1982).

In this regard, we must also question the ways in which technology and biomedical research, while continuing to make real advances, allow us either to "discover" more and more new risks or to label as risky what used to be considered natural. For example, women used to be advised to consume a great amount of milk in order to guarantee their intake of calcium as an essential element for fetal development: they are now being warned that too much milk can severely hinder the absorption of calcium. Thus, women are now advised to lower their milk consumption to one pint instead of one quart a day.[10] This broader definition of what constitutes risk creates, by the same token, new categories of women. To the categories of "high-risk" and "low-risk" women, the *Williams Obstetrics* added the new category of "growing risk" to their 1985 edition. Finally, or rather consequently, the normative field surrounding pregnancy never ceases to broaden as the boundaries of pathology continually expand:

> We thus reach the paradoxical situation where pregnancy is more than ever perceived as being a "risky business" in a context where, surprisingly, the mortality rate plunges to an all-time low and where we now have greater knowledge and tools that aim at further reducing even that mortality. (Renaud *et al.*, 1987: 199)

Subtle Social Control

Finally, the pernicious effect of the risk factor ideology and more generally of the preventive strategies surrounding the phenomenon of pregnancy lies in their failure to acknowledge how social control is being exerted. In this regard, my analysis clearly illustrates what is happening on a macro-sociological level in advanced industrial societies. Current policies concerning risk prevention are part of the psychologization of the modalities of the socialization process (Lipovetsky, 1983); they clearly reflect the replacement of direct forms of control by less obvious indirect ones (Barel, 1982), the development of various new choices, all in the name of growth and progress. This leads some people to say that the contemporary malaise is partly derived from the difficulties linked to the inflation of choice. The whole phenomenon of maternity is a good example. Women are currently facing, or rather are being forced to face, a growing number of choices (Katz Rothman, 1984). Thanks to contraception, we can now choose whether or not to have children, how many to have, when to have them, and (once pregnant) to continue or end the pregnancy, or to give the baby up for adoption. Some — not all — of us can choose where and how we will give birth. We may also choose the type of physician who will follow us through the process (female,

male, generalist, specialist). We are given the choice of undergoing ultrasound at the third or sixth month of pregnancy; sometimes we will
have to choose or refuse amniocentesis and, if the results indicate genetic problems, we may then choose to abort the pregnancy. Soon we
may be able to select the sex of the baby and, should a diagnostician's
"error" occur, we could again choose abortion. We may also someday be
able to choose between the anxiety of those risky first three months of
pregnancy or the comforting reassurance of a risk-free incubator for the
fetus. In other words, with the growing expansion of pregnancy-related
knowledge and techniques, choices are being offered and new needs are
being created.

The question remains whether these choices translate into greater
freedom for women. It might appear that the earlier submission to destiny and nature will be replaced by a growing dependence on science;
but it is likely that women will remain unaware of the limitations of this
science and of the socioeconomic forces that underlie it. It is in this
context that one could say that there occurs, during the first months
of pregnancy, a management of women's bodies in order to improve the
quality of their "product" — the child (Tabet, 1985). This control of the
body also means, in a more dubious way, the control of women. Indeed,
medical expertise today is no longer strictly centered around the mother
but rather around the fetus. The latter is becoming increasingly more
autonomous and, as outlined by Maier (this volume), is gradually being
perceived as the primary patient.

A Reduction in the Meaning of Pregnancy

It must not be assumed that in considering risk factor ideology I intend to
deny any of the possible effects of certain habits of pregnant women (such
as the abuse of tobacco or alcohol) on the newborn (lower birth weight,
for example). Rather, I want to question the way in which discourses on
risk factors and their related social effects are being conveyed. In this
respect, even though our knowledge of risks is based on established relationships between them, individual factors alone are generally presented
to women in the lay literature and the media, usually out of context.
This results, as we have seen, in the total loss of control over pregnancy
discourses by the subject who is not qualified to fully grasp the medical aspects of pregnancy and giving birth. Furthermore, the risk factor
ideology increases the growing concern about the fetus by reinforcing
women's exclusive responsibility for it throughout the pregnancy, thus
enhancing the "good mother" mystique, which states that the mother's
interests and personal needs should automatically be second to those of
her offspring (Friedan, 1964; Oakley, 1980, 1984). Furthermore, by this

use of risk factor ideology, those surrounding the women (spouse, parents, friends) may themselves tend to reinforce the shift of importance from the woman to the fetus. Throughout pregnancy this concern with the child-to-be-born is being reinforced by the use of various tests such as ultrasound, which tend to see the woman's body as a container for the uterus and to look through it, at the fetus. The same applies to medical consultations in which only the belly — as the intermediary to the fetus — is probed, touched, and observed. For many of those interviewed, this very dismissal of the women themselves, to focus on what is in their womb, creates a feeling of being less important than the baby, of being "ignored," "neglected," of being "merely the one who's bearing the child." This may explain, in part, the acute feeling of solitude that many respondents talked about.

More generally, this solitude seems to be due to both the process of "decollectivization" of the experience of pregnancy and to the failure to grasp it as a whole. Indeed, simultaneously with the medicalization of pregnancy, there has been a strengthening of its privatization, both concretely and symbolically. Being pregnant (and then giving birth) is increasingly becoming a private matter that takes place between a woman and her physician, in a relationship increasingly mediated by technology. Maternity as a social, collective process is losing ground. Therefore, in delegating birth-related matters to "experts" we are contributing to the reduction of pregnancy and childbirth to their merely biomedical dimensions and to putting aside the expectations and socioaffective experiences of both women and men.

In conclusion, the discourses about risk factors surrounding the phenomenon of maternity clearly reflect characteristics of our modern political system. There is a noticeable increase of "therapeutic work spreading widely to all social activities to such a point that we are forced to use medical metaphors in order to identify various social problems" (Jeudy, 1984). For example, we must "cure the illnesses" of the "social body," "heal" the "wounds" emerging from social conflicts. Furthermore, and particularly true for maternity:

> A great hygienic utopia plays on the sensitive chords of fear and security in order to impose the perverse rationality, the absolute reign of pragmatic reason and the no less absolute power of its agents, technocrats, planners, administrators of the happiness of life where nothing ever happens. (Castel, 1983: 123–4)

Notes

I gratefully acknowledge the competent and free help of Patricia Jobin who translated this paper from French. I wish to record my thanks also to Abby Lippman and Stephen Schecter who critically read the manuscript and improved the English.

1 See Ann Oakley (1980, 1984) and Barbara Katz Rothman (1984).

2 This research, conducted between 1983 and 1987, led to the preparation of my PhD dissertation (Quéniart, 1987) and ultimately to the publication of my book (Quéniart, 1988).

3 The interviews with the women, which lasted approximately two and one-half hours, were conducted four months after giving birth.

4 These observations were made at the Community Health Department of the Maisonneuve-Rosemont Hospital where I was working as a researcher.

5 Let us not forget that in France the word "accoucheur" (here loosely translated as "child deliverer") appeared only in 1677, and that in Great Britain this category of specialist was referred to as "male-midwives."

6 On the "depolitization" of health problems by making them the fault of individuals, see Crawford (1980).

7 In Quebec, though, it has been recognized since 1981 that working can involve some risks for the pregnant woman. Therefore an occupational health and safety decree has been issued under the title "The right to an early withdrawal from work for the pregnant woman and the nursing mother." This measure ensures a woman the right to withdraw early from her usual position at work if this work involves any health risks or hazards (ergonomical, biological, chemical, physical) for the woman or the child-to-be. The employer is therefore under the obligation to "reassign" to other functions any woman taking advantage of that right. When no such reassignment is possible, the woman may cease working until she gives birth and she may benefit from the program put forward by the CSST (Commission of Health and Safety at Work) that provides her with as much as 90% of her regular net salary. What is interesting about this measure is the way it recognizes precisely the fact that some tasks or even whole labour structures (for example, night shifts) may involve some risks for the fetus (Quéniart, 1986). It thus asserts positively the genuine possibility of any environmental impact on the pregnancy or health status of the fetus, thereby distinguishing itself from the dominant discourses (or rather, the most prevalent ones) on the risk factors solely centered around women's behaviour.

8 Within the present framework I cannot develop the thesis on the relationship between women and technology. For further details on that specific topic, see Quéniart (1987, 1988); Katz Rothman (1984); and De Koninck (1988).

9 While ultrasound does have its proper uses — checking for *spina bifida* or the presence of twins, for example — most women do not seem to know

that the technique can diagnose only gross abnormalities or that it poses some risks to the fetus.

10 Those examples were related by Renaud *et al.* (1987: 206) in their analysis of *Williams Obstetrics*.

Questions

1 Infant mortality rates in developed countries have decreased dramatically during the past century. Is this decrease attributable to the increased medicalization of childbirth?

2 What motivations lie behind the increased use of tests to determine the "normality" of the fetus?

3 What do the interviews in this chapter tell us about the ways in which the body itself is a cultural construct?

4 What do the interviews described in this chapter tell us about taking women's experiences as the "unmediated truth" about women's lives?

References

Arms, Suzanne. 1978. *Immaculate Deception: A New Look at Women and Childbirth in America*. Boston: Houghton Mifflin.

Barel, Yves. 1982. *La Marginalité sociale*. Paris: PUF.

Baudrillard, Jean. 1983. *Les Stratégies fatales*. Paris: Grasset.

Braun, Françoise and Hélène Valentini. 1984. "Échographie: un examen au-dessus de tout soupçon?" *L'Une à l'autre (la revue de Naissance-Renaissance)*, Vol. 1, No. 2 (printemps): 7–9.

Castel, Robert. 1983. "De la dangerosité au risque," *Actes de la recherche en sciences sociales*, Nos. 47–48 (juin): 119–27.

Crawford, Robert. 1980. " 'C'est de ta faute': l'idéologie de la culpabilisation de la victime et ses applications dans les politiques de santé." Pp. 481–512 in Bozzini, Renaud, *et al.* (eds.), *Médecine et société: les années 80*. Montreal: Saint-Martin.

De Koninck, Maria. 1987. "Multiplication des césariennes: phénomène chirurgical ou . . . officine de laboratoire." Pp. 239–59 in F. Saillant and M. O'Neill (eds.), *Accoucher autrement*. Montreal: Saint-Martin.

Ehrenreich, Barbara and Deirdre English. 1982. *Des Experts et des femmes*. Montreal: Éditions du Remue-Ménage.

Friedan, Betty. 1964. *La Femme mystifiée*. Paris: Gonthier.

Gélis, Jacques. 1984. *L'Arbre et le fruit: La naissance dans l'Occident moderne, 16e et 19e siècles*. Paris: Fayard.

Glaser, Barney G. and Anselm L. Strauss. 1967. *The Discovery of Grounded Theory: Strategies for Qualitative Research*. New York: Aldine Publishing.

Jeudy, Jean-Pierre. 1984. "Pour une critique de la notion de risque," *Action et recherches sociales*, No. 3 (novembre): 57–69.

Katz Rothman, Barbara. 1984. "The Meaning of Choice in Reproductive Technology." Pp. 23–33 in R. Arditti, *et al.* (eds.), *Test-Tube Women: What Future for Motherhood?* Boston: Pandora Press.

Lipovetsky, Gille. 1983. *L'Ère du vide: Essai sur l'individualisme contemporain*. Paris: Gallimard.

Morin, F. Edmonde. 1982. *La Rouge Différence ou les rythmes de la femme*. Paris: Seuil.

Oakley, Ann. 1980. *Women Confined: Toward a Sociology of Childbirth*. London: Martin Robertson.

Oakley, Ann. 1984. *The Captured Womb*. Oxford: Basil Blackwell.

Quéniart, Anne. 1987. "Le Façonnement social de la grossesse. Une analyse des diverses dimensions du vécu des femmes." Unpublished PhD dissertation, Université du Québec à Montréal.

Quéniart, Anne. 1986. "On mérite bien un congé." In *Rapport de recherche sur la mise en application du droit au retrait préventif de la travailleuse enceinte dans le secteur des hôpitaux et des services sociaux*. Montreal: Université de Montréal/DCS Maisonneuve-Rosemont.

Quéniart, Anne. 1988. *Le Corps paradoxal. Regards de femmes sur la maternité*. Montreal: Saint-Martin.

Renaud, Marc, *et al.* 1987. "Regard médical et grossesse en Amérique du Nord: l'évolution de l'obstétrique prénatale au 20è siècle." Pp. 181–212 in F. Saillant and M. O'Neill (eds.), *Accoucher autrement*. Montreal: Saint-Martin.

Scully, Diane. 1980. *Men Who Control Women's Health*. Boston: Routledge and Kegan Paul.

Images of Women in Canadian Social Policy: Em-bodying Patriarchy

Kathryn McCannell
School of Social Work
University of British Columbia

Claire McCarthy
Vancouver General Hospital

Barbara Herringer
School of Social Work
University of Victoria

Social policy plays an active — albeit often unrecognized — role in reconstituting relations of domination and subordination. McCannell, McCarthy and Herringer highlight the ways in which social policy not only reflects but reproduces patriarchal relations between men and women. It does so by benefitting women in their roles as wives and mothers, while neglecting women who remain outside the norm of the heterosexual, two-parent family. Despite increases in women's autonomy such as their increased economic independence, and despite their tendency to (at least) postpone marriage and often act as heads of households, Canadian social policy has failed to acknowledge women's new roles and needs. The authors illustrate this through examples of reproductive choice, taxation policy, and the neglect of never-married "spinsters."

Women in Policy

A 19-year-old First Nations woman living on a reserve discovers she is pregnant. Her white, male doctor pressures her to have an abortion, pointing out that as she is a single woman, her baby will in all likelihood be raised in poverty.

A 53-year-old working-class spinster is employed in a clerical position and grosses $25,000 annually. Her company offers minimal benefits and no pension scheme. She pays one-half of her monthly income on rent and has no savings.

A lesbian couple and three children are experiencing financial hardship due to extremely large dental bills. While one of the partners has an excellent dental plan through her place of employment, coverage is not available to her partner or to two of the children.

These vignettes illustrate the ways in which images of women in policy have an impact on our daily lives. What is and is not covered by social policy? What is seen as falling within the purview of the state, and what is left outside? Do gender, race, and class relations support patriarchy, and how is capitalism legalized and enforced? Such questions are of critical importance as the Canadian women's movement moves forward with an agenda for change.

Social policy, as it relates to the needs of women in Canada, for the most part, simply reflects the larger influence and power of the patriarchal state. Women continue to be marginalized on the border of a larger picture that treats men as the more important group. Mainstream social policy has done little to address a wide range of women's needs. Indeed, as Sapiro (1986: 231) states, "most social policy aimed at women has been designated explicitly to benefit them in their capacity as wives and mothers and more particularly, to benefit those who depend upon them for nurturance and domestic service: husbands, children, and elderly relatives." As a result, women continue to be invisible as individuals, and regarded primarily in terms of their relation to others. Even when they are seen in relation to others, social policy recognizes and supports only particular family models.

In this chapter we will examine how Canadian women's everyday lives are shaped by policies that embody images of women that serve the interests of our patriarchal and capitalist system. Examples will be drawn from three areas: reproductive choice, living and labouring in families, and economic policies affecting midlife women, particularly those who have never married.

Reproductive Choice

Much of the emphasis of social policy concerning women has focused on issues of reproductive choice. Because of women's unique contribution to reproduction, it is the last bastion of human experience not completely dominated by men. Nonetheless, society makes vast efforts in order to control *who* will reproduce, and *how* and *when* reproduction will occur, with fewer of these decisions being made by women.

Reproductive choice encompasses a broad spectrum of issues. These issues include the ideological aspects of the expectations of women to be mothers; a male-dominated medical profession that is able to control women's access to reproductive choice; and economic, political, and religious pressures on women.

Levine and Estable (1981) discuss the different social perspectives on motherhood. As they point out, the desired model is based on the heterosexual, Caucasian, middle-class, nuclear family. This societal agenda has a direct impact on women's access to reproductive choice. One has only to consider the limited availability to all women of safe and reliable contraception; and, more specifically, the pressures on white, middle-class women not to have abortions or not to be voluntarily sterilized. Compare this to the overwhelming coercion of women of colour, poor women, disabled women, immigrant women and First Nations women to have abortions or to be sterilized in order to prevent them from having what are seen to be less desirable children. The *Boston Women's Health Book Collective* (1984: 257) states that, "since 1974, women have revealed and studies have documented a terrible pattern of sterilization abuse. Victims of sterilization abuse are usually poor or black, Puerto Rican, Chicano or Native American." In 1981, statistics on the involuntary sterilization of minority women indicate that 54% of teaching hospitals in North America continue to require that a woman consent to be sterilized in order to obtain an abortion (Rich, 1986). Still further, we note that new reproductive technologies are being developed in order to enhance the potential of specific groups of women to bear children. Couples experiencing difficulties with conception are being offered techniques such as in-vitro fertilization or surrogacy arrangements. Other techniques allow for genetic manipulation and sex selection. Concerns about the research into and the availability of reproductive technologies have been expressed in recent years. Too little effort is being put into understanding what may cause infertility and sterility in the first place. As well, access to reproductive technologies is very much directed toward economically advantaged, white, heterosexual couples (Brodribb, 1988).

The patriarchal state's interest in women's reproductive powers has been well served by the medical community, which has overwhelmingly disempowered women and over-medicalized many of women's natural physical experiences (Ehrenreich and English, 1978). Such processes are central to physicians' training. For example, a relatively recent medical textbook states that "The vast majority of women have a basic need to have a home and children of their own" (Craddock, 1976: 48). Furthermore, in the recent past, women requesting sterilization were assessed for suitability based on a formula using the number of children they had and their age (Leiberman *et al.*, 1979). If age times number of children was greater than 120, the doctor would agree to sterilization. For example, in order for a woman of forty to be considered for the surgery, she would be required to have at least three children.

The patriarchal focus of social policy and its effects on women is perhaps best exemplified in the singular example of access to abortion in Canada. In 1969, the Canadian government legalized abortion for the first time, under three conditions. The government required that an abortion be performed in an accredited hospital and by a physician. The third condition required than an abortion be approved by a Therapeutic Abortion Committee, composed of a minimum of three physicians, which could approve the request if the pregnancy was likely to endanger the life and health of the woman (Dubinsky, 1985; Rapp, 1981). This law (Section 251 of the Canadian Criminal Code) gave rise to the abortion debate, which has seen two diametrically opposed groups attempting to change the law. McDonnell summarizes the problem:

> It became grimly clear in succeeding years that women in Canada did not win the right to abortion in 1969. The government's own Badgley Commission, set up in 1976 to examine the workings of the abortion law found it to be unworkable, a bureaucratic obstacle course that endangered women's health by prolonging the approval process and increasing their anxiety about the outcome. By the late 1970s, due to growing pressure from the anti-abortion movement and a political climate generally less favourable to women's rights, access to abortion actually dropped all across the country. (1984: 19)

In 1969, the Canadian law on abortion resulted in so many delays for women seeking abortion that, until 1988, Canada had the second highest rate of second-trimester abortions in the world, less only than India's (Singer, 1984). The high rate of second-trimester abortions suggests that society in general, and the medical profession in particular, had a great deal of difficulty allowing women to make their own decisions related to pregnancy.

In January 1988, the Supreme Court of Canada struck down the Abortion Law of 1969, declaring it unconstitutional with respect to the Canadian Charter of Rights and Freedoms. This decision was in response to Dr. Henry Morgentaler's appeal of a lower court's decision that found him guilty of performing abortions outside the regulations set in Section 251 of the Criminal Code. The court, in its five-to-two decision, found that Section 251 was "unconstitutional because it violated a woman's right to 'life, liberty and security of the person'" (Day and Persky, 1988: 13). This decision, and the abortion issue as a whole, raises the question of whether "women are autonomous, independent persons or, as Madame Justice Wilson says, 'passive recipients of a decision made by others as to whether [their bodies are to be used to nurture new life]'" (Day and Persky, 1988: 180).

Since the Supreme Court decision, access to abortion has been haphazard, depending on where a woman lives and her ability to pay for an abortion. This is particularly problematic because health care in Canada is administered provincially. Thus, although the *federal* government may dictate policy on abortion (through Criminal Code legislation, for example), *provincial* governments actually control access to abortion (through legislation governing health and welfare). For example, in Newfoundland a woman requires the consent of a gynaecologist, nurse, social worker, and psychiatrist prior to obtaining an abortion, which can be performed only during the first trimester. In Prince Edward Island, women have no access to abortion. In the Yukon and Northwest Territories, women can obtain abortions at major hospitals and have their transportation costs covered as well, although access to abortion sometimes varies depending on whether the woman is Inuit, First Nations, or white. Aboriginal women, more often than not, are encouraged to have abortions, while the reverse is true for white women.

In 1990, the Canadian House of Commons passed a bill regulating women's access to abortion through the Criminal Code of Canada; however, when presented to the Senate in 1991 this bill was narrowly defeated in a tied vote. While Canadian women have won a reprieve from having to fight the federal legislators on this element of reproductive choice, the struggle continues at other levels to ensure equal access to abortion for all women, regardless of race, geographic location, economic circumstances, age, or physical or mental ability.

Living and Labouring in Families

As Baker (1990) points out, misleading models of what is a 'family' abound. While one form of family is reinforced by policy — a heterosexual, nuclear, two-parent arrangement — the numerous and diverse ways of living-in-relation in which Canadian women participate are for the most part, invisible or unsupported by social policy. As an example, current policy does not adequately address the economic, social, and emotional needs of single-parent families, despite the dramatic increase in their prevalence. In British Columbia, one in five families is headed by a single parent, and approximately 60% of families headed by a single female parent live below the poverty line (National Council of Welfare, 1990). This Canadian reality can be viewed in an international context by comparing how other countries treat single-parent families headed by women. A recent study compared poverty rates for single mothers in seven developed countries (Kamerman, 1983; Smeeding, 1989). The results show that Canadian policies lead to very high rates of poverty for families of single mothers: in contrast to the Canadian rate of 60%, 11% of single mothers in Sweden live below the poverty line, while the comparable rate in Norway is 18%. These figures reflect a complexity of political choices and decisions with regard to child-care policy, the exclusion of caring from what is seen as work, the lack of enforcement of equal pay for work of equal value, and the lack of explicit family policies. Taxation policy reflects implicit views on family life, and it is in this area that examples of outdated patriarchal images (one of which will be described below) can be found.

In an attempt to enhance the quality of life for single-parent families, and to address housing and social support needs of this group, an innovative service called The Single Mothers Housing Network was established in the Lower Mainland area of British Columbia in 1986. Through this network, single-parent families could pair up to share housing. The emergent household could pool resources in whatever manner was mutually beneficial. It became apparent in 1988, however, that living in such an arrangement was being penalized by the income tax system. Section 109(b) of the Income Tax Act of Canada sets out personal deductions based on the premise that a minimum tax-free income is needed to maintain oneself and one's dependents. In 1987, single parents were allowed to deduct a $3700 "equivalent to married" exemption for supporting a dependent child, rather than claiming the $560 child exemption. This made a substantial difference to the financial status of some Canadian women by increasing the tax refunds they were eligible to receive. But, the guidelines stated that only *one* "equivalent to married" exemption could be claimed for each dwelling. The following excerpt is from the Income Tax Guidelines distributed to Canadians:

> Example: Kathy and Alison are both divorced. They have two children each, and they and their children live together in one house. Because only one equivalent to married exemption may be claimed for each dwelling, Kathy and Alison have decided that Alison will claim the equivalent to married exemption for one of her children.

Despite the fact that *neither* Kathy or Alison would have legal access to the other's resources (as in the case of marriage) because they are merely sharing a house, only one is being supported by the tax structure in her role as parent. The deduction as originally drafted was based on a model of a married couple in which one party worked outside the family home and one party worked within the home, without a wage. A married couple living with another person or persons would not lose the deduction. This policy therefore acts as a disincentive to some forms of family. Because of the statement that only one exemption is allowed per dwelling, many women were afraid to claim a child as "equivalent to married," although they felt entitled to the deduction. Some women chose to creatively establish dwellings, using for example, addresses such as 123A Patri Arky Lane and 123B Patri Arky Lane. Advocacy efforts to address this discrimination were initiated and are still underway.

Marital status is also important in determining whether or not older Canadian women are poor. At 75 years and over, 50% of unattached elderly women live in poverty (National Council of Welfare, 1990: 99), a conservative figure as it excludes people living in institutions. Rather than developing measures to address the economic hardships faced by elderly women, the federal government put forward new proposals for the Canadian Pension Plan in 1987 that suggested that the maximum pension go only to surviving spouses whose marriages had lasted 40 years or longer. If implemented, this would decrease surviving spouses' benefits in the majority of cases. At the present time there is *no* provision for payment of surviving spouses' benefits to former wives or husbands. Of course, survivor benefits are of little comfort to women who have never married, a group whose invisibility in policy is considered in a later section of this chapter.

While the Canadian Pension Plan and Quebec Pension Plan have drop-out provisions that allow continuous coverage to parents of children under the age of 7, allowing them to take time off from paid work without pension penalty, no such provision is made for people who leave the labour force to care for aging or disabled relatives. Middle-aged daughters often carry this burden of caring and are penalized economically in their old age for having left the labour force for a reason which is not "valid" in the eyes of policy makers. Thus the factors of low salaries, limited pension coverage, and restrictive drop-out provisions intersect with societal ideology that assigns women all responsibility for nurturance and caring, creating a complex web of inequality buttressed by policy.

The reproduction of labour in our economy requires ongoing service work which is most often performed by women. Within this gender-based division of labour, race and class further constrain opportunities. Immigrant and visible minority women are disadvantaged through racism and through the ways in which policy addresses "women's work." For example, consider the work performed by domestics. In a ten-year period ending in 1990, more than 55,000 women came to Canada with temporary permits to work as nannies, live-in housekeepers, maids, or companions to the disabled (National Council of Welfare, 1990: 123). The majority were from the Philippines. How does policy reinforce unequal relations within this domain? The policies of most financial import are provincial employment standards. British Columbia offers limited protection through a flat-rate daily minimum wage, regardless of hours worked. Quebec's employment standards exclude live-in domestics whose main duties are child care, and Alberta's law excludes *all* domestics. Only Ontario has laws on hourly minimum wage, overtime, and room and board deductions, and these treat live-in domestics almost as well as other employees. Enforcement of rights identified in policy is rare, and women may not be aware of standards or may fear conflicts with their employers.

In conclusion to the above, life within families and labour within families is inextricably linked to the economic well-being of women. In the next section we look at a specific group of women whose presence in policy has been virtually ignored: never-married women.

Never-Married Women in Midlife

Aging is another area in which social policy continues to rely on patriarchal assumptions of what roles women should assume. Despite feminist inroads, policy and research concerning women in midlife are often based on the assumption that women in this age group are, or were, married with children (Geile, 1982; King and Marvel, 1982; Gee and Kimball, 1987). As long as marriage and the nuclear family are seen as women's only acceptable options, those who do not follow such a path will continue to be either invisible or regarded as deviant.

The common experience (and image) of most women in their late forties and early fifties is that of homemaker. Although this trend is changing significantly as women marry later or not at all, have fewer or no children, and combine education and career, policy-making lags far behind. What of spinsters? This nonmarital state warrants little if any attention from researchers, let alone policy-makers. Rather than portraying self-sufficient women with jobs or careers and with social networks of family, friends and (perhaps) lovers, the very word "spinster" conjures up a passionless and dowdy woman, to be pitied because of her lack of husband or child. In contemporary jargon, spinsters are "never-married" or "ever-single," as opposed to "spouse-free." And, while spinsters may opt to raise children on their own, many are also child-free.

Many of the life events that spinsters face parallel those of most married women — career changes, health concerns, aging parents, and so on. One of the most crucial is that of retirement or loss of work. For many, the result of losing employment is also the loss of financial independence, since poverty is, by far, the most critical problem facing older women on their own. As the numbers of never-married women increase, we will need to break through the fears and stereotypes that prevent us from seeing these women who remain outside the mainstream. In order to increase our understanding of the experience of middle-aged spinsters, we must redefine their situations. To begin, we might ask "how are spinsters currently defined?"

According to popular usage, a spinster is someone still unmarried at 35, while historians define spinsters as those women over 50 who die celibate. The word *spinster* is derived from the female occupation of spinning thread. Originally, the term referred specifically to unmarried or widowed women who were hired by households to assist in the family-centred production of textiles. Over the years, it has come to refer to any unmarried woman, and is associated with "certain pejorative attributes — such as narrowness of spirit and a tendency to gossip over teacups" (Hufton, 1984). In the past, as is often the case today, the notion of independent women is not socially acceptable, making the spinster socially problematic. Nuns are still referred to as "brides of Christ"; healers/witches could not be allowed their own power without being said to be in league with the devil. Only prosperous widows enjoyed a degree of autonomy. Formerly, the notion of passionate female friendships was not questioned, because it was not believed that women experienced sexual desire (Faderman, 1981). Today, however, women without men are frequently pejoratively referred to as lesbian, regardless of their sexual orientation. In reviewing history, the irony is that little substantive change has occurred in attitudes toward independent women. As was the case two hundred years ago, the notion that women should have rights and lives beyond the patriarchal family appears to upset proponents of the new right. As outlined above, neoconservative attitudes and policies, exemplified in the abortion and pro-family debates, continue to oppose women's choice and control over their independent lives. The irony is that while the new right argues for dismantling the welfare state and the return of women to the home, capitalist expansion requires women workers for low-paying service jobs.

Policy towards the elderly, particularly elderly women, is a process of social construction linked to broad historical and contemporary social structural issues (Zones, Estes, and Binney, 1987). Others (Long and Porter, 1984) argue that policy needs to respond to the diverse needs of various groups, and that an overemphasis on women's family roles has led to characterizing midlife as a time of loss. We might question why the state remains unwilling to acknowledge that gender, race, and class, in addition to occupation and marital status, determine women's economic situation. Notwithstanding the numbers of unattached female elderly living below the poverty line, Russell (1987) states that most discussions of aging tend to adopt a genderless view of the process. The poverty statistics continue to reflect the ongoing subordination of women, through age discrimination and sexism — not to mention the burdens of race and class — at every level of society. While these statistics illustrate a terrifying future for the female elderly, education and long-term employment are factors in reducing poverty among women. Thus, because spinsters may not have as many interruptions during their work lives, they may — depending on their economic class or race — be in less danger of poverty in their old age than divorced or widowed women.

Recent interviews with contemporary spinsters (Herringer, 1988) indicate that the conditions facing these women have altered little in the recent past. In addition to implicit and explicit attitudes regarding their (so-called) unwomanly state, women outside marriage who work to support themselves continue to struggle with wage disparities, poor or nonexistent pensions schemes, lack of education, unaffordable or unavailable housing, threats to their personal safety, the possibility of taking care of aging parents, fears of growing old alone, and homophobia if they are lesbian. On the other hand, like those Victorian spinsters who rebelled against marriage and whole-heartedly embraced the risks of their autonomy, these women talked positively about the challenges that they face. Of central importance is the issue of independence: a woman's economic self-sufficiency is inextricably linked to her ability to work. A woman who, through either choice or circumstance, does not depend upon anyone else, must be able to support herself for her entire life.

Conclusion

It is important, then, that social policy address the significance of supports that allow women to maintain independent lives outside the societal construction of marriage. Access to education, wage and pension reform, housing, and social support development, must be at the top of the policy agenda in order to plan for the needs of the female elderly of varying backgrounds. Despite the numbers of social work practitioners, students, and social service consumers who are women, social policies still support assumptions about women that reflect the patriarchal interests of individual men, the economy, and the state.

The examples given above are selective illustrations of the ways in which the images of women currently reflected in social policy restrict our lives and maintain the existing inequitable economic structure. A feminist analysis is essential in making visible women's needs, and in raising the question of whom policy serves. As Segal (1987: 217) notes, feminism has put critical questions on the agenda, including the nature of human needs and how they are met (how we live, relate to and care for each other); the nature of work and how it is recognized and rewarded; and the nature of politics: how we organize for change and to what end. The link between private misfortune and public policy is increasingly clear to Canadian women, and resistance to the constraining images and their material consequences is strengthening. Groups such as DAWN (Disabled Women's Network Canada), the National Organization of Immigrant and Visible Minority Women of Canada, the Women's Legal Education and Action Fund, the Native Women's Association of Canada, and the National Action Committee on the Status of Women do important work in resisting the images which enforce inequality. It is our belief that, as women make visible the realities of their daily lives and claim authority to shape their futures, women's "struggle over the body" will take new shape in policies which support a diversity of choices and societal relations.

Questions

1 What types of conditions are necessary before Canadian women will have full reproductive choice? Can these conditions be achieved through social policy? If not, why not?

2 Why has the Canadian state been slow to respond to women's demands (if, indeed, it has responded at all)? Would having more women in positions of decision-making necessarily make a difference?

3 In what ways are young, single women treated as potential wives and mothers?

References

Baker, Maureen. 1990. "Perpetuation of Misleading Family Models in Social Policy," *Canadian Social Work Review*, Vol. 7, No. 2: 169–82.

Boston Women's Health Collective. 1984. *The New Our Bodies, Our Selves*. New York: Simon and Schuster.

Brodribb, S. 1988. *Women and Reproductive Technologies: Report Prepared for Status of Women Canada*. Ottawa: Status of Women Canada.

Canada. Revenue Canada. 1987. *Income Tax Guidelines*. Ottawa: Supply and Services Canada.

Craddock, D. 1976. *A Short Textbook of General Practice*. London: Lewis and Company.

Day, S., and S. Persky (eds.). 1988. *The Supreme Court of Canada Decision on Abortion.* Vancouver: New Star Books.

Dubinsky, K. 1985. *Lament for a "Patriarchy Lost"? Anti-feminism, Anti-abortion and R.E.A.L. Women in Canada.* Ottawa: Canadian Research Institute for the Advancement of Women.

Ehrenreich, B., and D. English. 1978. *For Her Own Good: 150 Years of the Experts' Advice to Women.* Garden City, N.Y.: Anchor Press.

Faderman, L. 1981. *Surpassing the Love of Men: Romantic Friendship and Love Between Women From the Renaissance to Present.* New York: Morrow.

Gee, E.M., and M.M. Kimball. 1987. *Women and Aging.* Toronto: Butterworths.

Geile, J.Z. (ed.). 1982. *Women in the Middle Years.* New York: John Wiley and Sons.

Herringer, B. 1988. "Never-married and Childless Women in Midlife: An Exploration of the Issues." Unpublished master's thesis, School of Social Work, University of British Columbia.

Hufton, D. 1984. "Women Without Men: Widows and Spinsters in Britain and France in the Eighteenth Century," *Journal of Family History*, Vol. 9, No. 4: 355–76.

Kamerman, Sheila B. 1983. "Women, Children and Poverty: Public Policies and Female-Headed Families in Industrialized Countries." In B.C. Gelpi, *et al.* (eds.), *Women and Poverty.* Chicago: University of Chicago Press.

King, N.R., and M.G. Marvel. 1982. *Issues, Policies, and Programs for Midlife and Older Women.* New York: Centre for Women Policy Studies.

Levine, H., and A. Estable. 1981. *The Power Politics of Motherhood.* Ottawa: Centre for Social Welfare Studies, Carleton University.

Lieberman, R.G., A. Kaufman, W. Heffron, P. DiVasto, J.D. Voorhees, K. Williams, and L. Weiss. 1979. "Vasectomy for the Single, Childless Man," *Journal of Family Practice*, Vol. 8: 181–4.

Long, J., and K.L. Porter. 1984. "Multiple Roles of Midlife Women: Case for New Directions in Theory, Research and Policy." In G. Baruch and J. Brook-Gunn (eds.), *Women in Midlife.* New York: Plenum Books.

McDonnell, K. 1984. *Not An Easy Choice.* Toronto: Women's Press.

National Council of Welfare. 1990. *Women and Poverty Revisited.* Ottawa: Minister of Supply and Services Canada.

Rapp, M. 1981. "The Role of the Psychiatrist in Canadian Abortion Law." In P. Sachdev (ed.), *Abortion: Readings and Research.* Toronto: Butterworths.

Rich, A. 1986. *Of Woman Born: Motherhood as Experience and Institution.* New York: W.W. Norton.

Russell, C. 1987. "Aging as a Feminist Issue," *Women's Studies International Forum*, Vol. 10, No. 2: 125–32.

Sapiro, V. 1986. "The Gender Bias of American Social Policy," *Political Science Quarterly*, Vol. 101: 221–38.

Segal, Lynne. 1987. *Is the Future Female? Troubled Thoughts on Contemporary Feminism*. London: Virago Press.

Singer, G. (director, writer, co-producer). 1984. *Abortion: Stories from North and South*. Film by the National Film Board of Canada, Studio D Production.

Smeeding, Timothy M. 1989. "Poverty, Affluence, and the Income Costs of Children: Cross-national Evidence from the Luxembourg Income Study (LIS)," *Journal of Post Keynesian Economics*, Vol. 11, No. 2 (winter): 232.

Zones, J.S., C.L. Estes, and E.A. Binney. 1987. "Gender, Public Policy and the Oldest Age," *Aging and Society*, Vol. 7: 175–302.

Section Three

Reclaiming the Female Body

Representation and Resistance:
Feminist Struggles against Pornography

Dawn H. Currie
Anthropology and Sociology
University of British Columbia

Once misogyny is revealed as a dominant theme in the cultural portrayal of women, censorship is raised as a potential strategy for resistance to the symbolic appropriation of women's bodies. Censorship has been recommended as a solution to pornography, in particular. As appealing as this recommendation may appear, however, it has divided feminists. While radical feminists advocate censorship on the grounds that pornography encourages violence against women, others emphasize the importance of free expression and sexual liberation. By using a semiotic approach to explore these debates, we can clarify the ways in which censorship is, in this author's experience, unable to produce the intended effect. This is because the problem of pornography does not lie simply in the consumption of pornography, but also in the conditions of its production.

The Problem: Pornography or Censorship?

Following Michel Foucault, the study of discourse reveals not truth, but ways in which the "true" and the "false" are differentiated, with effects attached to the alternative that we designate as Truth. "Discourse," in this context, includes not only text but attendant beliefs about reality which constitute the Subject of a particular discourse. In this chapter, pornography will be analyzed as a discourse that constructs sexuality, primarily through the portrayal of the female body. As text, pornography is constructed from the perspective of the male viewer and for the male consumer (albeit through the appropriation of women's labour). Debates about the regulation of pornography concern male practices which are imputed to arise from the pornographic text. As such, pornography is currently contested terrain. While sexual libertarians endorse it as the freer depiction of sexual diversity which challenges repressive proscriptions, in reaction conservatives claim that by providing vicarious experience of natural pleasure, pornography encourages a self-centered sexuality that threatens socialized behaviour. In contrast, feminist discourse links pornography to the sexist portrayal of women's bodies in a patriarchal culture, a portrayal which objectifies women and encourages male violence against women in general. Because feminists and reactionary moralists thus share the view that pornography creates an antisocial Subject, it is perhaps not surprising that they have formed an alliance in campaigns for censorship. This alliance has been particularly divisive for the Women's Movement, and a number of feminists who are against pornography have nevertheless identified themselves as "feminists against censorship" (see Burstyn, 1985).

My aim here is to explore the basis for these analytical divisions and political disagreements. By providing an alternative approach to the study of censorship, I suggest that the choice between the freedom of expression, which pornography is claimed to reflect, or censorship is a false one. Feminist analyses should concern the social context that makes possible both the production of pornography and pornographic readings. In doing so, we can transcend irresolvable struggles over the content of pornography by paying greater attention to its production, as made possible through the real (and not simply symbolic) appropriation of women's bodies.

Pornography as Fact or Fiction:
Liberal, Radical, and Conservative Discourses

In Canada pornography has been legally regulated since 1892 under the ambiguous and emotionally laden offences of "obscenity," "depravity," and "moral corruption." What constitutes the obscene has never been specified but is taken to mean any action which seems to offend established standards of decency. Thus, pornography is seen as a test of community tolerance. Over the past 30 years or more there have been several legislative enquiries and public actions in order to determine what the Canadian community will accept. Since 1959, the limitations have been established in the Criminal Code as the "undue exploitation of sex." Case law has established that "undueness" is measured in accordance with community standards, that the "community" means the aggregation of all Canadians, and that the "standards" may change over time (Rhodes, 1988: 133). The courts have emphasized that the test is tolerance, not taste. Historically, this tolerance has been based on the assumption that patriarchal standards are desirable. Legislation effectively reinforced the monogamous heterosexual family by giving male-dominated courts the power to censor images that do not conform to this model. The first major challenges came during the 1960s from sexual liberationists and second wave feminists.

A significant and lasting feature of the 1960s has been the establishment of libertarian discourses about sexuality and sexual behaviour. Following a doctrine that upholds the right to personal beliefs, liberals argue that society benefits from an open marketplace of ideas and opinions, a principle enshrined in the Canadian Charter of Rights and Freedoms. Since there is no infallible source of knowledge, we cannot know in advance what social, moral, and intellectual developments might be possible or necessary for human development and societal advancement. The individual's development includes sexuality, a complex psychological drive shaped by cultural processes, particularly by repression and sublimation. From this perspective, pornography is seen as encouraging sexual diversity and challenging repressive proscriptions. Further, as an intimate dimension of experience and expression, individual sexual conduct is considered to be a personal activity and therefore an arena of private morality. By equating pornography with fantasy, and because its use occurs within the private realm, the only justification for legal regulation is when it spills over into the public sphere, either by causing physical harm or by offending other people when on public display. As Thelma McCormack (1987, 1988) argues, for liberals the basic tenet of a free society is control of behaviour and not thought, regardless of how repugnant the latter might be. While individuals are held responsible for their actions, they are not publicly accountable for their thoughts. From this position, liberals argue that censorship of pornography constitutes a violation of civil liberties, an afront to the Charter which upholds "freedom of thought, belief, opinion and expression including the freedom of the press and other media of communication."[1]

In contrast to liberals who thus endorse pornography as the free depiction of sex as a private act between consenting individuals, feminists identify the social context of pornographic texts. In doing so, they do not focus on the depiction of natural pleasure but on violence and power. With *Sexual Politics* (1969), Kate Millett highlighted male domination and female subjugation as central to literary descriptions of sexual relations. Linking sexuality and misogyny to the maintenance of patriarchy, Millett argued that the sexual permissiveness and self-expression encouraged during the 20th century have simply given greater latitude to the expression of male hostility towards women (1969: 42–5). Pornography in particular represents the eroticization of patriarchal sexual relations. Following Millett, a number of writers link pornography to sexual vio-

lence against women, presenting violence as both the necessary theme
and the result of pornography. Against the dominant liberal view of
pornography as erotic fantasy, Andrea Dworkin (1974, 1981) claims that
it depicts the reality of patriarchal oppression throughout the ages, en-
capsulating the tenets of male supremacy: "the power of self, physical
power over and against others, the power of terror, the power of naming, the power of owning, the power of money and the power of sex"
(1981: 24). While these themes are easily identified in pornography, she
also links them to women's roles as housewife, sexual slave, prostitute,
low-waged employee, or rape victim. According to Dworkin (1981: 224),
pornography reveals the extent to which "male pleasure is inextricably
tied to victimizing, hurting, exploiting; that sexual fun and sexual passion in the privacy of the male imagination are inseparable from the
brutality of male history." It remained for Susan Brownmiller (1975) to
connect the violence of fiction to this history of male violence. Defining pornography as "the undiluted essence of anti-female propaganda"
Brownmiller equates its philosophy to that of rape. She maintains that
the open display of pornography in American culture actively promotes
a climate within which acts of sexual hostility are not only tolerated,
but ideologically approved. Both Dworkin and Brownmiller, therefore,
encouraged general acceptance of the slogan that "pornography is the
theory and rape the practice" of patriarchy.

From the 1970s onward, feminists began to challenge the liberal
distinctions between pornography as fantasy and pornography in the
reality of women's lives. Radical feminists in particular maintain that
women as a class are victimized in an ideological sense by pornography
and that this leads to the actual physical victimization of individual
women, as summarized by Catharine MacKinnon:

> Pornography . . . is a form of forced sex, a practice of sexual politics, an
> institution of gender inequality. In this perspective, pornography is not
> harmless fantasy or a corrupt and confused misrepresentation of an oth-
> erwise natural and healthy sexuality. Along with rape and prostitution in
> which it participates, pornography institutionalizes the sexuality of male
> supremacy, which fuses the eroticization of dominance and submission
> with the social construction of male and female. (1987: 148)

From this position it therefore seems reasonable to argue, as does Lorenne
Clark:

> On the theory that it is justified to prohibit whatever causes harm to
> others, either through the direct infliction or threat of physical harm, or
> through violation of their rights, it follows that it is justified to prohibit
> actions, and materials which display actions, which bring about harms
> of either of these types, whether or not they bring about a pleasurable

sexual response. . . . And it must also be acknowledged that if one gets sexually aroused from things which create a clear and substantial risk to the safety and/or rights of others, then one can justifiably be prohibited from getting one's responses that way. (1980: 4)

From this position, which links the ideas expressed by pornography to the practice of male violence against women, a feminist lobby for censorship has become a visible challenge to liberal discourse.

Perhaps paradoxically, feminist campaigns against pornography appear to be similar to those of reactionary moralists who object to the libertarian ideals of the 1960s, including those espoused by the Women's Movement. Both share fundamental premises about the translation of undesirable thoughts into antisocial behaviour. As we have seen, however, an important difference is that feminists do not see pornography as primarily about sex, and therefore as evil in itself. For conservatives, civilization represents a constant struggle to impose external limits on human passions. From a Freudian perspective, sexuality is the least socialized of human passions and has no self-regulating mechanism, no internally produced limits. It is only by means of an externally enforced repression (and the internalized superego) that unrestrained pleasure-seeking is transformed into civilized behaviour. Sexually explicit materials may undermine this repression by providing a vicarious experience of "natural" pleasures which may encourage the individual to revert to a "state of nature." Pornography, in particular, may unleash the unrestrained growth of sexual libido and result in a downward and irreversible sinking into more perverse and bizarre passions. Following from this, a number of "common sense" objections to pornography rest on what Marianne Valverde (1985) calls the "domino theory" of the passions. It is argued that exposure to pornography destroys the ability to feel shame, which is the key to sexual self-restraint. By removing self-restraint, pornography — like all sexually explicit materials — provokes regression to autoerotic and infantile sexuality which can become a permanent, self-reinforcing neurosis for the individual. Furthermore, by de-individualizing and dehumanizing sexual acts, materials which portray sexual relations as impersonal reduce or remove the feelings of mutual identification and empathy that keep us from treating one another as mere objects. Because this empathy is an internal barrier to nonconsensual acts, pornography encourages rape, torture and assaultive crimes in general. Thus conservatives promote the censorship of pornography on the grounds that it "blunts sensibility, leads to a society of selfish, disengaged, uninvolved individuals, results in sex without love, and violence solely for the pleasure it begets" (quoted in Padon, 1984). Following from this, all sexually oriented materials — including educational texts

— are identified as problematic, and censorship is promoted as necessary for the preservation of communal life; the state has not only the right, but the duty, to prevent behaviour that is contrary to tradition and that undermines established social institutions such as heterosexual marriage and the family. Because the legal code is symbolic of the "common good" conservatives, like feminists, justify laws that prohibit immoral behaviour even when this behaviour is freely chosen and cannot be shown to harm individuals. Within this view, harm includes the behaviour of individuals who, unwittingly, may act in ways which foster the moral disintegration of society.

From this overview it is clear that, while conservatives would ban the representation of all sexual acts, for feminists it has been sexist rather than merely sexually explicit materials which are problematic. Thus the feminist analysis that leads to an advocacy of censorship differs in several fundamental respects from that of conservatives. For feminists, societal power does not act to suppress pleasure but rather to create it. The content of pornography is not about sex but about power and violence as it relates to the real life experiences of women (see Diamond, 1980: 690).

The consciousness raising which accompanied readings of pornography as acts of male sexual aggression created a sense of outrage among many women which became the basis for anti-pornography campaigns. These women organized tours of porn districts of various cities to dramatize the commercial exploitation of women; they held "Take Back the Night" marches; and they boycotted products advertised with misogynist messages.[2] What began as a broad struggle against sexism, however, turned increasingly to focus on pornography as the *ultimate* source of sexism and violence against women. Over time, it has become increasingly difficult to distinguish between feminist and conservative factions of the lobby to restrict pornography. When the first public seminar on pornography was held in 1983, a number of feminists joined the Presbyterian-based Canadians for Decency in the call for censorship. At the same time, conservatives have co-opted much of the feminist discourse: they no longer talk about the "evil" of pornography and its immoral effects, but rather the "degradation," "objectification," "coercion," and excessive "violence" which it represents (Lacombe, 1989: 11).

The alliance of feminism and conservative moralists against pornography has been condemned by a diversity of civil libertarians, feminists, artists, gays, and lesbians. Opponents to censorship note that historically, restrictive legislation has been used to impede the liberation of women, for example by preventing the circulation of information on birth control. More recently, depictions of alternative sexuality — gay male sex in particular — have been routinely censored by police, while the owner of Page's Bookstore in Toronto was taken to court when a group of feminist artists displayed a variety of "obscene" objects in his store window.[3] Reflecting the deepening split within feminist ranks on strategies to combat pornography, a number of writers identify themselves as "feminists against censorship." In weighing the far-reaching effects of government-controlled censorship against the possible benefits for women, these writers emphasize that the consensus of the research community is that no causative linkage between exposure to pornography and the commission of sexual or other crimes can be demonstrated. The most common allegations by feminists — that the use of pornography leads men to become more sexually aggressive with women, more tolerant of sexual aggression in others, more callous towards women at the personal level, and less receptive to women's legitimate claims for equality and respect — are simply not supported by scientific studies. On the contrary, a number of inhibiting factors tend to keep our responses within culturally defined norms. However, in her assessment of this research for the Metropolitan Toronto Task Force on Violence Against Women, McCormack (1985) notes that while the link to direct physical aggression cannot be demonstrated, it is possible to argue that a cultural milieu in which women are always perceived as sex objects contributes to the devaluation of women and undermines the broader feminist goals of greater participation of women in public life and their equal treatment.

Given the importance that McCormack and others put on sex education and alternative imagery of sexual behaviour, anti-censorship writers remind us that neoconservatives would ban sex education from schools and restrict all sexually explicit materials. A further danger of law-and-order lobbies associated with rightwing politics is that they strengthen rather than challenge the male-dominated institutions of police and courts. There is no reason to believe that judges, for example, will interpret "community standards" with feminist goals in mind.[4] Finally, legislation against pornography is likely only to drive the material in question underground. While this will not seriously impede the distribution of pornography, it will convey the false appearance that the state has been responsive to feminist demands. In the final analysis, feminists against censorship argue that:

> censorship is about as effective as applying cardiopulmonary resuscitation to a mastodon, when what we need is a whole new system for creating and distributing cultural information in our society, a system that is able to more adequately reflect how we will live our lives, and is structured more democratically in terms of production and dissemination of imagery and information. (Steele, 1985: 59)

Most feminists against censorship are skeptical of the claim advanced by Dworkin and MacKinnon that "pornography is central in creating and maintaining the civil inequality of the sexes" (see Snitow, 1985). Given the dangers of censorship and the lack of concrete evidence that pornography causes measurable social harm, these writers suggest that we err on the side of caution. Also relegating pornography to the domain of fantasy, feminists against censorship join liberals in campaigns to uphold the fundamental liberal principle of freedom in thought and self-expression.

Beyond the Impasse: Rethinking Censorship

In effect, analyses of pornography are irreconcilable, so that a number of sociologists have identified the debates surrounding pornography as the phenomenon of greater interest (see Miller, 1987; Jarvie, 1987; Lacombe, 1989). As a feminist and a social scientist, the problem for me was that I can see the merits of both cases as presented. My interest in anorexia and bulimia among women (see Currie, 1990) has heightened my concern with cultural stereotyping and objectification of women. From this work, I do not share the view that a clear line exists between thought and action, belief and behaviour, fantasy and reality. At the same time, however, as an academic struggling for "legitimacy" within the still controversial domain of "Women's Studies," I am convinced that censorship would be used to stifle rather than foster revolution. While I have a healthy respect for the notion that we should support our claims with evidence rather than moral authority, I doubt that the liberal social sciences, with their legacy of sexism, will (if indeed they can) provide us with the "truth." I therefore fell between the two sides of the pornography and censorship debate, comfortably remaining out of the fray. At the same time, it seemed to me that the emotional nature of both sides of the debate hides the complexity of the issues. Looking back, I should not be surprised that it has been my practical involvement in struggles against pornography, rather than purely academic interest, that raised new questions for me and suggested that current discourses are constructing false choices for feminist practice. This practical experience is my membership in the British Columbia Periodical Review Board. For the remainder of this paper, I would like to put aside the question of whether or not we *should* have censorship — whatever its form — in order to explore why we cannot have censorship as a meaningful exercise of community standards.

The British Columbia Periodical Review Board (BCPRB) was formed in 1984 following the Vancouver hearings of the Fraser Committee on Prostitution and Pornography in Canada. Together with magazine wholesalers, a number of women's and church groups pressed the Attorney General to implement a process whereby the community would have a voice in determining the nature of "adult publications" that are available for public consumption. Strictly speaking, the BCPRB is not a censorship board *per se*; its purpose is to review pornographic periodicals prior to their circulation in order to determine whether, in the opinion of the Board, any of the written or pictorial texts "violate community standards" and therefore should be voluntarily withheld from circulation by distributors. The Board has no legal mandate and can more properly be viewed as a watchdog of community standards. This review process is independent of industry (although funded in part by it). It begins with the Attorney General's guidelines, which state that material depicting or describing sex with force, coercion, bodily harm or possibility of bodily harm; or sex involving children or young persons under the age of 18; or incest; or sex involving excreta, necrophilia and bestiality may be subject to prosecution. In addition to strictly legalistic criteria, materials are judged against community standards by taking into account current case law, the context in which the material appears, artistic or literary merit, the producer's intent, and the concerns of the Canadian public as reflected in the Fraser Commission. Jillian Ridington, an activist who was influential in establishing the BCPRB, emphasizes the feminist presence in this group. In consequence, she claims that the review process reflects the most common concerns of the major women's groups that appeared before the Commission. Ridington (1988: 4) describes the feminist perspective endorsed by the Board as accepting the argument "developed by activists and theoreticians that [publications involving] violent pornography are forms of violence against women and children, and promote and encourage acceptance of other violence." The majority of magazines that the Board recommends against (either in whole or part) contain material advocating sexual abuse of women and children. The Board advises against magazines featuring personal advertisements for sadomasochism and other violent activities. In her assessment of the Board's activities, Ridington claims that the Board has had a positive impact; almost all distributors in the province comply with Board recommendations so that the availability of materials which link sexual pleasure to the overt abuse of women has been reduced.[5]

On the surface, it might appear that the Board successfully fulfills the central goal of its mandate, and it is not my purpose here to assess the success of the BCPRB. While I whole-heartedly admire its efforts, my experience has led me to conclude that censorship will necessarily ensure that liberal principles of freedom of thought and expression override feminist claims to justice. The problem is that the obscene acts that are the major target of censorship — physical violence, incest, or intercourse with children or animals — are not literally depicted. Consider advertisements for erotic videos, which are a central feature of soft porn publications. While it is true that censorship prevents circulation of materials that use children as models or make direct reference to sexual acts between parents and children, these acts are implied through videos which are somewhat ambiguously titled (for example) "Playground Pussy," "Babysitter Blowjobs," "Pajama Party," or "Daddy's Darling." Clearly, no direct reference appears to objectionable acts themselves, despite the fact that appeal rests on the forbidden. In many cases, this appeal is reinforced by the use of adult female models portrayed as children, or by featuring animals in videos entitled simply "Taboo" or "Forbidden Acts." In this way, the uncensorable but everyday content of pornography concerns sex with children, incest, and bestiality. And yet this material can never be "pulled," specifically because these acts are never explicitly portrayed. In fact, the effect of the Review Board could well be seen as providing feminist support for the patriarchal eroticism that it identified as problematic in the first place. For this reason, it seemed to me that the practice of the Review Board was a contradictory one for feminists and that the effect of censorship has not been unambiguously positive for women. What interested me about censorship, therefore, was how this contradiction arises.

As indicated above, the problem of censorship is not the result of inadequate criteria or lack of rigour in their application. Rather, it occurs through the construction of meaning and, as such, can be understood through semiotics. As the study of how meaning is constructed, semiology emphasizes that it is not the message itself that communicates meaning, but rather its relationship to the viewer, who brings to the viewing memories, imagination, and cultural beliefs. Within any system of meaning, the sign as the object of analysis consists of two components: the signifier and the signified. While the former is the concrete material vehicle of meaning, the latter as an abstraction actually "is" meaning. Within any system of meaning, the sign as the effect or message represents the unity of these two elements. Roland Barthes gives the example of roses, which in our society signify romance. While a rose on its own is merely "a flower," a signifier devoid of necessary meaning, in our culture the giving of roses is perceived as "romantic." This is because as a sign this act brings together the concrete signifier — the roses — and the abstract meaning or that which is signified — passion. Hence the message which is created by the act of giving roses is one of romantic intent. In another culture and another system of meaning, this act could mean something totally different, perhaps even the opposite of passion. Thus semiotics emphasizes that images rely upon external belief systems in order to have meaning. Williamson (1978) refers to these systems of cultural meanings as "referent systems."

What this analysis implies is that, in terms of pictures or text, meaning itself does not exist on the page but must be actively constructed by the viewer, although the way in which imagery is employed will affect the way in which images are read. Technically, specific readings can be assisted in a number of ways: by associating an object with a person who is symbolic; through the context within which the object is placed; by the association of two objects; or by the association of feelings with objects (Leiss, Kline, and Jhally, 1986). While these techniques direct the way in which meaning will be constructed for the viewer, transference of significance is not complete within the given image itself; the viewer must make the connection. However, individual viewers are unlikely to complete idiosyncratic readings of identical imagery when that imagery draws upon *a priori* referent systems, a fact which is perhaps most evident in advertising. Williamson notes that in advertising every message contains two levels of meaning: what is said explicitly on the surface and what is conveyed implicitly. A message which visually links two objects, such as a car draped with a sexy woman, for example, implies that ownership of the product will make the consumer more sexually attractive to women, although this is not stated anywhere in the ad. We interpret it this way through internal and external transfers of significance. This is not the only interpretation possible; the message as given here relies upon a system in which the ownership of commodities is associated with social prestige and the viewer, as potential owner, is male.

Although these kinds of analyses tell us a lot about pornography, of interest here is what semiotics tells us about the regulation of pornography through censorship, specifically why it is bound to fail. As I discovered as reviewer/censor, while we can remove the signifier which acts as the vehicle of meaning which is offensive — and possibly harmful — censorship cannot affect the referent system necessary for pornographic readings of the sign. Let us consider an everyday example taken from a popular advertisement which appears regularly in soft porn magazines but which does not violate the criteria for restriction used by the Review Board. This ad is for a video entitled "Play With Me." While the title alone is sufficiently innocuous to pass unnoticed, the ad is sometimes accompanied by an illustration of a woman wearing pigtails and surrounded by nursery toys. Here a specific reading has been imposed:

it concerns sexual innocence and youthfulness as being attractive to the viewer. In terms of the construction of the message, what we see is the substitution of one signifier — a prepubescent girl, for example — for another — an adult woman juxtaposed with symbols of childhood. Despite the use of an adult rather than child model, however, the resulting process has not been substantively altered; arousal for the viewer is due to the idea/fantasy that the subject is a child. Otherwise the props to sustain this imagery would be redundant, or alternatively, the props themselves would be erotic and the human subject unnecessary. This system of meaning depends in large part on cultural stereotyping, which equates femininity with physical and social immaturity; otherwise the message could be either comical or repugnant. This belief about femininity, however, reflects the virtual absence of women from political decision-making and their association with secondary support work in the economic realm.[6] For example, imagine whether the erotic meaning could be sustained if the model were male. There is no referent system which would render the image of a naked adult man playing with a train set, for example, as an object of desire. On the contrary, the symbols of masculinity are those of both physical and social maturity: well-developed physique, athletic competence, greying hair — as long as the other status indicators are in place — the three-piece suit and briefcase or expensive car/boat/commodity. These are the things which both symbolically and literally give men their traditional sex appeal — just check any romance novel or afternoon soap opera.

I do not want to belabour the point in terms of the relative "meaning" of pornography, however, because that avenue is also full of pitfalls. What semiotics does suggest is that we should pay more attention to the way in which pornographic readings are constituted rather than simply to the literal content of pornography and how this relates to censorship. In order to produce a pornographic reading, pornography requires the separation of cultural objects — literally, the bodies of women — from a complexity of meanings (as signifier the female form can represent pro-creativity, maternal warmth, physical beauty, or desire, to give but a few examples) in order to reimpose a specific reading which draws upon a narrowed referent system of patriarchal heterosexist and misogynist values (see McAslan, this volume). In doing so, pornography also reduces the diversity of the female body to a uniform standard of male desire; for the large part, this body is young, slender, and usually white.[7] The problem lies, therefore, in what censorship takes for granted but semiotics reveals: the separation of the female body as cultural signifier from a diversity of meanings in order to reimpose a specific reading. This separation occurs during the production of pornography and as a consequence of the social, not technical, aspects of its production. When approached from this perspective, our inquiry moves away from pornography as an object consisting of representations of women used by predominantly male readers, to examine the process of production through which women are transformed from subjects into pornographic objects.

From the Consumption to the Production of Pornography

By focusing on the consumption rather than the production of pornography, current debates on censorship emphasize the use-value of pornography, or the "value" which it may, or may not, have for the consuming public. Anti-censors, for example, argue that pornography has the positive value of liberating individuals from repressive modes of sexual self-expression, while pro-censors point to the negative value — or harm — which pornography has specifically for women. When framed in this way, debates are likely to remain unresolved. What I suggest here is that we draw attention to pornography as a commodity, produced for profit or for its exchange-value. The production of pornography illustrates what Marx, writing in the 19th century, observed about the production of commodities through capitalist waged labour: because labourers no longer exercise control over production, the objects created by their labour no longer embody their needs or desires. To Marx, this process of alienated production robs workers of their distinctly human potential. Only when labour transforms human subjectivity and desires into concrete objects that satisfy the needs of their makers is work an exercise in creative self-expression. This is why he believed that commodity production under capitalist relations of production reduced workers to merely appendages of machines and condemned them to a life of purely physical labour which thwarted their intellectual potential. While this condition of the workers appears to arise from the new techniques of production, it is the result of relations of ownership of the means of production. It is the owner and not the workers of factories who determine what is produced, how production will take place, and what the products will be used for. Following from the separation of mental and manual labour in this way, two separate spheres emerge: that of production, where commodities are manufactured as having exchange-value, and that of circulation, where needs and desires for these products are continually created.

Understanding the production of pornography in this way as a commodity, we can see that women's labour as a group is appropriated during the production of a sexual culture which is linked to and perpetuates their oppression. As a multi-million dollar industry, pornography is produced through the waged labour of women: as models — or "porn queens" to use the industry's jargon — but also as workers in the print industry and as sales clerks in convenience stores where soft porn is sold. While women thus play an active role in both the production and the circulation of pornography, as feminists have noted, the content of pornographic culture is not about the sexuality, sexual needs, or desires of these same women. As I have outlined here, the production of pornography is a process which creates, and then *appears* to satisfy the natural, sexual desires of men. Although it may seem that the pornographic object itself is the source of women's oppression — and therefore the object of intervention — we are directed to an examination of the underlying social relations through which women's oppression by pornography is constituted. What this suggests is that the activity of monitoring community standards through concerned groups such as the BCPRB is a *symptom* of the problem of pornography and therefore can never be its solution. Both pornography as an industry and censorship as a response to that industry reflect the exclusion of women as subjects from the production of a mass "sexual" culture based on the objectification of women. The notion of community standards that reflect women's concerns and that can be applied after production arises only because women, as members of the community, have no say in the material production of culture. The exercise of censorship as the regulation of cultural production emerges with the separation of the community from the production of culture as a commodity for mass consumption, and as such is a contradictory solution.

From this perspective, it is not the behaviour of individual consumers that is the problem, but rather the production of culture for mass consumption. In this context pornography represents colonization of the female form (and masculine desire) for the economic benefit of those who own the means of cultural production through the appropriation of women's labour. Thus, I agree with Susan Cole (1989: 59) that pornography proves that there is no freedom of speech. This point is obscured by liberals who view the consumption of sexual culture (rather than its production) as an exercise in individual self-expression. However, from the analysis presented here I am not advocating alternative or women's publication of pornography. Under current economic arrangements, the production of pornography by women would suffer from many of the same problems; while we might postulate that it would be informed by real experiences of women's sexuality and thereby endorse an entirely different set of interpersonal values, it could not claim to represent the community of women.

Analyzing the social relationships through which the female body as an object of sexual desire is constituted also reveals the way in which women are differentially exploited and oppressed during the production of pornography. For example, women who are recruited as models and therefore visibly exploited are young and predominantly white. Less visible is the appropriation of women's labour during other aspects of the production and circulation of pornography as a process which creates other divisions and hierarchies between women. These latter divisions would be unaltered if we lobby simply for women's access to production under current conditions of commodity production. In all likelihood, relatively more privileged women would have access to the production of "women's culture" — in the same way that privileged women have greater access to the production of feminism through Women's Studies programs. The point for feminism is not to make pornography accountable only in terms of its content or images, but rather in terms of the processes of its production and the relations through which sexual desire/culture is produced. This cannot be accomplished through censorship.

Conclusion

In conclusion, a major problem with anti-pornography campaigns is that they currently focus upon the content of pornography. From this position, their concern arises from the meaning of the pornographic image which they find offensive and which they believe causes harm in the viewer/consumer. What I have suggested here is that we move away from a fixation on the consumption/circulation of pornography and concern ourselves with pornography as a process, beginning at the point of production. From this perspective we are led to an exploration of its form rather than only its *content* and thus to the social conditions that sustain both the material production of pornography and the referent system upon which it relies. These latter problems cannot be addressed by censorship or the regulation of images of women's bodies. Rather, solutions lie in the regulation of the conditions and relations of the pornography industry (see Cole, 1989) or the production of alternative sexual imagery (see Burstyn, 1985). The struggle to reclaim women's bodies, while occurring through discourse, takes us beyond and outside the cultural to the material realm. While this may make the problem of pornography appear more difficult to address, in my opinion, this cannot be avoided if our goal is to change the real and not simply the cultural position of women.

In the final analysis, although the equation of pornography with "violence against women" has helped to spark public indignation, this formulation does not foster the search for alternatives which extend beyond law-and-order campaigns. The danger is that once coercive representations have been eradicated, it may appear that the struggle against pornography has been won. Very little of the soft porn that I review deals directly and explicitly with physical abuse. However, this does not mean that pornography is not problematic. Rather, it suggests that what we need is a public discourse about pornography which more accurately reflects the everyday messages of pornography but moves beyond pornographic readings. While exegesis of the literal content of pornography is important to the Women's Movement, I believe that it has limited usefulness in general public campaigns. This is because there is some truth to the notion that pornography is in the eye of the beholder, given that the reading of pornographic texts relies upon the predisposition of the subject. Readings of pornography may politically mobilize individuals who recognize the subordinate status of women, but not those who fail to share this referent system. Since this referent system is the necessary beginning point for the development of any strategy of intervention, clearly the challenge is to promote a discourse which analyzes, rather than presupposes, the societal position of women. This is where Women's Studies, as a discourse by women about women's subordinate status, can make inroads against pornography. It is the beginning of a process through which women as subjects can reclaim the female body as cultural object.

Notes

1 At this point it is important to note that, unlike the United States where the First Amendment as an underlying premise of the American Constitution unequivocally upholds the right of freedom of expression, this fundamental freedom was not enshrined in the British North America Act. Reference to the freedom of expression first appears in Canadian legislation in the Canadian Bill of Rights in 1960 (see Beckton, 1982). This point is often overlooked in discussions, reflecting the American influence upon current debates.

2 Perhaps the best-known case here is the Rolling Stone's album cover: "I'm Black and Blue from the Rolling Stones and I Love It."

3 Rhodes (1988) describes these as a variety of objects related to female experience, including plaster penises and sanitary napkins stained with red paint. She maintains that it was the sanitary napkins which inspired the police to lay charges.

4 As a matter of record, numerous examples can be found in the application of criminal and family law which suggest serious resistance to the view that law should uphold the dignity of women. For examples, see *Gender Equality in the Courts: A Study by the Manitoba Association of Women and the Law*, 1988.

5 It is perhaps worth noting here that the BCPRB is likely to be disbanded as a review process after fall 1990. This follows a series of struggles surrounding the Wong decision (1989) during which BCPRB members appeared as witnesses for the prosecution, against distributors who subsequently (for whatever reason) discontinued funding.

6 References to racist stereotypes are likewise a common feature of pornography.

7 What I have observed as reviewer is a "specialty" market of pornography featuring women of visible minorities, especially Asian women. This latter market plays on stereotypical views of Asian women as both exotic and subservient.

Questions

1 What are some of the current definitions of pornography which you are familiar with? Are they adequate?

2 How can feminist protest against pornography be distinguished from conservative hostility to it?

3 What roles do women play in the production of pornography? Can pornography by/for women be envisioned as desirable?

4 What strategies are most effective to combat pornography?

References

Brownmiller, Susan. 1975. *Against Our Will: Men, Women and Rape*. New York: Simon and Schuster.

Burstyn, Varda. 1985. *Women Against Censorship*. Vancouver: Douglas and McIntyre.

Clark, Lorenne. 1980. "Pornography's Challenge to Liberal Ideology," *Canadian Forum*, (March): 9–12.

Cole, Susan. 1989. *Pornography and the Sex Crisis*. Toronto: Amanita Enterprises.

Currie, Dawn H. 1990. "Women's Liberation and Women's Mental Health: Towards a Political Economy of Eating Disorders." Pp. 25–39 in Dhruvarajan (ed.), *Women and Wellbeing*. Montreal and Kingston: McGill-Queen's University Press.

Diamond, Irene. 1980. "Pornography and Repression: A Reconsideration," *Signs*, Vol. 5, No. 4: 686–701.

Dworkin, Andrea. 1974. *Woman Hating*. New York: E.P. Dutton

Dworkin, Andrea. 1981. *Pornography: Men Possessing Women*. New York: Perigee Books.

Jarvie, I.C. 1987. "The Sociology of the Pornography Debate," *Philosophy of the Social Sciences*, Vol. 17: 257–75.

Lacombe, Dany. 1989. "Feminism and Pornography: Toward an Understanding of Repressive State Policies." Unpublished paper presented at the British Criminology Meetings, Bristol, England (July).

Leiss, William, Stephen Kline, and Sut Jhally. 1986. *Social Communication in Advertising: Persons, Products, and Images of Wellbeing*. Toronto: Methuen.

MacKinnon, Catharine. 1987. *Feminism Modified: Discourses on Life and Law*. Harvard: Harvard University Press.

McCormack, Thelma. 1985. "Appendix I: Making Sense of the Research on Pornography." Pp. 181–205 in Varda Burstyn (ed.), *Women Against Censorship*. Vancouver: Douglas and McIntyre.

McCormack, Thelma. 1987. "Feminism, Women's Studies and the New Academic Freedom." Pp. 289–303 in Gaskell and McLaren (eds.). *Women and Education: A Canadian Perspective*. Calgary: Detselig Enterprises.

McCormack, Thelma. 1988. "The Censorship of Pornography: Catharsis or Learning?" *American Journal of Orthopsychiatry*, Vol. 58, No. 4: 492–504.

Miller, Leslie J. 1987. "Uneasy Alliance: Women as Agents of Social Control," *Canadian Journal of Sociology*, Vol. 12, No. 4: 345–61.

Millett, Kate. 1969. *Sexual Politics*. New York: Doubleday.

Padon, Roger. 1984. "On the Discourse of Pornography," *Philosophy and Social Criticism*, Vol. 10, No. 1, (Summer): 17–38.

Rhodes, Jane. 1988. "Silencing Ourselves? Pornography, Censorship and Feminism in Canada," *Resources for Feminist Research*, Vol. 17; No. 3: 133–5.

Ridington, Jillian. 1988. "Confronting Pornography: A Feminist on the Front Lines." Unpublished paper, Vancouver, B.C. (available from author).

Snitow, Ann. 1985. "Retrenchment versus Transformation: The Politics of the Antipornography Movement." Pp. 107–29 in Varda Burstyn (ed.), *Women Against Censorship*. Vancouver: Douglas and McIntyre.

Steele, Lisa. 1985. "A Capital Idea: Gendering the Mass Media." Pp. 58–78 in Varda Burstyn (ed.), *Women Against Censorship*. Vancouver: Douglas and McIntyre.

Williamson, Judith. 1978. *Decoding Advertisements*. London: Marion Boyars.

Knowing Ourselves as Women[1]

Winnie Tomm
Coordinator, Women's Studies
University of Alberta

In order to transcend patriarchal knowledge, women need to develop new ways of knowing, based on integration of the rational and the emotional. Masculine binary oppositions set up a false dichotomy between mind and body, accepting as valid knowledge based only on the former. Patriarchal knowledge depends upon the concept of the 'autonomous' individual making 'objective' decisions based on 'abstract' judgement. Rather than persisting in attempts to accede to this type of knowledge and share in its production, some feminists are developing an alternative model based on reciprocal autonomy and mirroring. Positive value is assigned to women's desire for connectedness. It is necessary first to reject the sexual contract behind patriarchal domination. Aphrodite imagery, leading to new images of Beauty and Wisdom, is useful in enabling women to accept their own authority.

From Separated to Connected Knowing

Women's Studies challenges how we think about knowing, specifically that it requires the separation of mind and body. In this essay, we will examine ways of connecting knowing with sexuality, that is, with embodied social energy. A second purpose is to indicate how patriarchal society is organized around the assumption that men have a right of access to women's bodies and, therefore, to their consciousness. Third, we will show how goddess symbolism provides women with the possibility of knowing themselves more directly as subjects of independent female energy and how that imagery thereby counteracts institutionalized social practices of gender-based dominance-subordination.

The epistemology question was significantly demystified in *Women's Ways of Knowing* (Belenky *et al.*, 1986). Here the authors explore the question "What constitutes knowledge?" without explicitly referring to epistemology. Most readers can identify with some or all forms of knowledge presented in the study. The expression "ways of knowing" is preferred to "having knowledge" because the former emphasizes the dynamic nature of consciousness. The suggested ideal way of knowing in *Women's Ways of Knowing* is to construct knowledge through connectedness between intellect and feelings, both within oneself and between oneself and others. The two basic criteria for knowing are: first, a subjective, prereflective awareness; and second, the more public form of reflective, analytic discourse. Reliable ways of knowing require a good fit between these two dimensions of consciousness.

In Julia Kristeva's (1980) widely discussed view (as interpreted by Andrea Nye, 1987), the two essential ways of knowing are the underlying, uncontrolled semiotic urges and desires, on the one hand, and the structured, formal meaning-giving process of linguistic logic, on the other. According to Nye: "The semiotic is distinguished from the symbolic by Kristeva as the internal rhythms, the sonorous distinctiveness that does not yet signify anything and will be at the same time repressed and brought to light by articulated language" (1987: 673, fn. 33). These two forms of knowing, in Kristeva's view, do not blend together in a single person's consciousness. Both forms of discourse are seen to be functions of the patriarchal, phallocentric symbolic ordering of language. For Kristeva, women in patriarchal cultures do not have their own language and are therefore perceived as a group which constitutes a "disruptive and potentially revolutionary force for subjectivity of the marginal and repressed aspects of language" (Weedon, 1987: 68). This situation, as portrayed by Kristeva, creates a dilemma for women: they are either coopted or subversive in patriarchy. As a way out of the dilemma, Hélène Cixous (1981: 250) admonishes each woman to "Write your self. Your body must be heard. Only then will the immense resources of the unconscious spring forth." If we write the body it is impossible to separate the two basic features of consciousness, that is, felt awareness and analytic reflection. The inseparability of critical thought and bodily feelings is supported by Nye. She argues that language is invariably shaped by prereflective sensations and that all ideas are emotively toned.[2] As indicated by Belenky *et al.*, Cixous, Nye, and others,[3] there is reason to assume that a mutually inclusive relation exists between the semiotic (which underlies chaotic urges) and the symbolic ordering through language in an individual's consciousness.

Rejecting Patriarchal Authority

Intellectual specialists have traditionally associated authority with linguistic discourse, even though in their discourse there may be only a minimal connection with the subjective component of knowledge. The feminist thinkers I have quoted reject the strict dichotomy between the "dark wilderness" of prereflective, felt awareness, on the one hand, and the brightly lit and ordered clearing of analytic, procedural reasoning, on the other hand. This position disavows the "ethos of objectivity" (see Christ, 1987a), which favours the thinking "I" over the feeling "me," the "mind" over the "body." In addition, it argues against the claim that individuals operate freely according to the principle of rational self-interest through participation in institutionalized social contracts. Privileged men have benefited socially and economically from the imposition of their interests through legalized social contracts. This male privilege has depended upon women's lack of social freedom.

Because male authors have espoused analytic knowledge, it is associated with the male expert, even though it characterizes both male and female thinking in the patriarchal model. The normative dualism of Western rationality is fundamentally gender-based. Marsha Hanen (1988: 29) points out that our notion of objectivity includes "the assumption of a polarity between man and woman that structures our views of and investigations into what constitutes men's and women's natures"; more generally, it determines other binary dualisms characteristic of patriarchal language. Normative dualism entails the assumption that binary polarities are qualities of the "real" world rather than part of the analytic framework through which we perceive and give meaning to the world.

In contrast to normative dualism, the integrative approach to knowledge assumes the unity of mind and body. Knowing through our bodies as well as by intellectual reasoning is compatible with the paradigm of knowing according to an "ethos of passion and empathy" (Christ, 1987a), a notion which will be developed in the last part of this paper. Knowing with passion and empathy integrates knowledge and action. This model reflects the rejection of impersonal, analytic knowledge and the corresponding male authoritarianism of the "ethos of objectivity." According to Naomi Black (1988), our unwillingness to accept male authority, just because it is male, is probably the biggest act of insubordination in history.

The rejection of male authority just because it is male frees us from polarizing dualisms. "When language is seen dialogically, the goal is not the subversion of always reconstituted rationality but, rather, the achievement of understanding and commonality" (Nye, 1987: 683).

Knowledge is constituted through connections between the wildness of the body (nature) and the controlled structures of language (culture). Knowing ourselves as women includes ordering our realities in a language that reflects and nourishes our female subjectivity. The culturization of nature and the naturalization of culture are part of an integrated consciousness and lifestyle.

Universalist, ahistorical analyses of both male dominance and resistance to it should be connected to particular, historical analyses which explain localized social patterns. Ann Ferguson (1989: 6) claims that "specific societies must be analyzed as social formations whose forces of male dominance depend on the particular historical combination of the economic and social systems involved." According to Ferguson, our North American social institutions such as politics, economics, education, church, and family are largely organized around "sex energy." This energy paradigm of sex allows us to make connections between non-rational factors in our consciousness and rational self-interests which determine the organization of social patterns. Ferguson argues that "sex is a bodily energy which is gathered up and organized into social outlets by contextual social meanings" (1989: 52). In light of the way in which sexual politics permeate our society, it is reasonable to claim that our ways of knowing are shaped by our experiences of ourselves as sexual beings. We cannot know ourselves independently of the sexual energy that is part of our individuality and sociality. The social contracts into which we enter are shaped by the social meanings attributed to our sexuality.

According to Carole Pateman (1988), women's subordination in all respects — including that of authoritative knowing — stems from a male privilege. In Pateman's view, patriarchy derives from a hidden sexual contract that privileges male access to women's bodies. She calls this privilege the "male sex-right": the original social contract. An original contract "explains why exercise of right is legitimate" (1988: 1). This contract initiates the patriarchal right which is "the power that men exercise over women" (*ibid.*). The influence of the male sex-right does not stop at the bedroom door or in the brothel or in sexual harassment in the workplace. It extends to authority in the lecture room, the boardroom, the factory, and, indeed, throughout civilized society. Socialization in patriarchal cultures results in acceptance of the superior authority of men at the highest and lowest levels of society: that is the social meaning attributed to male sexuality in patriarchy.

Following from the assumption of a male sex right, female sexuality is valued primarily as a means of satisfaction for men's interests and desires with respect to such contracts as marriage, reproduction, and prostitution. However, the male sexual dominance that is assumed in the bedroom extends into the economy so that today we are addressing the major global phenomenon of the feminization of poverty (see Waring, 1988). Sexual politics are endemic to our patriarchal way of life, contributing to women's lack of authority and to their poverty both in the unpaid and paid labour forces.

According to Pateman, every social contract since the original one has been underwritten by the male sex right. If we look at the structuring of our society's institutions with the idea that they were shaped by a sexual contract, we can recognize the social relation of the sexes to be fundamentally one of dominance/subordination. A woman who enters into these relations and who does not accept their hierarchical nature (either implicitly or explicitly) commits an act of insubordination. It is from this perspective that feminist theory and the women's social movement are perceived by men as collective insubordination. However, we still have not dealt very effectively with our own sexuality, what it means with respect to our authority and, coextensively, with the ways in which we can know ourselves and others. I do not think we can move much further toward increased authority for women's knowledge unless we cut at the root of women's subordination: the male sex right that gives unquestioned privileges to men with respect to women's bodies and, correspondingly, their consciousness. In order to undercut the strength of the hidden sexual contract that organizes our society, we must take women's sexuality seriously, as a form of social energy and authority potentially free from the dominance of male sexuality. The female birthright, no less than that of the male, is the power over one's own sexuality.

Reclaiming Women's Sexuality

The work of Carol Christ (1989a, 1989b, 1987a, 1987b, 1979) is an example of a possible way of arriving at a more helpful view of our sexuality. In her book *Laughter of Aphrodite* (1987b), she describes her journey out of traditional religion and into goddess reverence. She emphasizes how important it is for a woman to have a connection with a spiritual source that she herself can identify with as an embodied female. For Carol Christ, Aphrodite symbolizes the ability to laugh at oneself as a woman for having been taken in by the patriarchal dominant/subordinate story of the relation between the sexes. She allows us to laugh at the ridiculousness of patriarchal assumptions about male dominance and to rise above the humiliating and painful submission that results from them. There is the realization, according to Carol Christ, and also Jean Shinoda Bolen (1984), that through the goddess, we can live from within our own power and enter into relations from a position of strength. In her song, *I Love Women Who Laugh*, Canadian songwriter Heather Bishop declares that "We have to learn to love ourselves first." Christ claims that the study of goddess symbolism and experiences of the presence of the goddess help us to do just that. She claims that identification with a spiritual source such as an Aphrodite archetype is a means of personal reclamation and a way of knowing with assurance.

Goddess imagery assists us in identifying female sexuality as central to our perception of women as self-determining social agents. It is not uncommon among those who acknowledge a spiritual dimension of the self to refer to a "metaphorical hole" (see Macquarrie, 1983) within the self, a vessel which is filled with a spiritual power. It is a space that we can come home to in ourselves and from which we can move out to others. It is our "re-membering place" where we remember our heritage and we re-member ourselves: put ourselves together. Knowledge and action are believed to be empowered through grounding the self in that "metaphorical hole." It is an integrative power which is re-evolutionary, directing social action away from a dominator model and toward an evolutionary process characterized by connection and integration (see Eisler, 1987). If women are to participate significantly in the symbol-making system which shapes social evolution, then their sexual identity must be integrated constructively in the symbol-making system. In order for us to accept our own authority and that of other women, it is important that our sexual identity be incorporated into our individual and collective consciousness in an affirming way. We need to affirm both the uniqueness of women, as distinct from men, and the normality of women as persons.

A social reality, in which the subjectivities of women and men are given equal weight, is supported by a theory of human nature which includes a sex-specific account of human beings. To ignore sex specificity is to play into the hands of "received wisdom," which defines an "individual" as an owner of property in "his" own person (Locke); knowledge as being independent of non-rational factors (Descartes); and morality as the application of universal principles of freedom upheld by male rationality (Kant). Women were intentionally excluded from those accounts of the nature and function of autonomous individuals who could freely enter into social contracts that would protect rational self-interest to the greatest degree.

If the agency of women is to be acknowledged fully, it is not sufficient simply to enlarge such an inadequate account of individuals, knowledge, and morality to include women. Rational self-interest and non-rational concerns for connectedness have to be integrated in ways in which we know ourselves as persons in relation to each other and to our environment. Both women's and men's rational self-interests and emotional needs are inseparable from their respective sexualities. If we give positive social meanings to women's independent sexuality, then a single woman would not be considered suspect, as she often is in patriarchal societies in which men's sexuality is privileged. Most particularly, her sexuality would not be governed by a morality that separates respectable women from disreputable ones, according to socially sanctioned relations with men. Judging a woman immoral because her sexuality is not circumscribed by a socially approved relation to a male would itself be regarded as immoral if women had a real independent status as persons. In the place of a morality based on the male sex right, morality could be about self-care and care for others. This would require that we take ourselves and other persons (as well as the rest of nature) seriously.

A Feminist Moral Vision

In many ways, life is largely a conversation; we contribute to the perceived nature of reality through the conversations we have. We talk about ourselves and others in ways that encourage integrative growth or in ways that minimize it. We have the power to enliven others or to shrivel them. We do the same to ourselves, depending on the kinds of conversations we have. The ability to transform ourselves and others is reflected in our ways of knowing. Such transformation depends on the ability of subjects to elicit strengths from each other through openness and receptivity.

Our society is characterized largely by the interaction of separate, dominating individuals and soluble, subordinate ones. The interests of the latter dissolve into those of the heroic figures (see Keller, 1986). The hidden sexual contract, as discussed above, contributes to the social organization of separate and soluble selves along sexual lines. Between the two extremes of a separate or soluble self lies the possibility of a permeable self: the existence of receptivity and responsiveness in relationships. If we know ourselves in that way, it is probable that our form of knowing is characterized by being-in-relation. This means that one receives oneself and the other, as well as being received by the other (Ulanov, 1981). It means that the use of women as "goods" according to the hidden sexual contract underlying patriarchal social relations will cease to be a feature of dominant morality and social practice (see Irigaray, 1981).

Riane Eisler (1987) and Gerda Lerner (1986) suggest that there probably was a social and cultural drift away from egalitarian social relations between the sexes toward dominant-submissive ones prior to the time of recorded history (around 3500 BC). Historically, we learned to "know" according to the cultural assumptions that supported the rise and continuation of patriarchy. As Christ points out, "the androcentric perspective functions to legitimate a patriarchal society, to make it seem 'obvious' . . . that elite men have always held the power in the world and always will" (1987a: 53). The competitive man of reason, whom Genevieve Lloyd (1984) describes so adequately, is complemented by the maternal, supporting woman. She has been (and often continues to be) rewarded for knowing her restricted place, not for knowing herself as a person with the capacity to expand in unlimited ways. Mandatory gender roles were institutionalized in social contract theory, as we saw above. In the patriarchal paradigm, we learned not to take a stand for our own power and destinies.

To know otherwise requires a paradigm shift, a shift in consciousness. We have to expose the hidden sexual contract and resist seeing ourselves in terms of the dominant-subordinate patterns which arise from its assumption. The shift includes "a questioning of fundamental and unquestioned assumptions about canon, ideas, value, authority, and method" (Christ, 1987a: 53), which govern the ways in which we seek to know. With a paradigm shift toward integrative knowing, we erode the assumptions of a perspective that privileges the intellectual way of knowing in terms of Western rationality, which depends on the separation of rational self-interest and emotive drives to connectedness. Integrative knowing is directed by an ethos of connectedness, of eros and compassion. To be human in the new paradigm is to "understand our connection to other people and to all other beings and to rejoice in the life that has been given to us" (Christ, 1989b: 322). The essential self is a process of becoming: of opening ourselves to the mirroring of others through listening.

As women, we have largely lost touch with our "re-membering place," the place where we locate our connections to our female heritage. We often do not remember about the intricacy of beauty and wisdom, which lies in the intensity of energy reflecting the subjectivity of a person. The "re-membering place" is the metaphorical space inside where desire for connection arises and where passionate engagement with ourselves and others is made possible (see Benjamin, 1986). Beauty is having the passion that comes from identification with oneself and others in a powerful way. Wisdom is living with moral passion that comes from the realization of connectedness through subjectivity. Both come from the creative matrix of which we are a part (see Allen, 1989).

In light of this process of re-membering, we are redefining the notions of beauty and wisdom and recognizing the inseparability of one from the other. We experience and understand beauty in terms of its transformative power. We express beauty through wisdom. Beauty is the power that enlarges the self through relationship. Knowledge of oneself, others, and the environment — a knowledge resulting from openness and receptivity — constitutes a form of wisdom that renders the knower beautiful. The power of the knower lies in the ability to enhance others. This is the beauty of the knower and it is also her wisdom. Both are located in the permeable self and are expressed through social action directed by the desire for connectedness. This view of the self and relations with others contrasts sharply with the notion of self as an independent property owner, whose strength lies in his power to dominate the other through the promotion of rational self-interest in the context of social contracts.

The freedom of female embodied knowing that comes from re-membering our own powerful subjectivity is transformative. It is the power that any individual has to contribute to another and to expand through the presence of another. It is also the power to be present to oneself. That kind of being present to oneself is a form of autonomy (self-determination), a way of knowing oneself that shapes one's thoughts and activities. At the same time, it is depends on our mirroring or coaching of those around us. In this way of knowing, the self is a permeable self, rather than a soluble or separate one. Accordingly, one's way of knowing is a connected way of knowing that includes the two components of felt experience and reflection. It is a way of knowing that is bold and courageous, on the one hand, and gentle and responsive, on the other — the kind of knowing that is reflected in Aphrodite symbolism, as described by Christ and Bolen. It transforms both the self and others. It engenders boldness and courageousness through commitment to oneself and others. Most importantly, it includes commitment to women.

Conclusion

As outlined above, the notion of ways of knowing distinct to women significantly challenges the patriarchal approach to knowledge, which emphasizes the separation of cognitive and affective dimensions of our being. In its place, a number of writers posit the construction of knowledge through connectedness between intellect and feeling, both within oneself and between oneself and others. Connected knowing implies a shift away from a hierarchical to an egalitarian view, both in our relations to subjects of inquiry and in our relations with others. In the final analysis, commitment to women is required for this paradigm shift away from dominance and toward equality. As we have seen, the disempowerment of women in patriarchal societies is reflected in our ways of knowing and behaving. It is reflected in the stories we tell and internalize. Aphrodite, for example, was depicted as a sort of dumb blond sexpot in hellenic mythology, a mythology shaped by the domination of Zeus. When we examine the heritage of females,[4] it becomes clear how the lineage of goddesses associated with Aphrodite was dismantled and the story was retold to suit patriarchal assumptions. The importance of retelling the story of the heritage of women's self-determining power, and eliminating the negativity with which it is imbued, cannot be overemphasized.

Following Carol Christ, I believe that in order to know the desires of our re-membering places, it is helpful to have symbols upon which we can reflect and whose power we can call upon. Aphrodite symbolism is one such source. Bolen (1984) refers to Aphrodite as the alchemical goddess. Alchemy was the medieval science of turning a base metal into gold. Aphrodite symbolizes the ability to transform oneself and others from something perceived as of little worth into something of inestimable value. This ability develops through the practice of drawing out the strengths of oneself and others through openness and receptivity — being present to oneself and to others. The depiction of beauty as wisdom, including courage and vulnerability, is a guide in Aphrodite symbolism for women developing new and powerful ways of knowing ourselves, others, and our connectedness to the earth. In this way we contribute to a paradigm shift away from domination toward connectedness in which our sexuality as vital energy characterizes our individual and collective ways of knowing and interacting.

Notes

I wish to thank the following people for generously commenting on earlier versions of this paper: Dr. Wendy Donner, Department of Philosophy, Concordia University, Ms. Aileen Quinn, student and research assistant, Dr. Peter Schouls, Department of Philosophy, and Dr. Pat Valentine, Faculty of Nursing: the last three are at the University of Alberta.

1 Portions of this paper are included in my forthcoming article, "Goddess Consciousness and Social Realities," in *Women and World Religions*, a new journal edited by A. Sharma and K. Young, to be published at McGill University.

2 The inseparability of ideas and sensations in consciousness and moral agency is discussed at length in Tomm, 1984.

3 For an excellent analysis of Luce Irigaray's account of how women might be represented as autonomous and self-defined subjects through the female body, see Elizabeth Grosz, 1990.

4 See, for example, Adler, 1979; Downing, 1984; Plaskow and Christ, 1989; Stone, 1976, 1979; and Weaver, 1989.

Questions

1 In our experience, do women "know" in ways which are different from men? If so, what does this imply for current academic definitions of "knowledge"?
2 In what ways are these "women's ways of knowing" related to our bodies? Are images such as "reciprocity," "openness," "permeability," justified in this context?
3 How can women modify the sexual contract underlying the patriarchal mind/body dichotomy?
4 In what ways might Beauty and Wisdom, and the relation between them, be redefined by women?

References

Aiken, Susan Hardy, *et al.* (eds.). 1988. *Changing Our Minds: Feminist Transformations of Knowledge*. New York: State University of New York.

Adler, Margot. 1979. *Bringing Down the Moon*. Boston: Beacon Press.

Allen, Paula Gunn. 1989. "Grandmother of the Sun: The Power of Woman in Native America." Pp. 22–8 in Plaskow and Christ (eds.), *Weaving the Visions: New Patterns in Feminist Spirituality*. San Francisco: Harper and Row.

Belenky, Mary Field, *et al.* 1986. *Women's Ways of Knowing: The Development of Self, Voice, and Mind*. New York: Basic Books.

Benjamin, Jessica. 1986. "A Desire of One's Own: Psychoanalytic Feminism and Intersubjective Space." Pp. 78–101 in de Lauretis (ed.), *Feminist Studies / Critical Studies*. Bloomington: Indiana University Press.

Bishop, Heather. 1982. *I Love Women Who Laugh*. World Records for Mother of Pearl Records Inc., Woodmore, Man.

Black, Naomi. 1988. "Where All the Ladders Start: A Feminist Perspective on Social Science." Pp. 167–90 in Tomm and Hamilton (eds.), *Gender Bias in Scholarship: The Pervasive Prejudice*. Waterloo, Ont.: Wilfrid Laurier University.

Bolen, Jean Shinoda. 1984. *Goddesses in Everywoman: A New Psychology of Women*. San Francisco: Harper and Row.

Christ, Carol P. 1989a. "Embodied Thinking: Reflections on Feminist Theological Method," *Journal of Feminist Studies in Religion*, Vol. 5, No. 1 (spring): 7–17.

Christ, Carol P. 1989b. "Rethinking Theology and Nature." Pp. 314–25 in Plaskow and Christ (eds.), *Weaving the Visions: New Patterns in Feminist Spirituality*. San Francisco: Harper and Row.

Christ, Carol P. 1987a. "Toward a Paradigm Shift in the Academy and in Religious Studies." Pp. 53–76 in Christie Farnham (ed.), *The Impact of Feminist Research in the Academy*. Bloomington: Indiana University.

Christ, Carol P. 1987b. *Laughter of Aphrodite: Reflections on a Journey to the Goddess*. San Francisco: Harper and Row.

Christ, Carol P. 1979. "Why Women Need the Goddess: Phenomenological, Psychological, and Political Reflections." Pp. 273–87 in Christ and Plaskow (eds.), *Womanspirit Rising: A Feminist Reader in Religion*. San Francisco: Harper and Row.

Cixous, Hélène. 1981. "Utopias." Pp. 245–64 in Marks and de Courtivron (eds.), *New French Feminisms*. New York: Schocken Books.

Culpepper, Emily Erwin. 1987. "Philosophia: Feminist Methodology for Constructing a Female Train of Thought," *Journal of Feminist Studies in Religion*, Vol. 3, No. 2 (fall): 7–16.

Downing, Christine. 1984. *The Goddess: Mythological Images of the Feminine*. New York: Crossroad.

Eisler, Riane. 1987. *The Chalice and The Blade: Our History, Our Future*. San Francisco: Harper and Row.

Ferguson, Ann. 1989. *Blood at the Root: Motherhood, Sexuality and Male Dominance*. London: Pandora.

Gilligan, Carol. 1982. *In a Different Voice: Psychological Theory and Women's Development*. Cambridge, Mass.: Harvard University Press.

Grosz, Elizabeth. 1990. "Irigaray's Notion of Sexual Morphology." Paper presented at "Imag(in)ing Women: Representations of Women in Culture" (Conference), University of Alberta, Edmonton, 5 April.

Hanen, Marsha. 1988. "Feminism, Objectivity, and Legal Truth." Pp. 29–45 in Code, Mullett, and Overall (eds.), *Feminist Perspectives: Philosophical Essays on Method and Morals*. Toronto: University of Toronto Press.

Irigaray, Luce. 1981 "Demystifications." Pp. 107–10 in Marks and de Courtivron (eds.), *New French Feminisms*. New York: Schocken Books.

Keller, Catherine. 1986. *From A Broken Web: Separation, Sexism, and Self*. Boston: Beacon.

Kristeva, Julia. 1980. *Desire in Language: A Semiotic Approach to Literature and Art*. New York: Columbia University Press.

Lerner, Gerda. 1986. *The Creation of Patriarchy*. Oxford: Oxford University Press.

Lloyd, Genevieve. 1984. *The Man of Reason*. Minneapolis: University of Minnesota Press.

Macquarrie, John. 1983. *In Search of Humanity: A Theological and Philosophical Approach*. New York: Crossroad.

Nye, Andrea. 1987. "Woman Clothed with the Sun: Julia Kristeva and the Escape from/to Language," *Signs*, Vol. 12, No. 2 (summer): 664–86.

Pateman, Carole. 1988. *The Sexual Contract*. Oxford: Polity Press.

Plaskow, Judith, and Carol P. Christ (eds.). 1989. *Weaving the Visions: New Patterns in Feminist Spirituality*. San Francisco: Harper and Row.

Stone, Merlin. 1979. *Ancient Mirrors of Womanhood: A Treasury of Goddess and Heroine Lore from Around the World*. Boston: Beacon.

Stone, Merlin. 1976. *When God Was a Woman*. New York: Harvest/HBJ.

Tomm, Winnifred. 1990. "Sexuality, Rationality, and Spirituality," *Zygon*, Vol. 25, No. 2, (June): 219–37.

Tomm, Winnifred. 1984. Spinoza, Hume, and Vasubandhu: The Relation between Reason and Emotion. Unpublished PhD dissertation, University of Calgary, Calgary, Alta.

Ulanov, Ann Belford. 1981. *Receiving Woman: Studies in the Psychology and Theology of the Feminine*. Philadelphia: Westminster Press.

Waring, Marilyn. 1988. *If Women Counted: A New Feminist Economics*. San Francisco: Harper and Row.

Weaver, Mary Jo. 1989. "Who is the Goddess and Where Does She Get Us?" *Journal of Feminist Studies in Religions*, Vol. 5, No. 1 (spring): 49–64.

Weedon, Chris. 1987. *Feminist Practice and Poststructuralist Theory*. Oxford: Basil Blackwell.

Unhiding the Hidden:
Writing during the Quiet Revolution[1]

Anne Brown
Department of French
University of New Brunswick

During the Quiet Revolution in Québec (1960s) an unprecedented number of women writers published novels. Many of these focus on women's experience of their bodies in an oppressive regime based on Catholic conceptions of woman as responsible for Original Sin, and the flesh — particularly that of women — as Evil. Physical functions such as menstruation, pregnancy, and childbirth are perceived in these novels as reminders of female deficiency. Women, having internalized guilt, view their physiology with shame and disgust. Although dominant views are not necessarily denied, women do find a voice to express their anguish, preparing the way for subsequent feminist writing in Québec.

"Unhiding the Hidden"

During the decade that predated the resurgence of feminism in Québec, novels written by women could be characterized by their aim to explore a strictly female reality. During the Quiet Revolution, a decade also known as "l'âge de la parole,"[2] women wrote seventy-four novels. Prior to that, relatively few female voices were heard in Québec's literary scene. The winds of freedom blowing over Québec thus gave flight to women's literary aspirations. Writing at a time when feminist consciousness was not yet generalized, they nevertheless clearly concerned themselves with breaking the silence on women's private experiences. In this they foreshadowed the second wave of Québécois feminism. The position they now occupy in the female literary tradition of Québec is a remarkable one. By boldly paving the road leading to the repossession of the Word, they have bridged the gap between the more traditional women writers of the past and the more radically women-centered ones to come. Perceiving women as both source and center of their writing, the authors of these texts have been among the first in Québec to undermine the ruling androcentric model, according to which women are mere adjuncts to plot and theme. Having displaced the phallic subject with the female subject, these novelists began to inscribe women's physical experiences in writing.

Since they focus on the lives of contemporary women, what is often foregrounded in the narratives is the fundamental alienation of women, an alienation resulting in large part from our culture's denigration of the female body. Indeed, society's opprobrium for femininity is a motif which recurs in many of these novels. Given the vast array of novels written in the 1960s, I have chosen to highlight those texts in which the hatred of the female body is explicitly described. Bent on "unhiding the hidden" (Godard, 1987: 19), they provide us with a hitherto unwritten description of women's bodily functions and women's perceptions of these functions. This description testifies to the fact that women — having internalized the ruling male culture's intermingling of the notions of evil and female sexuality — are psychically wounded. Out of touch with their own experience and that of other women, the protagonists appear unable to reject the distorted image of the female body — the vessel of all evil and of all vices — presented to them as the word of God and the wisdom of man.

It should be emphasized that feminist critics such as Douglas (1970: 65) have argued that "the social body constrains the way the physical body is perceived." This is particularly true in Québec where, until fairly recently, the female body and its functions — menstruation, pregnancy, and giving birth — were the most taboo dimensions of women's situation. Dominated by a male-centered, sex-negative conservative Roman Catholicism, in which evil was associated with sex and sex with women, this society ideologically manipulated women into believing that their bodies were linked to all that is lower and should therefore remain hidden, unspoken.

Supported by the liberal principles of modernization and secularization that took root in Québec during the Quiet Revolution, women writers broke the silence on women's private experiences. Their narratives — which both describe and interpret the impact of a systematic denigration of the female body on women's lives — provide valuable insight into the mutilated femininity of women in such a society where denigration is internalized by its victims. A heroine embraces self-hatred born of her abhorrence of the female body, for example. What interpretation can one venture of this self-destructive act? Can she divest herself of this alienating force? If so, what are the conditions that enable her to redefine herself as a being worthy of self-love?

In her analysis of the intrinsic 'value' that is traditionally attached to the female body, the French psychoanalyst Luce Irigaray (1974: 142) argues that "la femme n'a pas . . . l'organe sexuel qui monopolise la valeur."[3] She further proposes that phallocentric societies' refusal to validate the female body has left profound scars on the feminine psyche. In their desire to underline this fact, the writers in question almost exclusively portray women who are plagued with feelings of existential worthlessness similar to the self-disdain of the colonized. This self-disdain is most clearly expressed in their hatred of the body.

Hatred of the Female Body

In Michèle Mailhot's *Le Portique* (1967), for example, Soeur Josée's hatred is typified by an obsessive aspiration: the destruction of her body. The anguish that she feels at the thought that her soul is imprisoned in a female body not only borders on the neurotic but comes within a hair's breath of a profound death wish. By subjecting her body to various forms of self-inflicted torture, this cloistered postulant hopes to eradicate her physical essence. As she so clearly states: "Le tuer [son corps]. Etre une âme, rien qu'une âme" (1967: 20).[4] Her death wish stems from her acceptance of the Roman Catholic ethos according to which matter and spirit are separate. In this dualistic thought, man is associated with spirit and matter with woman. Matter is also thought to corrupt spirit. This gynophobic, manichaean perception of woman, circulating freely in Soeur Josée's culture, leads to the disintegration of her identity. The more severe aspects of her emotional instability are exemplified in the severe disorder of her thoughts. These range from ecstasy and mystic salvation to extreme despair coupled with hallucinations and delusions as, for example, when she is convinced that God is an impatient lover who complains about her lateness in joining Him in "un jardin de délices" (1967: 22).[5]

It is interesting to note that Soeur Josée's story ends on a positive note. Unable to suppress her life force, which is in constant rebellion with her role as a martyr, she becomes increasingly aware that her acts of physical degradation and of sexual deprivation are akin to a form of mental illness. This insight leads her to abandon her cloistered life in favour of a secular existence, the latter symbolizing the beginning of her quest for wholeness. Viewed in a certain light, Soeur Josée's metamorphosis seems designed to illustrate the rise in consciousness of Québécois women, who, during the Quiet Revolution, began to question the validity of their Roman Catholic upbringing and its stifling rules, which were bent on perpetuating the myth of a universe dually controlled by opposing forces of good (male) and evil (female), a world in which the female body is consistently identified with the realm of sin and chaos.

One of Marie-Claire Blais's most popular novels, *Manuscrits de Pauline Archange* (1968), also features a young heroine, Louisette, who is unable to take pride in her femininity. Educated by nuns who taught her that her genitalia embody "le lieu du péché" (1968: 64)[6] *par excellence*, Louisette quickly succumbs to an all-pervasive hatred of her sex coupled with a great admiration for the opposite sex. As she so readily admits: "Je déteste les filles . . . , tandis que les garçons . . ." (1968: 64).[7] Characterized by her inability to perceive females in a positive light, Louisette becomes a problem student who laughs in the face of authority, disrupts her classes, and takes inordinate pleasure in instructing some of her peers in the fundamentals of masturbation. Louisette's rejection of authority, compulsive masturbation and hatred of women symbolize the rage that inhabits her: a rage nourished by the inescapable fact that her culture justifies its refusal to validate the female experience by equating women with evil. Instinctively, Louisette senses that, because of her sex, she may be trapped forever in the periphery of her culture. Her delinquent behaviour, motivated primarily by her desire to distance herself from the conventional values of a culture that stultifies true freedom, must therefore be interpreted as her only hope of escape. For, as she herself insists: "c'est question de vie et de mort" (1968: 71).[8]

Yolande Chéné's *Au Seuil de l'enfer* (1965) offers an interesting variation on the theme of women's hatred of their bodies. Her protagonist, Marthe, displays a variety of psychosomatic illnesses. Subject to insomnia, depression, fainting spells, and seizures, Marthe's life slowly unfolds before her like an endless nightmare. Enough clues are dispersed throughout the text to allow us to conclude that the source of her ill-health lies mainly in her hatred of her gender. Having internalized the myth of male superiority and its counterpart, female inferiority, Marthe is unable to rejoice in her femininity. Convinced that the female body is riddled with diseases, while the male body is synonymous with health, she emphatically rejects her bodily nature: "[J]e ne veux pas être femelle" (1965: 135).[9] By rejecting the very essence of her being, she condemns herself to a life dominated by the spectre of insanity. In the novel's final scene, Marthe is interned in a mental asylum following a failed suicide attempt. Her case differs from Soeur Josée's and Louisette's in that there is very little hope that she will one day transcend her alienation.

In the protagonists mentioned above, the portrayal of female alienation is further intensified by the fact that all are characterized by dissimilar social situations yet are similarly consumed by a strong hatred of their bodies. Practising or lapsed Roman Catholics, they move about in a society coloured by a repressive brand of Christianity bent on perpetuating a particularly insidious myth identified by Simone de Beauvoir (1949: 232) as the following: "La chair qui est . . . l'*Autre* ennemi ne se distingue pas de la femme."[10] If a positive self-image is paralyzed in them, it is also because, like all Roman Catholics, they are unable to reject the Paradise myth as told in Genesis. According to this ancient myth, it is a woman, Eve, who first introduced sin into the world. It is she who ate the fruit, experienced sexual desire, seduced Adam, and brought about the Fall of Man. Thus the female body was transformed into an organ of danger, incarnating the soul's eternal enemy.

Women novelists go on to show, subtly or bluntly, that it is through patriarchally fostered cultural views that women so readily attach negative labels to natural bodily events such as menstruation, pregnancy, and childbirth. By ending the silence which had traditionally surrounded these events in our literature, they bring out of the shadows and into the spotlight an important insight of feminist psychology: the tendency in most women to deprecate the physical manifestations of their femininity. Through direct or indirect references to their protagonists' rejection of the body, women writers expose the sexist biases underpinning the image and the perception of the female body in our culture. In addition, they provide the reader with an insight into the traumatizing effects that menstruation, pregnancy, and childbirth can have on the feminine psyche when social, cultural, and religious conditions are such that women cannot help but internalize an external negative perception of these biological realities. In sum, unable to celebrate the body, women are transformed into fragmented beings whose experiences tear them apart. Their sexual alienation thus becomes a powerful expression of their overwhelming human alienation. These, then, are texts of denial and mutilation, texts which are framed by an existential threat to women's personal identity. The aesthetic dimension of these stories, in which female self-hatred dominates the textual surface, appears, at different levels, to be structured as a critique of our society as a whole.

Indeed, various dissimilar fictitious women are similarly affected by the myths and taboos that surround the female body and that are allowed to circulate freely in their society. For some of them — Françoise in Louise Maheux-Forcier's *Une forêt pour Zoé* (1969), Mme Marchand in Nellie Maillard's *La Nuit si longue* (1960), and Mme Archange in Marie-Claire Blais's *Les Apparences* (1970) — the hatred of the body is captured in their belief that the menstrual flow is the indisputable sign of women's infamy. In their minds, this blood is cursed blood, a defiled and defiling liquid, a symbol of Divine punishment which they must bear in shame, for in the eyes of God they are, as Marie-Claire Blais's (1970: 100) heroine says, "des animaux inférieurs."[11] Descendants of Eve, whose sin of disobedience all women have been condemned to expiate, these protagonists are equally convinced that their salvation, and that of their daughters, rests on their ability to imprint in the latter's minds the mythical belief that menstruation is first and foremost the physical proof of their sex's unworthiness, uncleanliness, and inferiority.

The Pregnant Body

If these women are alienated from their bodies because of the menstrual taboos under which they have been placed, still others see their pregnancy and childbearing as shameful, disgraceful experiences. Among these protagonists, many loom large. In Jacqueline Tremblay's *Marie-Anne ma douce* (1964), for example, the repressive nature of Québécois society in all matters pertaining to the female body shows in the neurotic reactions attributed to the properly married protagonist, Marie-Anne. Bearing the burden of a psychological scar directly related to a religious upbringing that engrained in her a belief in the female body as the root of all evil, Marie-Anne's dormant self-hatred is awakened soon after she discovers that she is pregnant. Recurring references to her feelings of shame and loathing attest to her psychological struggle in dealing with her pregnancy. Convinced that her body is repulsive, she refuses to receive visitors and voluntarily incarcerates herself in her home. Her femininity, visibly expressed by her pregnancy, leaves her reeling with shame. She confesses to her husband: "Cela me gêne tellement" (1964: 82).[12] Her first pregnancy is therefore a tremendous source of anguish rather than a joyful affirmation of her female power.

Another novelist, Paule Saint-Onge, develops this same theme of pregnancy as a state of pure shame and anguish. Isabelle, the protagonist of *Ce qu'il faut de regrets* (1961), is a mother of four. Her complete lack of pleasure at the thought that she is once again with child has nothing to do with the number of children she has already borne. Indeed, she has endured her pregnancies in a state of self-loathing and alienation. For this protagonist, pregnancy is nothing more or nothing less than an "atroce et humiliante déformation" (1961: 20).[13]

The shame and humiliation that dominate the protagonists' emotional landscape during their pregnancies rapidly escalate into acute revulsion and horror during labour. Gilberte in Claire de Lamirande's *Le Grand élixir* (1969), for example, is so horrified by the birthing process that she loses all control and indulges in a fit of screaming. Hoping to shame her into silence, the attendant nurse orders her to "Pensez à

Jésus sur la croix" (1969: 162),[14] to which Gilberte screams all the more loudly: "Pourquoi cette disgrâce, pourquoi cette laideur?" (*ibid.*).[15]

It is this question — about the disgrace and ugliness of the female body — that women novelists attempt to answer. In their fiction it becomes clear that, if women equate menstrual blood with "des ordures" (Blais, 1970: 101),[16] pregnancy with a shameful process that deforms the body, and childbirth with a debasing experience which reduces them to the level of "une bête" (de Lamirande, 1969: 162),[17] it is primarily because in Québec, as in other patriarchal societies, women must live the various moments of their female condition under the signs of modesty, silence, discretion, shame and disdain. Having been taught that the menses are "stigmates d'infériorité" (Mailhot, 1967: 34),[18] that the penalty for forgetting to destroy all evidence of this blood is to be ostracized and/or beaten "à coups de règle" (Blais, 1970: 102),[19] that the pregnant body must be hidden because the sight of it brings to mind the sexual act, and finally, that labour pains are "ce qu'on mérite à cause d'Eve" (Blais, 1970: 101),[20] the protagonists eventually fall prey to a sickness that characterizes all oppressed groups. This sickness can be identified as a self-hatred so inclusive that it often extends to encompass all of womankind.

The Female Body as a Commodity

This self-hatred is further shown to be exacerbated by a consumer society in which the female body is systematically and unabashedly used to promote the sale of goods. The imaginary world of Madeleine Ferron offers us a salient example of the pain that the appropriation of the female body inflicts upon women. In *La Fin des loups-garous* (1966), she portrays a young woman, Rose, who is repulsed by her body mainly because she lives in a world that thrives on advertisements which, implicitly or explicitly, define the female body as a commodity. The narrator thus describes Rose's loss of self-esteem: "depuis que la peau de la femme se vendait au pied cube pour augmenter la vente des autos, des brosses à dents, même des journaux, elle était gênée de la sienne" (1966: 52).[21]

Laure, one of Michèle Mailhot's principle characters in *Dis-moi que je vis* (1964), has a lot in common with Rose. Like the latter, her female pride has been shattered and her sense of self distorted by a consumer society in which the female body is used to fan men's desires to buy. The author repeatedly shows that, in a culture that fetishizes the female body and distorts its image, women tend to be defined by their lovers or husbands as mere objects to be abused or disposed of at will. Suffering from what Jacques Derrida (1976: 141) defines as "speculary dispossession," Laure drowns her anguish in a bottle and becomes increasingly obsessed with the twisted hope that one day "une grosse bombe atomique" (1967: 88)[22] will be dropped on the society that has robbed her of her true identity, and therefore of her power.

Conclusion

Through the study of the troubled self-hood that plagues Québécois heroines during the 1960s, we have seen that, on the one hand, women are ordered to cover their bodies because they are a source of sin while, on the other hand, they are made to disrobe to increase the sale of goods. In both cases, the female identity is defined solely in terms of the body. By exposing the hypocrisy inherent in our culture in matters pertaining to the body, women writers have also shown that mental experiences reflect bodily ones. Their narratives thus confirm Rubenstein's (1987: 4) observation: "the body is . . . a template for figurative expressions of experience." What then is this experience? To summarize, it is one in which the mind is torn asunder because the body is fragmented. This fragmentation is responsible for generating an overwhelming feeling of dispossession which, in turn, gives rise to women's torn experience. Overcome by man's contempt for women, clearly expressed in society's devaluation of their physical experiences as well as in its appropriation/reification of their bodies, the protagonists succumb to alcoholism, insanity, psychological suicide, self-hatred, compulsive behaviours, masochistic tendencies, psychosomatic complaints, and deep-rooted neuroses.

Nevertheless, these novels are not as pessimistic as they might at first appear to be. By representing what women find repulsive in themselves, the writers — consciously or not — recognize that the human experience is gender-based. This recognition symbolizes the first step that all women must take on the journey leading to the repossession of their bodies and to the construction of a positive self-image. By unveiling the myth of women's unworthiness supported by social and religious conventions, the writers move toward a second recognition, that of the misogynous nature of that claim. The underlying message of these novels is, therefore, that full restoration to women of the ownership of their bodies depends on the elimination of sexual classes. This elimination can only come about if women, following Soeur Josée's example, decide to free their bodies from the Christian hatred of the flesh and if, following Louisette's example, they openly defy patriarchal authority. For it is by acting on this hatred and this authority that our society has been able to reduce woman to the level of a mere thing, a marketable product. Since, however, the deep-rooted self-hatred that informs these texts is, almost without exception, coupled with the protagonist's inability to transcend it, the novels' main function seems to be to testify to the following fact: during the 1960s, the struggle to reclaim the body was still in its embryonic stage. It follows that, by breaking the silence on women's private experiences, by naming the fears and hatreds that women associate with the body, and by clearly identifying the phallocentric myths and taboos under which the body has been placed, these writers broke new ground. In so doing, they opened the way for a future generation of Québécois women writers (Nicole Brossard, France Théoret, Louky Bersianik, and Madeleine Gagnon to name but a few) whose writings clearly map out strategies destined to empower women and to lead them into the ultimate struggle for the repossession of the body.

Notes

1 Sections of this text first appeared in an article entitled: "La Haine de soi: le cas du roman féminin québécois," *Studies in Canadian Literature*, Vol. 14, No. 1, 1989: 108–26.
2 Trans.: "The Age of the Word," an expression coined by Roland Giguère.
3 Trans.: "Women do not have . . . the sexual organ that monopolizes value."
4 Trans.: "To kill it [her body]. To be but a soul, nothing but a soul."
5 Trans.: "a garden of delights."
6 Trans.: "the site of sin."
7 Trans.: "I hate girls . . . whereas boys . . ."
8 Trans.: "it's a question of life and death."
9 Trans.: "I do not want to be a female."
10 Trans.: "The flesh that is . . . the enemy *Other* is indistinguishable from woman."
11 Trans.: "inferior animals."
12 Trans.: "It [the pregnancy] makes me feel terribly embarrassed."
13 Trans.: "atrocious and humiliating deformity."
14 Trans.: "Think of Jesus on the cross."
15 Trans.: "Why this disgrace, why this ugliness?"
16 Trans.: "garbage."
17 Trans.: "a beast."
18 Trans.: "marks of inferiority."
19 Trans.: "with a ruler."
20 Trans.: "what we deserve because of Eve."
21 Trans.: "ever since female flesh has been peddled by the cubic foot to increase the sale of cars, toothbrushes, even newspapers, she has been ashamed of her body."
22 Trans.: "a big atomic bomb."

Questions

1 What features of Québec society before the Quiet Revolution made it particularly repressive to women?
2 By perceiving female bodily functions negatively, are women allowing themselves to be co-opted to a male view or accepting an unpleasant reality?
3 Do misogynist attitudes illustrate a masochistic tendency in women who accept them?
4 In what ways did the publication of these novels contribute to the changes brought about during the Quiet Revolution?

References

Beauvoir, Simone de. 1949. *Le Deuxième Sexe: Tome 1*. Paris: Gallimard.

Blais, Marie-Claire. 1968. *Manuscrits de Pauline Archange*. Montreal: Éditions du Jour.

Blais, Marie-Claire. 1970. *Les Apparences*. Montreal: Éditions du Jour.

Chéné, Yolande. 1965. *Au Seuil de l'enfer*. Ottawa: Le Cercle du Livre de France.

Derrida, Jacques. 1976. *Of Grammatology*. Tr. Gayatri Chakravorty Spivak. Baltimore: Johns Hopkins University Press.

Douglas, Mary. 1970. *Natural Symbols: Explorations in Cosmology*. New York: Pantheon.

Ferron, Madeleine. 1966. *La Fin des loups-garous*. Montreal: HMH.

Godard, Barbara. 1987. "Mapmaking: A Survey of Feminist Criticism." Pp. 1–30 in Godard (ed.), *Gynocritics: Feminist Approaches to Canadian and Québécois Women*. Toronto: EWC Press.

Irigaray, Luce. 1974. *Speculum de l'autre femme*. Paris: Éditions de Minuit.

Lamirande, Claire de. 1969. *Le Grand Élixir*. Montreal: Éditions du Jour.

Maheux-Forcier, Louise. 1969. *Une Forêt pour Zoé*. Ottawa: Le Cercle du Livre de France.

Maillard, Nellie (pseudonym Anne-Marie). 1960. *La Nuit si longue*. Ottawa: Le Cercle du Livre de France.

Mailhot, Michèle. 1964. *Dis-moi que je vis*. Ottawa: Le Cercle du Livre de France.

Mailhot, Michèle. 1967. *Le Portique*. Ottawa: Le Cercle du Livre de France.

Rubenstein, Roberta. 1987. *Boundaries of the Self*. Urbana and Chicago: University of Illinois.

Saint-Onge, Paule. 1961. *Ce qu'il faut de regrets*. Ottawa: Le Cercle du Livre de France.

Tremblay, Jacqueline. 1964. *Marie-Anne ma douce*. Montreal: Centre de Psychologie et de Pédagogie.

Black Women's Reality and Feminism: An Exploration of Race and Gender[1]

Noga A. Gayle
Department of Sociology
Capilano College

Within feminist discourse, women are presented as a homogeneous group, sharing a common oppression. In accepting this view, there is a tendency within feminist analysis to ignore the oppression of race and class experienced by many women. By exploring Black women's relationships to White-dominated feminism, this chapter offers a challenge to mainstream feminism to broaden the definition of feminism in order to take into account the diverse experiences of women.

The dominant Women's Movement in North America is increasingly being criticized for its exclusion of the experiences of women designated as "Other." This exclusion has become so ensconced in our consciousness that we tend not to see it as problematic. The very notion that this paper is exploring the relationship of Black women's reality to feminism is a clear indication that women as a whole do not represent a homogeneous group. So too, Black women are not a homogeneous group, and to treat us as such negates the cultural differences that exist among us.

This situation has persisted because earlier studies of feminism tended to present women as if they were a homogeneous group. The notion that Black women or other women of colour could be culturally heterogeneous remained unconsidered. For instance, Blacks in the Diaspora came from various parts of the world, and in many cases the only attribute we share in common is skin colour. In many instances we are miles apart linguistically and culturally. It poses many problems when we are perceived as a homogeneous group and expected to work together smoothly in achieving certain goals. It needs to be understood that the differences within the various groups, and those within the wider society, need to be addressed before any meaningful dialogue can take place. While I strongly believe that this is possible, we need to see our differences in order to plan our strategies around them.

So far, an articulate group of White middle-class women has dominated North American feminist discourse, which has been constructed from the new consciousness (i.e., of second wave feminism) shaped by the structures of White male hegemony. This appears to have had a stifling effect, in that it placed barriers on how far women could move. The restrictive situation has been appropriately expressed by Audre Lorde (1983) in her statement that "the master's tools will never dismantle the master's house." Given this context, it was taken for granted that the experiences of White middle-class women were representative of the experiences of all women. Because of this, there has been little criticism of the impact of race, class, and culture. Reflecting patriarchal idealizations within feminist discourse, "femininity" and "womanhood" continue to be constructed from a Eurocentric perspective. The focus has been on the notion of a "common oppression" which, as Bell Hooks (1984) argues, disguises, and mystifies the varied and complex social reality of women. She advises us that solidarity among women can only be sustained by the removal of barriers that divide us.

From Feminism to Feminisms

An exploration of Black women's experiences in Canada in relation to feminism represents an attempt to deviate from the one-dimensional approach that has dominated feminist discourse. Within this approach, there tends to be a strong focus on the notion that feminism is a Western construct. This idea has entered into the current debate as to whether feminist movements presently recognized in many non-Western societies are the result of the imposition of ideological structures from the West. Jayawardena sheds some light on this notion by pointing out that:

> Feminism is generally thought of as a recent phenomenon, rooted in Western Society and people tend to overlook the fact that the word was in common usage in Europe and elsewhere in the 19th and 20th centuries, to signify agitation on issues concerning women. (1984: 2)

In terms of Black women articulating their concerns, one can look at the significant roles they played in resistance movements during slavery in the Caribbean and the United States, in liberation movements in Africa, and in the Civil Rights movement in the 1950s and 1960s in the United States. For the most part, these contributions have been hidden in history and as such are not reflected in such dominant institutions as education, politics, and the media. Nor were these contributions ever used as a model by those who were at the forefront of the second wave of feminism in North America. As an example, Ora Williams (1982: 298) points out that although "the celebrated eighty-five year old Dr. Eva Jessye, composer, educator, conductor of many Porgy and Bess choruses, lives on the Pittsburg (Kansas) State University campus, a few hours away from Lawrence, Kansas, the site of the 1979 National Women's Studies Convention, she was neither invited to be part of the Convention nor mentioned at it except by me." This is a recurring situation in terms of the relationship of Black women to the dominant White middle class Women's Movement. It is therefore my contention that the lack of interest in constructing a model based on these contributions has been facilitated by a racist ideology that continues to permeate our culture. Racism, like any ideology, is unconscious and it certainly is not unique to the dominant feminist movement. Dominant North American feminism is a product of a society that is both racist and sexist at the core; hence the tension that exists in the relationship between members of the dominant feminist movement and Black women or other women of colour. In order to understand this tension, one has to be at least cognizant of the reality of Black women in Canada.

Blacks have been in Canada since 1628 (Winks, 1971), with our numbers growing through natural increase and different spurts of immigration. It is estimated that the Black population today is less than 2 per cent of the total. Our history in Canada is one fraught with racism and there still exists a legacy of this today, the impact of which is felt within the areas of education, employment, politics, media and day-to-day relationships. One just needs to look at recent racist incidents in Montreal, Nova Scotia, and Toronto to recognize that the situation still exists, although in a more subtle form.

History has shown that most people will resist oppression in a variety of ways and Canada's Black population is no exception. In an effort to combat racism and its negative impact, Blacks formed into various religious, social, and political organizations. Most of these organizations, like others of their kind, were male-dominated, and as is common in a patriarchal society, a mythology developed around this domination. Nonetheless, by the early 1900s some Black women's organizations were formed across the country. In Montreal, for example, the Phyllis Wheatley Art Club was formed to give Black women a sense of purpose. The Women's Club and the Women's Charitable Benevolent Association were also formed and were very active in the 1920s and 1930s (see Winks, 1971). Although these Black women's organizations were not transformative in their objectives, they played a significant role in terms of alleviating some of the harsh conditions Black people faced.

Many Black women in Canada today are originally from the West Indies; their numbers have increased significantly since the 1950s, when the colonies were being dismantled and many of the colonized were led to believe that the industrialized countries held great opportunities for themselves and their children. Many West Indians migrated to Canada, Great Britain, and the United States. By the middle of the 1950s, West Indians arrived in Canada to study at various universities. These students, who were predominantly male, encountered racism, particularly in housing. During this same period, Canada initiated a program with various West Indian governments to recruit women to work as domestics. Under this program, wages were low and the working conditions of the women were deplorable. The women were isolated in middle-class Canadian homes and many, ignorant of their legal rights, found their very movements controlled by their employers.

Some of these experiences have been well documented in Silvera's *Silenced* (1983); she calls this situation "legalized slavery." In referring to the situation of Black women working as domestics in the United States, Davis (1989: 45) points out that "Black women have been repeatedly the victims of sexual assault committed by the white men in the families for which they worked." Similar situations in Canada are revealed in some of the accounts in Silvera's interviews. In many of these cases the victims said nothing to the wives of their abusers, out of fear of the repercussions (that is, the threat of deportation); often when approached, the wives tended to react with accusations that the women were either lying or seducing their husbands. These White women were therefore collaborators with their male counterparts in the oppression of these women. Silvera (1983: 124) elaborates on this oppression by pointing out that "The (usually) white female employers of Black and Asian domestic workers, although themselves members of a subordinate group because of their sex, are also members of the dominant group by virtue of their race and class, and quite 'normally' share the assumptions on race and class held by their (usually) white male counterparts."

This example puts the dynamics of the interplay of race and class into proper perspective. The employer/employee relationship for domestic workers is an intimate one in that it is located within the household, and thus it presents certain contradictions. At one level, domestics are perceived as part of the family in terms of the duties they perform, while at another level they are treated as a unit of labour to be exploited to its fullest. For instance, there are still cases in which live-in domestics find the length of their workday irregular; after completing a "day's work," they are often called upon in the evenings to babysit without prior arrangement or extra pay. This situation is taken for granted because, given the structure of their "workplace," they are often seen as being available on a 24-hour basis. Their structural relationship to their employers and the Immigration Department is a factor which reinforces their silence. As Epstein (1983: 229) suggests, "the employment visa system thus creates a workforce of people so vulnerable and insecure that they are guaranteed not to make waves."

In the late 1970s and 1980s there has been a shift in the domestic program. Most of these women now come from Southeast Asia. As Calliste (1989: 50) shows "Filipinos comprised 42% of the 8,175 new entrants in 1987, with Jamaicans comprising only 2%." Other Black women arrived from the West Indies and Great Britain in the late 1950s and mid 1960s as nurses, teachers, doctors, clerical workers and students on visas (many of whom remained in Canada after completing their schooling). This signified a change in the occupational configuration, and racist and sexist attitudes were being challenged from a wider arena.

Female labour was recruited to fill particular labour shortages in Canada, and state policies such as restrictions to certain occupations were used to ensure the satisfaction of these needs. The State also had to ensure that the influx of immigrants of colour would not create racial tension, and so it was necessary to perpetuate an assimilationist ideology during this period. This did not discourage racism, however, and new streams of immigrant Black women who were highly skilled found themselves constantly underemployed. This situation created feelings of alienation because these women were socially and psychologically dislocated from their indigenous culture on one hand, while their new environment was not very welcoming, on the other.

The dominant feminist movement at this time was so consumed by its own class interests that the concerns of women outside the confines of this class have been ignored. This has been a pattern of the movement since the beginning of the second wave of feminism in the United States in the 1960s. The emphasis has been on women finding work outside the home. According to this ideology the condition of the "housewife" had become so unbearable that it began to manifest itself in certain symptoms that could not be diagnosed medically. This became known as the "problem that has no name" or the "housewife's syndrome" (see Friedan, 1963). Although Friedan's work was important, in reality it only addressed issues that were of concern to a small, privileged group of women. The Black woman's reality was rendered invisible since historically most Black women worked outside the home. Ironically, in the U.S. many Black women worked in the homes of some of these middle-class women who were beginning to articulate their own experiences of oppression, and at that time many Black women were struggling in other low-paying jobs. Davis (1983) argues that most Black women have worked outside the home and that housework has never been the central focus of their lives. She argues further that:

Black women, however, have paid a heavy price for the strengths they have acquired and the relative independence they have enjoyed. While they have seldom been "just housewives," they have always done their housework. They have thus carried the double burden of wage labor and housework — a double burden which always demands that working women possess the persevering powers of Sisyphus. (1983: 2301)

The inability of the feminist movement then, and to some extent now, to recognize that there are different concerns based on race and class is a clear indication of how these factors can limit the progress towards equality for all women.

From Objects to Subjects

The recognition of our marginalization within both patriarchal culture and the dominant Women's Movement has motivated women of colour in North America to organize among ourselves. These organizations have taken many forms; some have succeeded while others have failed for a variety of reasons. In the case of Canada, one such group which has survived is the Congress of Black Women which was formed in the early 1970s. Its objective has been to make the concerns of Black Women in Canada a priority. It is a national organization with one or more chapters in each of the provinces and a biannual conference focusing on current issues. There is also a National Organization of Immigrant and Visible Minority Women, formed in 1986, in which Black women are represented. Members of these groups recognize the importance of having their voices heard, even though they continue to be met with opposition from the wider society which is aware of the powerful force that their coming together could create.

The suppression of these voices of Black women is maintained, for the most part, through a massive assault on the North American consciousness with negative images of women of colour. These images are orchestrated through films, advertisements, cartoons, television sitcoms and fiction (see O'Neale, 1986). Throughout the media, our reality is constantly being defined, the dominant images being the Black woman as victim. Her life experiences are usually presented as a social pathology, and she is constantly being maligned as responsible for the "crisis" in the Black family. This, of course, detracts attention from the economic, social, and psychological forces that are the root causes of various social crises. The unfortunate outcome is that we, as Black women, have in turn internalized this definition and have accepted the image that has been imposed on us. If we see ourselves as victims, we will eventually become victims. Hooks (1988: 42-3) puts this problem in the context of the politics of domination and argues that "as subjects people have the right to define their own reality, establish their own identities, name their history. As objects, one's reality is defined by others, one's identity created by others, one's history named only in ways that define one's relationship to those who are subject."

As long as Black women remain objects, they will not be able to emerge from the mould in which they have been cast. As objects, we have allowed ourselves to be manipulated by the dominant society to the extent that race has superseded gender in most situations. This is carried out through the tendency to isolate women's issues from our agenda. This occurs among Black dominated groups as well, and is exemplified by Stokeley Carmichael's sexism; when confronted with the subordinate position of women in the Black Liberation movement during the 1960s, his retort was that "The only position for women in the SNCC (Student Non-violent Coordinating Committee) is prone" (Giddings, 1984: 302). We are reminded by Ginette Castro (1990) that this is common practice within male-dominated groups in general. As she points out:

> It is interesting to note that black and white male radicals had similar reactions to the demands made by their female fellow militants. The men of both SNCC and SDS, independently of each other and without discussion, fell back on the same insults, presenting a united front of sexism in which "machismo" transcended ethnic differences. After the insults, both groups hurled the same accusations at their female companions, saying they were guilty of diverting the revolutionary struggle to the profit of selfish and futile goals. (1990: 20)

For Black women and other women of colour, the notion of race is complicated by the difficulty in making a distinction between gender oppression and racial oppression. Some writers in this context refer to themselves as women of colour (see Hull, Scott and Smith, 1982; Moraga and Anzaldua, 1981), or womanist (see Walker, 1983). It needs to be reiterated that our ethnicity cannot be separated from our gender; the two are entwined. Preoccupation within feminist discourse regarding this artificial separation detracts from the real issue of the impact of race and class upon gender, and how this impact in turn affects the lived experience of Black women. "Portraying African American women as stereotyped mammies, matriarchs, welfare recipients, and hot mommas has been essential to the political economy of domination fostering Black women's oppression" (Hill-Collins, 1990: 67).

The feminist agenda needs to be restructured so that Black women can articulate their concerns in the effort to bring about social change. Both Black women and White women have a common goal in terms of social equality, but the achievement of this goal is hindered by inherent contradictions in the strategy. These contradictions reflect the construct of domination/subordination that characterizes the wider patriarchal society. Carried into the feminist movement, this construct places the Women's Liberation Movement in a unique structural position: in relation to women of colour, White women are in a dominant position while simultaneously being made subordinate in relation to the patriarchal structures. This latter point is fully emphasized by Smith (1987) and Christiansen-Ruffman (1989). This contradiction is further complicated by structural racism, in which the hierarchy of privileges is based on race. Failure to confront this fundamental problem is an abdication of responsibility in terms of the objectives of feminism.

The Challenge for "Women's Studies"

Arguing from the perspective of women of colour, Audre Lorde (1983: 98) points out that "it is a particular academic arrogance to assume any discussion of feminist theory in this time and in this place without examining our many differences, and without a significant input from poor women, black and Third World women, and lesbians." She suggests that we should take a look, for example, at how most conference panels are organized. When women of colour are included, they are usually called at the last minute, and when confronted about this, the excuse usually given is that the coordinators did not know whom to call. Following upon this attitude, she also expresses resentment towards the trend of many journals to offer publications as a "special issue" when dealing with women of colour, whether it is our art or writings. She further points out that the same situation applies to Women's Studies Programs; in many instances, the works of women of colour are not even on the reading list, much less required texts. She calls this a form of subtle racism.

It is interesting to note that advocates for Women's Studies Programs in high schools do not envision a multidimensional approach. It would appear that the agenda is to get Women's Studies into the schools; *after* this is accomplished, the issues of "others" will be added. History has shown that this has always been a problem. In her 1989 Vancouver lecture, Angela Davis expressed similar concerns. She stated that the structure of domination/subordination within the feminist movement is so entrenched that dominant feminists do not even recognize the power relationships involved when they invite women of colour to participate in events that result from activities that should have been collaborative in the first place. Feminists from the dominant class tend to set the politico-feminist agenda; there is no toleration for deviation at either the conceptual level or the level of peoples' experiences. If the goal of feminism is social transformation as social justice for *all* women, there must be a better understanding of the diversity of women's concerns and women's experiences. The centrality of class and race in feminist analysis must therefore be given top priority. We must strive to develop a feminist epistemology that encompasses the divergent trends in women's experiences. This process will have to start with the demystification of constructs through which "universal woman" is equated with "white woman." Given the historical relations of power, Whites are perceived as those having power whereas non-Whites are perceived as powerless. Most White feminists have appropriated these perceptions, which have become so embedded into their consciousness that they tend not to acknowledge their privileged position, limited as it may be in a White male-dominated reality. This is reflected in analyses of women's social condition which take White women's experiences as the reference point for all women. As Hooks (1984: 14) points out:

> Privileged feminists have largely been unable to speak to, with, and for diverse groups of women because they either do not understand fully the inter-relatedness of sex, race and class oppression or refuse to take this inter-relatedness seriously. Feminist analyses of women's lot tend to focus exclusively on gender and do not provide a solid foundation on which to construct feminist theory. They reflect the dominant tendency in Western patriarchal minds to mystify women's reality by insisting that gender is the sole determinant of woman's fate. (1984: 14)

This approach is clearly far too narrow and subsequently excludes vast areas of experiences that are influenced in varying degrees by factors such as class, race, age, sexual orientation, geographic location, and religion — to name a few.

The reality of the impact of these factors on gender must be recognized, and the complexities of this impact need to be explored and analyzed. This can only be achieved by listening to the voices of those who have been left out, with a serious commitment to their meaningful involvement in the transformation process. This is crucial for society as a whole. In the words of Hills Collins:

> As the "Others" of society who can never really belong, strangers threaten the moral and social order. But they are simultaneously essential for its survival because those individuals who stand at the margins of society clarify its boundaries. African American women, by not belonging, emphasize the significance of belonging. (1990: 68)

This situation is relevant to the Canadian context, but is further compounded by the multiplicity of racial and ethnic boundaries among women within the overarching class structure.

If the goal of the feminist movement is better social conditions for all women, certain assumptions and stereotypes inherent in feminist discourse about different groups will have to be abandoned if the movement is to survive. These assumptions and stereotypes continue to perpetuate exclusion and act as barriers to social change. Given this reality, it is imperative that these assumptions and stereotypes be challenged on all levels.

Note

1 Revised version of a paper presented at the Canadian Sociological Association Conference held at the University of Victoria, May 1990.

Questions

1 To what extent has the "liberation" of white middle-class women been at the expense of minority women?
2 Do all feminists want to "dismantle the master's house"? What tools could be used?
3 Within the North American context, how can the experiences of women of colour and other minority groups be incorporated into the university curriculum?

References

Calliste, Agnes. 1989. "Canada's Immigration Policy and Domestics from the Caribbean: The Second Domestic Scheme." Pp. 133–65 in Jesse Vorst (ed.), *Race, Class, and Gender: Bonds and Barriers*. Toronto: Between the Lines.

Castro, Ginette. 1990. *American Feminism: A Contemporary History*. Trans. Elizabeth Loverde-Bagwee. New York: New York University Press.

Christiansen-Ruffman, L. 1989. "Inherited Biases Within Feminism: The 'Patricentric Syndrome' and the 'Either/Or Syndrome' in Sociology." Pp. 123–45 in A. Miles and G. Finn (eds.), *Feminism from Pressure to Politics*. Montreal: Black Rose Books.

Davis, A. 1983. *Women, Race and Class*. New York: Vintage Books.

Davis, A. 1989. *Women, Culture and Politics*. New York: Random House.

Epstein, R. 1983. "Domestic Workers: The Experience in B.C." Pp. 222–37 in L. Briskin and L. Yanz (eds.), *Union Sisters: Women in the Labour Movement.* Toronto: The Women's Press.

Friedan, B. 1963/1974. *The Feminine Mystique.* New York: Dell Books.

Giddings, Paula. 1984. *When and Where I Enter: The Impact of Black Women on Race and Sex in America.* New York: Bantam Books.

Hills-Collins, Patricia. 1990. *Black Feminist Thought.* Boston: Unwin Hyman.

Hooks, Bell. 1981. *Ain't I a Woman? Black Women and Feminism.* Boston: Southend Press.

Hooks, Bell. 1984. *Talking Back: Thinking Feminist — Thinking Black.* Boston: Southend Press.

Hooks, Bell. 1984. *Feminist Theory: From Margin to Center.* Boston: South End Press.

Hull, G., P. Scott and B. Smith (eds.). 1982. *All the Women Are White, All the Blacks Are Men but Some of Us Are Brave: Black Women's Studies.* New York: The Feminist Press.

Jayawardena, K. 1986. *Feminism and Nationalism in the Third World.* London: Zed Books.

Lorde, A. 1983. "The Master's Tools Will Never Dismantle the Master's House." Pp. 98–101 in C. Moraga and G. Anzaldua (eds.), *This Bridge Called My Back: Writings of Radical Women of Color.* New York: Kitchen Table, Women of Color Press.

Moraga, C., and G. Anzaldua (eds.). 1983. *This Bridge Called My Back: Writings of Radical Women of Color.* New York: Kitchen Table, Women of Color Press.

O'Neale, S. 1986. "Inhibiting Midwives, Usurping Creators: The Struggling Emergence of Black Women in American Fiction." Pp. 139–56 in T. de Lauretis (ed.), *Feminist Studies/Critical Studies.* Bloomington: Indiana University Press.

Silvera, M. 1983. *Silenced.* Toronto: Williams-Wallace Publishers Inc.

Smith, D. 1987. *The Everyday World as Problematic: A Feminist Sociology.* Toronto: University of Toronto Press.

Walker, A. 1983. *In Search of our Mothers' Gardens: A Womanist Prose.* San Diego: Harcourt Brace Jovanovich.

Williams, O., D. Wilson, T. Williams, R. Matthewson. 1982. "American Women Composers: A Selected Annotated Bibliography." In G. Hull, P. Scott, and B. Smith (eds.), *All the Women Are White, All the Blacks Are Men but Some of Us Are Brave.* New York: The Feminist Press.

Winks, R. 1971. *The Blacks in Canada: A History.* Yale University Press.

*Daphne Marlatt and Betsy Warland are both writers, living to-
gether on Salt Spring Island in British Columbia. At the time of
the conference at which these readings were given, Daphne had
just completed a year as Ruth Wynn Woodward Professor of
Women's Studies at Simon Fraser University. She is the author
of several books, including* Ana Historic *(1988), the first one
that she calls "a novel," which she discusses here. In the same
year, she published a poetic collaboration with Betsy entitled*
Double Negative. *Betsy has also published three other works
of poetry. Both writers seek to undermine the masculine use of
language — especially the authority attributed to the authorial
"I." Daphne's "i" and the dual authorship of* Double Negative
*convey their refusal to conform to male models, in writing as in
"life." The two texts presented here provide a sampling of what
has been termed "writing in the feminine" — a form of writing
which does not deny women authors' experience of their (and in
this case, each other's) bodies.*

Self-Representation and Fictionalysis

Daphne Marlatt
Writer
Vancouver, British Columbia

For the critic, the question behind autobiography seems to be first of all
"how does the writer represent herself?" For the writer it is "how do
you represent others?" An interesting differential which, in either case,
brings up the notion of truth and how or whether it differs from fiction.
The writer worries about the difference between how she sees the people
she writes about and how they see themselves. The critic looks at the
self that is being presented and its difference from what is known about
the writer's life (the facts, say). Or "the (f) stop of act" as Annie puts it
in *Ana Historic*, isolating fact like the still photo as a moment frozen out
of context, that context which goes on shifting, acting, changing after
the f-stop has closed its recording eye. The fact a still frame. The self
framed she suspects, caught in the ice of representation.

As if there were a self that existed beyond representation as some sort of isolatable entity. And then, for company's sake, your self-representation, your self and your self-representation sitting side by side or better yet, coinciding. And without that coincidence someone will say, "Oh, she's making herself out to be . . ." Oh dear, fiction as falsity.

Fiction, however, has always included the notion of making, even making something up (as if that something had never existed before), and goes back to a very concrete Indo-European word, *dheigh*, meaning to knead clay. In many creation myths, a goddess or a god moulded us and made us, touched us into life, made us up. Out of nothing, out of whole cloth, as the saying goes. And so, this nothing-something, or this something that is nothing, we insist, as a species, on hanging desperately onto our Somethingness.

Fact or photo or figure (even clay), separate from ground, but not ground, not that . . . facelessness. *Women* are ground, *women* are nature . . . Well, we know all this, how for us it's no small feat to be Something, given the ways our culture reinforces the notion that we are less Something than men. And yet we continually demonstrate our abilities to generate something out of almost nothing: a whole baby, a whole book, the whole cloth of a life.

To pick up that phrase "out of whole cloth" is to find an odd reversal, given that "whole" means healthy, undivided, intact, the whole of something. How is it that the whole phrase has come to mean pure fabrication, a tissue of lies? Whole the other side of hole, w (for women?) the transforming link. We can't seem to avoid the notion that making and the thing made — tissue, or text for that matter, since they come from the same root, have, at root, nothing: "you made it up," or more usually, "you just made it up" (as if making were easy). In our culture of ready-mades, making anything is an accomplishment, making something of yourself even more so, but add that little word "up" and you add speciousness, you add a sneer. Children learn that dressing themselves is an achievement but dressing up is only play, child's play, as they say of something easy. Yet as children we know that play is not only easy; it is also absorbing and immensely serious; that play is the actual practice (not factual but act-ual) of who else we might be.

A powerful put-down, that word "up." Does it imply we're trying to imitate the gods and have no business reaching a notch higher on the scale of creation, especially when it comes to creating ourselves? Or is that scale fictional too, and "up" merely indicates we're getting close to something non-hierarchical but just as significant, as in "i'm waking up"?

Perhaps what we wake up to in autobiography is a beginning realization of the whole cloth of ourselves in connection with so many others. Particularly as women analyzing our lives, putting the pieces together, the repressed, suppressed, putting our finger on the power dynamics at play. It is exactly in the confluence of fiction (the self or selves we might be) and analysis (of the roles we have found ourselves in, defined in a complex socio-familial weave) — it is in the confluence of these two that autobiography occurs, the self writing its way to life, whole life. This is the practice of the imaginary in its largest sense, for without vision we can't see where we're going or even where we are. Autobiography is not separable from poetry for me, on this ground i would call fictionalysis: a self-analysis that plays fictively with the primary images of one's life, a fiction that uncovers analytically that territory where fact and fiction coincide.

In *Ana Historic*, Annie and Ina discuss the difference between story and history, between making things up (out of nothing) and the facts, those frozen somethings of evidence. But what is evident to Annie is not always evident to Ina, because in each of them the seeing occurs in differently informed ways. Clearly, there are different kinds of seeing, as evidenced by another little word, "through": seeing through, which isn't prepared to take things at face value. For Annie the facts are "skeletal bones of a suppressed body, the story is," and that suppressed body which can be resurrected by dint of making up, is the unwritten story of who (else) each of the women in the book might be. It is through analysis, analysis of the social context each of them inhabits, that Annie can write her way through the bare bones of who they apparently are to the full sense and the full sensory body of who each of them might be, *if* they could imagine themselves to their fullest.

And why isn't the imaginary part of one's life story? Every poet knows it is, just as i know that in inventing a life for Mrs. Richards, i as Annie (and Annie isn't me, though she may be one of the selves i could be) invented a historical leak, a hole in the sieve of fact that let the shadow of a possibility leak through into full-blown life. History is not the dead and gone; it lives on in us in the way it shapes our thought and especially our thought about what is possible. Mrs. Richards is a historical leak for the possibility of lesbian life in Victorian British Columbia, which like some deep-packed bedrock continues to underlie the leather shops and tinted glass of our highrise 1990s. We live in that context: the actuality of both. Just as we also live in the context of salmon rivers polluted with dioxins, harassed abortion clinics, Hong Kong's historic jitters, eco-islands of Sitka spruce, half-hidden memories of child abuse, and whatever hungry ghosts still pursue each one of us

— to pull only a few threads of the whole cloth. The context is huge, a living tissue we live together with/in.

To write a whole autobiography — i mean autobiography in its largest sense of self-writing life, not the life of the self but the life self writes its way to, the whole cloth — is to reach for what is almost unwriteable, a hole in that other sense. Yet autobiography until recently was set aside as a minor form, a sort of documentary support, like letters or journal-writing, for the great texts. Its significance lay in its veracity, the faithfulness with which it followed the lifeline, the overall narrative of its writer's life, without leaving any holes or gaps, certainly without contradiction. The "life-line" after all represents a single line, just as the writer's representation of herself should be a true likeness — like *what*? Given the whole cloth, the truth of ourselves is so large it is almost impossible to write. It is full of holes, pulled threads (multiple lines), figures indistinct from ground.

Here we run up against the reductiveness of language which wants to separate — what do you mean threads? ground? Get your metaphors straight for god's sake, no, for your reader's sake. Who's the creator here anyway? Maybe language after all, despite itself. But that's only if we can subvert its mainline story, that black stands to white as woman to man; that is, for the sake of definition (which language is all about) as ground to figure. Language defines Something, the subject, let's say, as *different* from any thing and any other who is merely undifferentiated object. We begin to see the bias of the subject operating here, and that this subject who so dominates the stage of representation is white, heterosexual, middle-class, monological, probably Christian and usually male. Wherever we as women overlap with any of those aspects, we inherit that bias. It leaks out everywhere in the most familiar of colloquial phrases, of idiomatic usage, in the very words that fall out of our mouths. Yet these are the words we have — very, indeed — and only by varying them (disrespectfully, the subject might say, intent on the singular line of his story), only by altering them infinetisimally, undermining what they say, bending them into knots, into not's and un's, can we break the rigid difference between figure and ground which preserves that figure's hegemony, his "truth." No wonder women have such difficulty with the truth — such a single-minded, simple-minded truth it is, with no sense at all of the truth of the ground, of that which bears us in all our harrowing complexity: context.

Autobiography has come to be called "life-writing" which i take to mean writing for your life[1] and as such it suggests the way in which the many small real-other-i-zations can bring the unwritten, unrecognized, ahistoric ground of a life into being as a recognizable power or agency.

This happens when we put together the disparate parts of our lives and begin to see the extensiveness of that cloth of connectedness we are woven into. Then we begin, paradoxically, to weave for ourselves the cloth of our life as we want it to be. For it is in the energetic imagining of all that we are that we can enact ourselves. Every woman we have read who has written about women's lives lives on in us, in what we know of our own capacity for life, and she becomes part of the context for our own writing, our own imagining.

When text becomes context, when it leaves behind the single-minded project of following a singular lifeline, when it drops out of narrative as climax and opts for narrative as interaction with what surrounds us, then we are in the presence of a writing for life, a writing that ditches dualistic polarities (good guys vs. bad guys, gays, bitches, blacks — you see how many of us there are), dodges the hierarchies (the achieved, the significant or the inessential, the failed, which goes to the root of our fear about life: was it all for nothing ?). It's all there in the so-called "nothing."

Note

1 See Gillian Hanscombe and Virginia L. Smyers (1987).

Reference

Hanscombe, Gillian and Virginia L. Smyers. 1987. *Writing for Their Lives; The Modernist Woman, 1910–1940*. London: Women's Press.

moving parts

Betsy Warland
Writer
Vancouver, British Columbia

The struggle for the self-determined body is absolutely crucial to all women. Yet, in our "house-bound" minds, we are uncertain about our practical, worldly knowledge. Even though we may be "professionals," our mind's muscles have been trained to push down; against. Our self-recognition is all too frequently rooted in what we are not: "I can't do that"; "I'm not like them"; and "I'll never know what that's like." The I-crises: self more a matter of what we *are not*, as women, than what we *are* and *can be*. It's as if we are caught in a suspended state of labour and our identity is locked at that point in the struggle. If we do "leave home" (figuratively or literally), we are no longer the birther but the birthed. In leaving our father/husband/boyfriend's "house," however, we place ourselves at risk: we live in the world "unprotected." Although we know our notion of security to be false — that our most intimate protector is frequently our violator — we still find the prospect of self-responsibility terrifying.

For lesbians, who are twice defined by our feminine gendered bodies, this struggle is doubly crucial. As our bodies propel us away, inciting a desire which is greater than fear — we take a leap into the unknown, which is the unnamed. With our desire we rename everything: slowly; passionately. And with the gathering of our words we own ourselves: become self-responsible. This takes years. This takes a lifetime.

In the process of becoming a self-named lesbian, any woman must find her way through a myriad of fears. As she does, she becomes less afraid. As she does, *she* becomes the focus of fear within the heterosexual world. Although inevitably mediated (to varying degrees) by patriarchal socialization and economics, she-the-lesbian has nevertheless gotten out of hand! For hetero-he, she is no longer manageable. For hetero-she, she is no longer a companion in resentment.

Given this, do lesbian-defined perspectives and imagery speak to or include non-lesbian women?

Considering that language and the canon (as we know them) are central in the maintainance and perpetuation of the values of male-dominant white culture, where does the lesbian writer, and the lesbian body, stand in relationship to the generic reader?

And, where does the reader stand in relationship to the lesbian writer and the lesbian body?

I have recently reread my four books with these questions in mind, and will briefly trace the evolution of these three positions by quoting from and reflecting on each of my books. I will also refer to the work of other lesbian poets and theorists associated with the making of my texts. In this self-examination, I will be working on the shifting edge between reading and writing and writer and critic, for the process of self-determination inevitably restructures how we see and go about our work.

My first book, *A Gathering Instinct*, was published in 1981. Among other topics, this text records the shift from the final years of my marriage to my first lesbian relationship.

    this circular force

    i must tell you
    i have held the sun in my arms
    i must tell you
    i have held the sun in my arms
      have become its burning reflection
          its hot shadow
      have become its definitive horizon
      have become the lids of this burning eye
          opening like a flower
          closing like a mouth
    opening wildly like a flower
    closing knowingly as a mouth

    i must tell you
    i have held the sun in my arms
      have made love to this circular force
        more times than i can remember
      have risen more powerfully than the sun
        more powerfully than the sun itself
        it has shrunk in my shadow
               shivering

    i must tell you
    i have held the sun in my arms

Within this poem the lesbian body remains obscured, non-gendered, and hidden behind the illusory veil of universality. As the lesbian writer, I associate woman with nature and the mystical. The erotic female writing body is searching for a language which is not forged by the heterosexual, male experience. Typically, I opted for the vocabulary of nature, which has been woman's only rightful turf of representation.

The lesbian writer's position is secret. The poem is written in isolation from the relationship: in solitude, as is often the male poet's tradition. It is from this position of apartness that objectification of the woman lover in the lyric poem can spring. The poem (and the relationship) is also isolated from the peopled world.

Although the generic reader may identify with the sentiments of the poem, she or he, in fact, is not trusted by the writer. The reader can either transpose the facade of universality onto her/his life (which represents a kind of imperialism), or the reader must attempt to read between the lines: sleuth out whose bodies these are.

As a young lesbian writer, I chose this tangentiality for self-protective reasons. At that time, I knew of no poet who was publishing her books as a self-identified lesbian writer in English Canada. The only models were writers such as Adrienne Rich, who published *Twenty-One Love Poems* (1976) well into her writing career, or writers like Pat Parker [*Pit Stop* (1974)], Judy Grahn [*edward the dyke* (1971)], and Alta [*Burn This* and *Memorize Yourself* (1971)], whose books circulated essentially within the American lesbian underground. Olga Broumas's *Beginning With O* (1977) — winner of the Yale Series of Younger Poets competition — was the first book (to my knowledge) by a beginning writer, to be published in the American poetry malestream. In his introduction to *Beginning With O*, Stanley Kunitz writes that because of her "explicit sexuality and Sapphic orientation, Broumas's poems may be considered outrageous in some quarters." Somehow I knew that the CBC Literary Competition wasn't about to promote feminist lesbian lyrics in Canada! Nor is it still.

My second book, *open is broken*, was published in 1984. By this time I had fallen deeply in love with another feminist, who was also a writer — Daphne Marlatt. Throughout the first year of our relationship we wrote a series of poems to one another. Although during their writing it had not occurred to us that these poems would be published, our manuscripts were subsequently solicited by a publisher (Longspoon Press). It was then that we began to realize the importance of creating a literary space for books like *open is broken* and *Touch to My Tongue*. In the years since *A Gathering Instinct* I had read, and been deeply provoked by Audre Lorde's *Uses of the Erotic: The Erotic as Power* (1978), by Helen

Cixous's essay "The Laugh of the Medusa" (which I read in translation in 1981 in *New French Feminisms*), and by an eloquent talk given by Mary Daly on the subject of presence and absence. Still, bringing our love poems "out" into the public was a terrifying thought. But publishing and reading from our books together not only made it possible, but empowering.

III

(from the "open is broken" suite)

> the leaves witness you unsheathing me
> my bud my bud quivering in your
> mouth you leaf me (leaf: "peel off")
> in front of a window full of green eyes we climb
> the green ladder: "clitoris, incline, climax"
> on the tip of your tongue you flick
> me leaf: "lift" up
> to tip tree top
> point of all i am to the sky
> "roof of the world"
> leaves
> sink slow into darkening
> with my resin on your swollen lips
> leave us in our
> betrothal: "truth, tree"

In *open is broken* the lesbian body becomes site-specific; her body cannot be easily appropriated. Through the use of explicit erotic imagery, the act of lesbian self-naming begins the process of deconstruction of woman as object. Woman's relationship to nature is no longer a passive/receptive or symbolic state but rather an intensely interactive, interconnected state in which boundaries blur. The lesbian body, through the the use of word play and etymology, reclaims the existing sexual vocabulary of intimacy. As the body breaks out and opens itself, so too the language opens up — revealing not only the patriarchal codes embedded within our most intimate words, but also revealing how these codes can be broken open: how the language can be inclusive — not exclusive.

My position as the lesbian writer of this text has changed dramatically. Homophobia is confronted directly (in another poem in the book), and as the writer, I affirm my sexuality, which is no longer a source of deception but a source of creativity and power. Here, the lesbian writer chooses to publicly name the terms of her reference; chooses not to remain mute — having them misnamed by the uneasy reviewer or critic. With our books together, objectification is further disrupted by the equal, active presence of both lovers/both lesbian writers. Our two books seem to have been the first of their kind to be published in North America. Suniti Namjoshi and Gillian Hanscombe published a joint collection of their love poems, *Flesh and Paper*, in 1986.

The reader's position has also shifted dramatically. Confronted explicitly by the presence of the lesbian body and the lesbian writer, the reader is admitted openly into the text. The code that the reader is now active in breaking (along with the lesbian writer), is the code of patriarchal language — not the code of an underground deviant language from which most readers automatically disassociate themselves. Subtexts surface and familiar surfaces are turned inside-out.

serpent (w)rite was published in 1987. This book represents my most intensive work in decoding and analyzing language as the bedrock of The Great White Fathers' value system. Dale Spender's *Man Made Language* (1980) was a crucial source of confirmation about the necessity of this language-deconstruction project, as was Nicole Brossard's deconstruction of woman in *These Our Mothers* (published in translation in 1983). Eve and Adam, the original moulds of gender indoctrination, are also deconstructed as is the experience of being lost (our post-Garden condition). As the writer, I submerge myself in the experience of being lost: through relentless deconstruction of clichés and decodifying of language; through the interruption by other voices excerpted from a wide variety of material I was reading during the writing; and through the resolution to not go back over and read any of the writing until the text came to its resting point. Consequently, the writing wanders in circles (as one does when one is physically lost), sometimes with recognition of earlier passings but more often with no conscious recognition of the textual landmarks — and so another perspective is laid down in the groove. There are no page numbers, and only in the latter editorial stage did I set the text into eight "turns" which function as indicators of the text's inherent movement (which also evokes women's cyclical orgasmic movement).

turn eight

we are open circle
word without end
a well-comed
break down in communication
breg-, suffrage + down, from the hill

over the hill
we are split subject
split, slit, *slot,*
hollow between the breasts
no longer divided against our/selves
we are the subject of two mouths
which now *face, form*
words of our own
prefix and suffix in dialogue
no longer waiting to be heard
no longer eating our hearts out

my word!
eating pussy

        cat got my tongue

we make love in the company of four

two Eves four mouths
refuse, refundere, to pour back
the scent/se of opposition
dis-cover

       language, lingua, tongue
has many sides
dialects,
a variety of languages that with other varieties constitutes
a single language of which no single variety is standard

Although the lesbian body continues to be site-specific in *serpent (w)rite*, it is no longer foregrounded. Out of 128 pages, there are only eight erotic lesbian passages. In essence, the lesbian body now becomes the ground from which the writing in *serpent (w)rite* is generated. Having established the terms of the speaking voice in *open is broken* as lesbian, I am centred and prepared to speak of the world as I know it beyond the lesbian littoral.

In breaking the greatest taboo of naming myself in *open is broken*, I am now free to address topics (such as war and new technologies) from which my status of woman has previously disqualified me. The search for an integral language is no longer sidetracked by Mother Nature metaphor. It is now situated solidly in the deconstruction and redefining of the very language itself. The lesbian writer's relationship with her lover, however, still functions essentially in resistance to, and as a retreat from, the world.

In *serpent (w)rite* the reader and the writer are both thrown out of the garden. Both are lost; both must be acutely present, for the role of non-participatory observer is no longer viable. Through the use of numerous quotes from disparate sources, as well as meditative white spacing throughout the book, the reader is compelled to enter the text and play an active role in its interpretation. With the emerging concept of dialects, the text embraces any reader whose life and perspective have been marginalized and oppressed.

Double Negative, my most recent book, was written in collaboration with Daphne Marlatt and was published in 1988. The first section of the book, "Double Negative," is a lyric collaborative poem which we wrote during a three-day train ride across Australia. We were motivated to write this text out of our curiosity to discover how our process of collaborative writing had evolved since we had written the poems in *Touch To My Tongue* and *open is broken*. We were also inspired by the beauty of the Australian desert that we were passing through, and we felt challenged to re-vision the traditional phallic symbolism of the train. The second section of the book, "Crossing Loop," is composed of a discussion we had after we returned to Canada about the constraints we experienced by staying on the literal and narrative track. In the third section, "Real 2," we broke the lyric and narrative frame by alternately taking a phrase from one another's poetic entries and running away with it — going off track into our own idiosyncratic associative prose reflections.

Perhaps one of the most remarkable things about *Double Negative* is that thus far it has received practically no reviews. Collaborative writing seems to be a radical and unnerving approach for the North American critical mind, which champions individualism. It is likely that reviewers' analytical processes have been disturbed by the fact that our individual authorships are not clearly marked in the text. In *Flesh and Paper*, although Hanscombe and Namjoshi's individual poetry entries are not specified, the reader can identify their individual voices in relation to their differences of race, culture and country.

"he says we got to stay on track" (from "Real 2")

well trained he is we are the only difference being it's his job he profits from it stopped for twenty minutes desert beckoning through conditioned glass he doesn't make the rules — just enforces them dissociative division of labour no one directly responsible for anything fill out a form someone will get back to you form letter replying to form (form is form) she looks out the window what she longs for is the absence of the symbolic to lose track of disappear into this emptiness (his key ring tight around her neck) why this vigilance it's not survival of the fittest (he no dingo she no emu) hand to mouth not their relationship no their hunt is on another plain food for thought word to word fight for defining whose symbolic dominates whose (Adam complex) she wants to migrate she wants to mutate she wants to have no natural predators be nothing looking at nothing thrive in her own absence be out of focus out of range of The Gaze hide out from The Law under assumed names but there's no way out even the desert cannot escape imagin-a-nation of the imaginations of 113 billion who have lived and recorded their mindscapes (real to reel) she reads the "Percentage of those whose memory survives in books and manuscripts, on monuments, or in public records: 6" she calculates possibly 1 per cent represents her gender's memory wonders how woman has even survived the wedge-tailed eagle circles above and the train begins to roll as her hand moves across the page spiral movement (imagin-a-nation) here she can rest here she can play encounter her anima(l) self pre-sign pre-time touching you i touch kangaroo words forming then shifting desert dunes her desire to untrain herself undermine every prop(er) deafinition she throws the switch on train as phallus ("bound for glory") train as salvation leaves it behind at the crossing loop feels words falling from her like the 50 million skin scales we shed each day breathing stars, moon saltbush scrub your hand moves across my body (imagin-a-nation) and we settle into this motion once again settle into the beginninglessness the endlessness of this page this desert this train this shared desire wholly here with a passion that humbles us what is woman (in her own symbolic?)

In *Double Negative* the lesbian body (although still site-specific) enlarges its symbolism to embrace any woman who is impassioned with her own quest for self-naming and self-determination. Society's negativism toward lesbians is understood to be symptomatic of the larger patriarchal attitude, which sees woman as negative space. In this text not only does the lesbian body locate itself intensely in the present, but it interacts publicly with "the world," because escape from the patriarchal grid of symbols and values is neither practical nor possible. For even in the desert, which is considered *the* earthly symbol of negative space, the oppressions of race, sex, and class are relentlessly carried out; nuclear testing, war games, and archeological thievery thrive.

The lesbian writers' position is now one of writing in the *presence of* and *with* each other as contrasted to writing in the *absence of* and *to* each other. As the private interaction between us (writers/lovers) is documented and embraced, so too is the inherent collaborative process at work in all writing. This acknowledgement calls into question the notion of one authoritative voice (version) crying out in the wilderness. By her existence the lesbian challenges one of the basic concepts of property: she belongs to no man. So too, we-the-lesbian-writers in *Double Negative* defy a basic patriarchal principle of the written word: individual ownership. The collective and collaborative essence of oral communication (the language of the mother and the language of love), is infused into the written word, and the fluvial movement between the us engenders a new in*her*textuality.

The lesbian writers also dismantle another literary formal fence — the division between writer and reader. We-the- writers also become we-the-readers of our own text: we discuss (and document in "Crossing Loop") our reactions (as writers *and* readers) to the first section, and then, we integrate what has resonated with us as readers into a new contexture ("Real 2"). The reader is not isolate and passive but partnered. But — there's the rub! Because love poetry (particularly erotic love poetry) has been essentially the tradition of male poets, the reader's familiar "entrance" to the poem has been "through the eyes of the beholder": the subject; the viewer. With the presence of both lovers, who are speaking, seeing/writing and receiving, the reader's former position is rendered obsolete. The gaze is up for grabs! It is no longer a fixed position of author/ity and control. Because our writers'/lovers' roles are in a continual state of flux and redefinition, the reader's role is also unhinged. No longer standing at the door of voyeurism, the reader must now dive into the unpredictable currents of the text and assume all the varied writers'/lovers' roles. The reader must pass through the initial fear of intrusiveness into the pleasure of inclusiveness. No safe text here. At the outset, often the non-lesbian reader is disoriented by being in the swim of lesbian sense-ability and vision and/or the lesbian *and* non-lesbian reader is disoriented by the flow of the language and form. Here is the irony, for in its defamiliarizations, *Double Negative* is the most faithful and therefore the most open text I have written — for fixed roles can only be dispensed of when we are able to move into a state of shared power and trust.

What this is all about is movement. Our clinging to roles (gender, heterosexual, literary, whatever) is an expression of our fear of the immense mass of energy we are and are in. Recently, I had such an intense experience of this movement that I thought I would explode. When I relaxed into it, I passed beyond motion sickness (fear) into this fierce beauty. As women, we have this body knowledge that we will not explode: that we can move through labour and fear; move through that crucial point in the struggle of pushing against and identification by resistance.

In every reader, there exists a deep-seated longing for the self-named body. Just as a writer's work is often generated out of a sense of absence (of the particulars of *their* story, *their* vision), so too, most readers are driven by *their* sense of absence. Except for practical or information needs, our sense of absence is perhaps our greatest motivation for reading: every reader is in search of *their* self-named body. Not that readers are only attracted to texts that reflect their own lives — quite the contrary; often we find a voice for our absence in "unlikely" places. The writers to whom I am referring are those whose life-long quest is to grasp how their particular understanding (of their story, their vision) might be a needed source of revelation and healing. This writing stance is very different from those writers whose work is fueled by the dominator's desire to control and profit from the fate of others who are less privileged.

The lesbian writer is passionate: she has risked, and will risk, a great deal to love. She knows she is not alone. She believes that when you never manage to get around to reading or reviewing or teaching her books, you erase essential parts of yourself.

Reading, perhaps more than writing, is an act of faith: faith in the future. Lesbian writers, along with other marginalized writers, are the voices of the future (which is the present) simply because our voices have been so absent in the past. We are the source of the knowledge that has been repressed, and it is that very repression that has put the world at such risk.

As women, we have listened and watched for a very long time. And the need for our "quiet" knowledge is greater and more urgent than even we can imagine. As a lesbian writer, I call up those parts in you which have been absented by ownership, roles, language, and fear — for these are the *perpetrators* (*perpetrare, to completely perform in the capacity of a father*) of my own absence. As women, this is our common ground; it is here that we can listen faithfully to each other, urge one another to speak. It is here that our disassociative isolations fall away. The motion sickness of *re-* is shed; the power of *active* said, and read.

Questions

1 Do we read texts by women as more (necessarily) autobiographical than those by men? Why?
2 What aspects of these texts illustrate the attempt to "write in the feminine"?
3 How does the heterosexual female reader read lesbian writing, and vice versa? Does reading texts by women challenge distinctions between heterosexual and homosexual women?

References

Alta. 1971. *Burn This*. Washington, N.J.: Times Change Press.

Alta. 1971. *Memorize Yourself*. Washington, N.J.: Times Change Press.

Brossard, Nicole. 1983. *These Our Mothers*. Toronto: Coach House Quebec Translations.

Broumas, Olga. 1977. *Beginning With O*. New Haven, Conn.: Yale University Press.

Grahn, Judy. 1971. *edward the dyke*. Oakland, Cal.: The Women's Press Collective.

Lorde, Audre. 1978. *Uses of the Erotic: The Erotic as Power*. Brooklyn, N.Y.: Out & Out Books.

Marks, Elaine and Isabelle de Courtivron. 1981. *New French Feminisms*. New York: Schocken Books.

Marlatt, Daphne. 1984. *Touch to My Tongue*. Edmonton: Longspoon Press.

Namjoshi, Suniti and Gillian Hanscombe. 1986. *Flesh and Paper*. Charlottetown, P.E.I.: Ragweed Press.

Parker, Pat. 1974. *Pit Stop*. Oakland, Cal.: The Women's Press Collective.

Rich, Adrienne. 1976. *Twenty-One Love Poems*. Emeryville, Cal.: Effie's Press.

Spender, Dale. 1980. *Man Made Language*. London: Routledge and Kegan Paul.

Warland, Betsy. 1981. *A Gathering Instinct*. Toronto: Williams-Wallace.

Warland, Betsy. 1984. *open is broken*. Edmonton : Longspoon Press.

Warland, Betsy. 1987. *serpent (w)rite*. Toronto: The Coach House Press.

Warland, Betsy and Daphne Marlatt. 1988. *Double Negative*. Charlottetown: Gynergy Books.

Habeas Corpus: Anatomy/Autonomy in Relation to Narcissism

Valerie Raoul
Department of French
University of British Columbia

French feminist theorists, notably Cixous, Irigaray, Kristeva, and Wittig, have been responsible for audacious attempts to destabilize and subvert the discourse of patriarchy, Lacan's "symbolic order." Well-versed in Lacanian psychoanalysis and Derrida's theory of "difference," these writers assert the capacity of women to speak as autonomous, self-defining subjects, by means of a form of writing which incorporates the female body. They revalorize feminine narcissism, both as a positive relationship to the body and as mutually empowering communication among women.

Writing in the Feminine

Several papers in this volume refer to various aspects of "French feminist theory," but the latter is far from easy to define.[1] Sometimes elaborating on concepts developed by male French post-structuralist thinkers (mainly Derrida and Lacan), sometimes pursuing a parallel path, some contemporary women writers in France have produced texts that are creative and philosophical as well as both personal and polemic. They do not constitute a cohesive "school." Some of them reject the feminist label, and others are opposed to the concept of theory. What they have in common is that, focusing on the problematic status and function of a female 'subject' position in relation to language, their texts have contributed to a debate around what has been termed "l'écriture féminine," "l'écriture femme," or, in Québec (Nicole Brossard), "writing in the feminine." This debate is inseparable from the revision of Freudian psychoanalysis and the emergence of "difference" or "otherness" as a central concept in the process of "deconstruction." Although it originates in France, this current of modern thought is marked by the contribution of writers living in France but not of French origin (including Cixous, a Jew from Algeria, and Kristeva, a Bulgarian) who are aware of ethnic and linguistic as well as gender difference. It is also significant that deconstruction has been more widely accepted in North America than in Europe,[2] a fact attributable in part to the fascination of its perceived "difference." My purpose here will be to clarify the background to the debate around difference, situating French concepts in relation to Anglo-American feminist theory and to my own work on "feminine narcissism" as a psychoanalytic and literary phenomenon.[3]

Psychoanalysis and Sexual Difference

In *Le Deuxième Sexe* (1949) Simone de Beauvoir cast a critical eye on Freudian theory and produced a feminist analysis of feminine "narcissism." Like other women interested in psychoanalysis, including analysts such as Karen Horney, Melanie Klein, and Clara Thompson, de Beauvoir balked at the concept of penis envy attributed by Freud to all little girls. Interpreted as an unalterable deficiency, the absence of the male organ is not perceived in Freudian theory as compensated for by the presence of other reproductive organs or even more visible protuberances, such as breasts. The "envy" in question is deemed also to be aroused by the organ itself, not by what it represents in a particular society (power, prestige, freedom). The girl child is supposed to assume that she has been castrated. Freud believed that the development of a moral sense (super-ego or internalized code of behaviour) in the male child depended on castration anxiety, occurring at the Oedipal stage, when the boy learns that he may not desire the mother for fear of castration by the father. The concept of the female child being already castrated — that is, having nothing to lose — was held responsible by Freud for the 'inferior' moral development of women.[4] It accounts, in his theory, for women's failure to achieve intellectual or artistic greatness. This belief appears to justify a radical form of biological and psychological determinism that dooms women for ever to subservience to men. De Beauvoir interprets Freud's analysis as an example of the way in which patriarchal thought assumes that male anatomy and male behaviour are the norm, in relation to which everything female is not simply different (with an implied potential for egalitarian complementarity) but deviant or deficient — that is, condemned. A physical feature of the male body becomes, paradoxically, the sign or symbol of male transcendence of the body, of masculine superiority.

This aspect of Freudian theory was to become the centre of Lacan's revisionist analysis, when he designated the Phallus (not the penis) as the ultimate Signifier of what is unattainable but always desired —

transcendental meaning. Feminist psychoanalysts, Juliet Mitchell and Jane Gallop in particular,[5] have more recently seen Lacanian theory as useful to women, since it relegates men also to a state of 'lack,' as the Phallus is inaccessible even to possessors of penises. Like women, they are subjected to the "Nom" (Name) or "Non" (No) of the Father, source of both the Word (Logos) and the Law. These two elements constitute what Lacan calls the Other (l'Autre), with a capital letter — the domain of preexisting structures (language, the unconscious which is structured like a language) from which we subsequently cannot escape: the symbolic order. This order is what humans accede to when they emerge from the pre-Oedipal phase, which Lacan terms the imaginary — the period during which the child is identified with the mother. Separation (recognition of identity and of difference) is brought about through the "mirror stage," when the child recognizes both what it is (in the mirror image) and what it is not (the mother), becoming conscious of the gap between both self and other and self and image.[6]

De Beauvoir, without access to all of Lacan's writing, designated in 1949 the ways in which psychoanalytic theory can explain patriarchy and the oppression of women, and intimated that rather than rejecting this theory out of hand (as Kate Millett, for example, did in 1970), women should gain access to its insights in order to better analyze their situation in relation to men, both personally and politically. Feminist criticism of her ideas (for example, Evans, 1985) focuses on her apparent assumption that, since the subject of language as it exists is always male (that is, the positive and the norm in relation to which female is negative), in order to speak as subjects, women must adopt a male position — or at least a masculine one, an important distinction. In practical terms, they must refuse to be objects of exchange for men by becoming financially independent and rejecting the limitations imposed by child-bearing. In many ways, de Beauvoir shared the pejorative male view of everything "feminine," including female body functions, and promulgated the male-oriented domain of reason and intellect over emotions, instinct or intuition and physicality. She valued autonomy over connectedness and assumed that equality for women implied competing successfully on men's terms, rather than attempting to change the rules underlying the system and structures of patriarchy (see Nye, 1988: 73–94).

For de Beauvoir (1949, Vol. 2, part 2, chapter 1), Freud's description of women as narcissistic was justified, an inevitable outcome of the definition of the feminine as other and as object. Since no subject position is available to woman, she identifies with the desire of the male, seeing herself as the desired object. Her energy is diverted from obtaining what *she* might desire to being desirable to men. The social system uses women as objects of exchange in a male economy which Irigaray, like Lacan, terms *hommo-sexual* (from "homme," meaning man, rather than "homo," which means the same); a woman's value lies in her attractiveness to the male consumer.[7] This does not eliminate male narcissism, since the man chooses a woman in function of the image he wishes to project: he loves her as an extension of himself and because she reflects him. His subjectivity is based on her subjection, on her acceptance of passivity and dependency as an inseparable part of being feminine. Mutual narcissism seems to be the only kind of rapport possible and excludes desire for the other as other. Within this system, de Beauvoir's view that women must become de-feminized — that the concept of 'woman' is in itself problematic — is entirely logical.

Psychoanalysis and the Women's Movement in France

De Beauvoir herself modified her position when she later became involved in the 'MLF' (Mouvement pour la Libération de la Femme) in the 1970s. Paradoxically, she finally accepted the designation 'feminist' at a time when other members of the movement, particularly those influenced by psychoanalysis, were rejecting it. One group, calling themselves Psych et Po (Psychanalyse et Politique — the order was later reversed) eventually broke away from the rest (appropriating the abbreviation MLF for their own use), because they saw the challenge of re-thinking the basis of western philosophical thought as ultimately more important than practical measures such as changing the laws on abortion or enforcing maintenance payments (Duchen, 1987). Antoinette Fouque of the publishing house Editions des femmes, speaking for this group in 1980, stated that they wanted *out* of the phallocracy rather than access to it, and that their fight was primarily against the masculinity in women's minds, rather than the men in power (Duchen, 1987: 50–54).

These views were expressed in the 1970s in women's writing in France, notably that of Hélène Cixous (1975, 1977) and Annie Leclerc (1974). Cixous, an anglicist by training, set out to destabilize the system of binary oppositions that dominate western thought, based on the primordial one of male/female, masculine/feminine. Her texts, which combine elements of autobiography, philosophy, and creative lyrical writing, are vehicles for the revalorisation of the feminine as representing multiplicity rather than unity or binarity, fluidity and flexibility rather than rigidity and firmness, a woven pattern rather than linearity, fertile receptivity rather than destructive violence, nurturing connectedness rather than exploitative domination, laughter and "non-sense" rather than logocentric rationality. Cixous attempts to illustrate a Derridean concept of *différance* as the deferral of meaning,[8] of simultaneous and shifting relationship to many "others," rather than one polarized and hierarchical opposition to an antithesis: yet the above list of opposed values confirms the difficulty (if not impossibility) of avoiding such dichotomies. She has also been accused of affirming, contrary to Derrida, the primacy of (feminine) voice (presence, implicating the body) over (masculine) writing (absence, the trace); but paradoxically she does this through writing, and through writing in a style reminiscent of male poststructuralists and postmodern poets.

According to Cixous, male writers may also produce "feminine" texts. She cites Genet (a homosexual) as an example. Most previous writing by women, on the other hand, is perceived by her to have been "masculine" (Colette and Marguerite Duras are two notable exceptions). It might appear, then, that "feminine" comes to designate any iconoclastic, ludic or subversive form of writing, regardless of the author's sex. Yet this assumption is belied in Cixous's own works by the predominance of imagery based on the female body. The metaphor of writing with "mother's milk" rather than with ink is one which is often cited. It is striking for its rolling together of physical (natural) and aesthetic (cultural) functions, of the feminine (the maternal breast) and the phallogocentric (writing, the pen/phallus), also for the colour reversal from black (ink/active production) on white (paper/absence, receptivity) to white on white (over the existing black?). Writing is perceived, like breast-feeding, as providing food (for thought?) and as both active and passive. It is a form of "jouissance," related to Barthes' "plaisir du texte,"[9] closely associated with the similarly forbidden (for women) act of masturbation (Cixous, 1975: 39–40), where subject and object roles also narcissistically combine. This seductive image fails to acknowledge, however, that men also produce a white fluid, and that not all women are mothers.[10]

Female body imagery as a basis for a new ontology has been taken even further by the psychoanalyst and philosopher Luce Irigaray. In her critical rereading of Freud, *Speculum de l'autre femme*, she reevaluates women's physical experience of interiority and the diversity of erogenous zones in female anatomy. The "speculum" is both a mirror, projecting what is inside toward the outside, and an instrument allowing penetration from the outside to within; "l'autre femme" refers to both the other as woman / woman as other (in Freudian theory) and to the new voice of another woman — one who refuses this definition — who projects a revolutionary image in the text. The concept of the feminine as a different way of relating to space and to physical otherness is further developed in her *Ethique de la différence sexuelle*. Woman's body is open, whereas man's is closed; she experiences a physical permeability which he does not, and has the capacity to relate to the other (mother or child) as both container and thing contained. In a short poetic text entitled, "Et l'Une ne bouge pas sans l'autre," Irigaray expresses the interconnectedness of pregnant mother and child, a relationship that serves as a paradigm for the impossibility of defining the limits between self and other. This emphasis on the pre-Oedipal phase of non-separation is an aspect developed also by other feminist psychoanalysts.

Primary Narcissism: Self and (M)other

Julia Kristeva, who began as a linguist and semiotician and has moved into psychoanalytic practice, is another very influential writer who avoids categorization as a feminist belonging to one group or another. Her experience with the publishing company "des femmes," as recounted in fictionalized form in her recent novel *Les Samouraïs*, seems to have alienated her from the women's movement. Unlike Irigaray, who was expelled from the Lacanian school of psychoanalysis and has attempted in her way of writing to convey her nonconformism to academic models, Kristeva is the only woman to have achieved the (perhaps questionable) honour of acceptance by the French literary and intellectual establishment.[11] Cynics might attribute this at least in part to her relationship with novelist Philippe Sollers, a leader of the *Tel Quel* group, but this would grossly underestimate the originality of her own work. Like Leclerc (in *Parole de femme*), Kristeva's intellectualism is tempered by her experience of pregnancy and childbirth. This is related to her re-valorisation of the pre-Oedipal primary narcissism associated with what she terms the semiotic, comparable to the realm of Lacan's Imaginary, before access to language produces separation and domination by the symbolic order (Kristeva, 1974; also see Weedon, 1987: 88–90).

Kristeva's analysis of the acquisition of gender difference, as it relates to identification with the mother, links up with the conclusions of American object-relations analyst Nancy Chodorow (1978). Feminist psychoanalysis corroborates Freud's opinion that the sexual development of the girl is more complicated and more difficult to achieve (if one accepts the heterosexual norm as desirable) because it involves reorienting object desire from a female object (the mother) to a male one (see Kristeva, 1987: 38–41). While the boy must renounce the mother, he nevertheless retains the female body as the focus of sexual attraction. The girl is required to learn to desire the male body, which in traditional western culture is not associated with close physical contact in infancy. Freud assumed that the girl, on recognizing that the mother is not phallic but castrated, blames her for her own lack of a penis and rejects her on these grounds, while also resenting her as a rival for the father's affection. Identification with the mother is only reestablished when the girl replaces her desire for a penis by the desire for a child. Her relationship to the mother then becomes one of imitation (becoming like her, on the vertical axis of replacement), rather than one of possession (incorporating her, or being one with her on the metonymic plane).[12]

Psychoanalysts agree that women have a basic bisexuality that men do not share, since their attraction to a female body is never completely erased. Their narcissistic attachment to their own bodies is related to this. Freud claimed that the infant is initially asexual, since gender identity is not established until the Oedipal phase. In fact, he posited both boys and girls as having a male sexuality to begin with, as he defines all libido as active and therefore masculine.[13] The girl's penis envy is attributed to her recognition of the clitoris as an inferior version of a penis. For Freud, mature femininity depends on a transfer from the clitoris to the vagina as the main source of erotic pleasure. Some of his patients (and even a disciple, the psychoanalyst Marie Bonaparte) underwent painful operations in the attempt to produce this result. Modern studies of female sexuality have exposed this dichotome as a myth: sexual pleasure is not derived from *either* the clitoris or the vagina, but from both, and other areas as well (as Irigaray emphasizes). Women do not have to choose between a "masculine" and a "feminine" mode of sexual enjoyment, just as they do not have to reject and hate their mothers in order to be attracted to other sexual objects.

Female Narcissism and Homosexuality

In Freudian theory, any woman who persists in wishing to think and behave in the same way as a man (that is, who does not accept the prescribed feminine role) is fantasizing that she has a penis and is likely to be attracted to other women as sexual objects rather than to men. Clinical cases of what are termed "narcissistic personality disorders" reveal that women exhibiting narcissistic symptoms tend to imagine, when being made love to by a man, that they are making love to themselves (Reich, 1953). If they do form a relationship with a man, it will be to act through him; he is perceived as an extension of the self. Other women perform a similar manoeuvre by living vicariously through a child, especially a son. The boundaries between self and other are blurred. While in extreme cases this may lead to a form of megalomania, narcissism is always the result of a "narcissistic injury" — that is, at some point during the period of individuation the self is perceived as defective, and subsequent behaviour tries to compensate for this deficiency. Female narcissism is thus attributable to the trauma of discovering that one is not a male; this negative self-evaluation is "normally" followed by the determination to obtain approval from a male, and acceptance of the feminine role in order to do so. Alternatively, some females "abnormally" persist in denying their difference and acting in the same way that males do; they may even seek approval from other women, rather than from men.

Freud's negative assessment of this phenomenon has been reversed by lesbian feminists, including those in France who proclaimed "we are not women" and "we are all lesbians," regardless of sexual orientation (Duchen, 1987: 38–40). Both Cixous and Irigaray at some point in their texts state or imply that a lesbian position (politically, at least, but also sexually) is the only valid one to adopt, once the mechanisms of gender construction have been recognized. Here they join American writers like Andrea Dworkin (*Intercourse*, 1987), who maintains that egalitarian heterosexual relations are impossible, and that the (hetero)sexual act is the basic paradigm for sado-masochistic oppression.

Lesbian writing has come to represent the ultimate refusal to be evaluated by men, the logical conclusion of the 'subject' position for women. Those in the MLF who were convinced that nothing can be gained from working within the (male) system accused heterosexual feminists of being collaborators or hypocrites. The tendency to exclude men from women's meetings had already created a great deal of controversy. A fiery debate ensued, and the women's movement in France was irremediably split between those who saw lesbian separatism as the only possible outcome and those (including some lesbians) who refused to eliminate the majority of (non-lesbian) women from their concerns; both sides evoked psychoanalysis as target or support.

On both sides there were those who feared that by becoming exclusive and dogmatic, women were behaving in a phallocratic fashion, that the denial of difference among women was tantamount to abolishing women's difference. Both sides promoted this difference as a strength. The lesbians celebrated feminine culture and history, reevaluating previously denigrated feminine qualities and strengths; heterosexuals linked these qualities and strengths to motherhood, involving a man's participation and the production of sons as well as daughters. These debates are found also in North America, in the work of Mary Daly in the U.S., Nicole Brossard and others in Québec,[14] and writers such as Daphne Marlatt in English Canada. In France, the strongest lesbian position was adopted by Monique Wittig, in *Les Guérillères*. In this poetic narrative she depicts a society composed entirely of women, with a culture based on symbols of the female body, at war with men; the narrative tech-

niques and use of language are themselves turned into weapons against the male symbolic order. Yet at the end the young men join the women. Wittig has stated elsewhere that the category of "woman" must disappear (see Duchen, 1987). In texts by Cixous and Irigaray, there is also an increasing tendency to express the need to include men in any final utopian solution.[15]

Female homosexuality has been condemned as an immature type of sexual development, as basically narcissistic, implying love for the same (the mother; the double or self-extension) rather than for the other, the different. Yet paradoxically, in psychoanalytic theory, it supposes identification with the father (rather than Oedipal desire for him). The designation "narcissistic" in the diagnosis of "borderline" neuroses is pejorative, but this judgement is justified only if normal femininity is considered both desirable and attainable. Lesbian feminists reject this assumption and rehabilitate this form of narcissism as a positive way of regulating self-esteem. Popular psychology reflects this logic, when it claims that in order to love someone else we must first learn to love ourselves. Yet it also maintains that "opposites attract one another."

Androgyny, Anatomy, and Autonomy

The opposition between male and female which sees the one as necessary to the other and both as complementary parts of a lost "whole," found its expression in Aristophanes' story of the androgyn, as told by Plato in the *Symposium*. Lacan invokes this legend to explain the "lack" which defines the human subject (see Silverman, 1983: 151). It posits original whole beings with both sexes (hermaphrodites), who were bisected. This division left each half yearning for the other, for the lost wholeness, resulting in copulation and reproduction in the vain hope of producing a new whole. Plato, defending homosexuality, supposes that some wholes were totally male or female, resulting in beings who also seek their other — similar rather than different — half. Human beings, whatever their sexual orientation, are seen as incomplete, as seeking connection to another. The longing for a former symbiosis may be interpreted as nostalgia for the primitive state of primary narcissism, but oneness with the whole can ultimately be achieved only through death (Green, *Narcissisme de vie, narcissisme de mort*, 1983).

Physical union with the other in life is necessarily temporary, illusory, or both, since the self is defined by the limits of its own body. The individual anatomy is constituted by the joining of its parts to form a discrete unit, which is autonomous. The word *anatomy*, ironically, has its Greek root in the verb meaning "to cut up"; it relates to dissection, rather than to articulation (joining together). Autonomy — separateness, the cutting of the umbilical cord — is synonymous in western culture with maturity, independence, and full subjecthood, but for males only. Auto-nomy also signifies "self-naming." In our culture, women do not have their own name, and have not participated in the naming process. Marked (like sons) by the Name of the Father, they have not been allowed (like sons) to take the father's place and pass it on.

The French writers associated with "writing in the feminine" challenge this apparently immutable situation on two fronts: that of the body's anatomy in relation to writing, and that of self-naming as the function of writing, or of any "prise de parole" (literally "taking the word"). A closer look at the myth of Narcissus throws light on the philosophical questions raised by their re-vision of the foundations of subjectivity and of representation.

Narcissus and Echo

In the version recounted by Ovid, Narcissus is loved by the nymph Echo but ignores her because he is fascinated by his own reflection in the pool. Unable to seize the image, which disintegrates as he approaches, he pines away. His body is replaced by a flower, a type of lily, associated with the name of his mother, Leriope. In another version, Narcissus is engulfed by the water in his attempt to join his double. The desire to be united with the Other that is the Same has obvious associations with a "return to the womb," to a state of fluid primary narcissism.

Narcissus' obsession is due to two misconceptions. First, he does not recognize that the image is a reflection of himself. He fails to complete the "mirror stage" of self-identification. Secondly, he does not recognize that the image is a two-dimensional representation, not a living human body; he mistakes a sign for a real referent, confusing the imaginary and the symbolic. In the legend, Narcissus continues to speak to himself despite his disincarnation, and his words are repeated by Echo, who loses not only her body, but the ability to pronounce her own words in her own voice.

French feminist writing addresses both aspects of the myth. First, the body is to be reinstated as the recognizable source of representation. Secondly, a feminine voice and language are to replace the ventriloquism of echolalia. Masculine emphasis on the visual (which Irigaray attributes to the external, visible nature of the male organ) is to be replaced by an emphasis on (physical) touch and (verbal) sound. As Cixous (1975) puts it, woman will speak from the other side of the mirror (see Silverman, 1988). Furthermore, Echo not only refuses to duplicate Narcissus' messages to himself; she discovers the other nymphs. Irigaray maintains in "Les marchandises entre elles" (in *Ce Sexe qui n'en est pas un*) that the whole economy of gender dichotomy is subverted when women value relations with other women as much as those with men, and if they set out to speak their own sexuality, rather than allowing it to be defined by men.

Habeas Corpus?

Male definitions of sexuality belong to the symbolic order. According to Lacanian theory, once the subject is constituted by its acquisition of (and by) language, any unmediated relationship to the physical world is ruled out (see Silverman, 1983: 172–3). Kristeva has contested this assumption, by maintaining that the order of the imaginary (associated with the feminine) continues to co-exist with the symbolic. Lacan concedes that women are not as alienated as men from the real (see Silverman, 1983: 186), precisely because female sexuality is not, and cannot be, represented within the male symbolic order, where it stands for the unknown. Male accounts of it are bound to be self-projections, and the female body is construed as irremediably other, an object to be used, exchanged, and discarded.

The legal concept of *habeas corpus* is useful to distinguish between the two concepts of the body. In the first instance *habeas corpus* refers to the ability to produce a body (or some-body) as evidence or proof. The body in question is regarded as passive and dissociated from any subjectivity. The other use of the term refers to the right of an individual to the freedom of "his" own body, which is self-propelled and inseparable from "his" identity. The first use is related to anatomy: the body as thing/ object available for dissection; the second to autonomy: the body as self-propelled person. Only a female subject can (re)claim the full personhood of the female body by giving it a voice. This female subject speaks (articulates) from a "different" place, from the margins of phallogocentric discourse. Her writing of the female body supposes the necessity of articulation, of connectedness, of bridges between self and other. When these writers say "I," as woman, they also imply "we," preferring identity in plurality over the singular "I/you" opposition.

Postscript

This theoretical approach to women's paradoxical situation in the male symbolic order has not gone uncriticized. A conception of all phenomena as signs or representations unknowable outside the "prison-house of language" (to use Fredric Jameson's term) runs the danger of ignoring the very real problems of the material world, especially for women. After writing, what? Yet the premise of modern philosophical thought is that discourse precedes individual or collective consciousness, and it therefore follows that changes in discourse can effect as well as affect other types of change. Women's Studies may appear to be narcissistic, as we concentrate on the study of women by women, but this is a necessary stage (as for other oppressed groups) in reconstructing a self-defined individual and group representation. In the case of feminist literary studies, some men are even beginning to echo the words of women. This reversal, the appropriation of women's discourse by men, is also necessary for any real change in the perception of sameness and difference, for the establishment of a genuinely polymorphous polylogue.

Notes

1 *New French Feminisms* is a useful anthology of extracts from French feminist writers, as is the one edited by Toril Moi. Moi's *Sexual/Textual Politics* includes sections on Cixous, Irigaray, and Kristeva. See also Suleiman's introductory essay, "(Re)Writing the Body: The Politics and Poetics of Female Eroticism" and Gallop, "French Theory and the Seduction of Feminism."

2 See Jardine, *Gynesis*, and the special issue of *Yale French Studies* (Vol. 62, 1981) devoted to French feminist theory.

3 The basic texts on narcissism are collected in Morrison (ed.), *Essential Papers on Narcissism*. My research involves the application of this theory to diaries by women and fictional journals by both female and male characters in the Québec novel.

4 Freud in 1925: "I cannot evade the notion (though I hesitate to give it expression) that for women the level of what is ethically normal is different from what it is in men. Their super-ego is never so inexorable, so impersonal, so independent of its emotional origins as we require it to be in men." He adds, "We must not allow ourselves to be deflected from such conclusions by the denials of the feminists" (who were claiming at that time equality rather than superiority for women) and (grudgingly) "but we shall . . . agree that the majority of men are also far behind the masculine ideal and that all human individuals, as a result of their bisexual disposition and cross-inheritance, combine in themselves both masculine and feminine characteristics" (Strouse, 1985, 25). The feminine characteristics in men are still implied to be inferior.

5 See Mitchell (1974), Mitchell and Rose (1982), Gallop (1982, 1985), Gallop and Burke (1980), and Schor (1981).

6 Lacan, "Le Stade du miroir" in *Écrits I*: 89–97.

7 *Ce Sexe qui n'en est pas un* (Irigaray, 1977: 168).

8 Derrida's 'difference' owes much to Saussure's linguistic concept of differences as non-hierarchical and non-binary. Derrida adds the notion of

difference as deferral ("différance," a pun in French): that is, each signifier is defined by difference from another one, which is in turn defined by difference from others, etc. "Meaning" (the ultimate signified) is unattainable, but we follow its traces. The absence of meaning is comparable to Lacan's designation of the Phallus as the signifier of "lack."

9 See Schor (1987: 100) "Dreaming Dyssymetry: Barthes, Foucault and Sexual Difference." "Plaisir" (pleasure) and "jouissance" (enjoyment) have connotations in French of sexual arousal and orgasm.

10 See Stanton (1989) and Lindsay (1986).

11 Cixous made an unsuccessful attempt to start a Women's Studies program at the University of Paris VIII in 1980 (see Sellers, 1986: 446).

12 Saussure distinguished between the vertical axis of selection (categories based on resemblance) and the horizontal axis of combination (based on contiguity) in the structure of linguistic grammar. These two axes are analogous to metaphor (identification by similarity) and metonymy (association by connection). Masculine and feminine modes of imagery have been perceived as privileging one or the other of these two poles, but the distinction is not always easy to maintain (see Silverman, 1983, Chapter 3).

13 Lacan punningly describes the pre-symbolic ungendered being as an "homme-lette" (formless but incipiently male).

14 Other Québec writers who express the same concerns as those in France are Louky Bersianik, Madeleine Gagnon, and France Théoret. See Drapeau (1986).

15 The liberal feminist view, that there will ultimately be no gender distinctions as parenting becomes shared and sex-roles indistinguishable, was also expressed in France by Badinter (1986) in *L'Un est l'autre* ("The One is the Other").

Questions

1 Does philosophical feminist theory establish new barriers for women by its abstract intellectualism?

2 Does "writing the body" challenge or merely reaffirm the male-centred definitions of Woman identified in Section One?

3 Is the expression to "write the body" a contradiction in terms, and the project therefore doomed to failure?

4 Does the split among feminists in France illustrate the impossibility of accepting difference as non-conflictive?

References

Badinter, Elisabeth. 1986. *L'Un est l'autre. Des Relations entre hommes et femmes*. Paris: Odile Jacob.

Beauvoir, Simone de. 1949. *Le Deuxième Sexe*. Paris: Gallimard.

Brossard, Nicole. 1983. "Pourquoi j'écris," *Québec français*, Vol. 47 (octobre): 31.

Brossard, Nicole. 1985. "Un Féminisme de préférence," *La Vie en rose*, Vol. 24 (mars): 29, 56.

Chodorow, Nancy. 1978. *The Reproduction of Mothering. Psychoanalysis and the Sociology of Gender*. Berkeley: University of California Press.

Cixous, Hélène. 1975. "Le Rire de la Méduse," *L'Arc*, Vol. 61: 39–54. Trans. Cohen, Keith and Paula, as "The Laugh of the Medusa," *Signs*, Vol. 1 (Summer): 875–99.

Cixous, Hélène. 1977. *La Venue à l'écriture* (with Annie Leclerc and Madeleine Gagnon). Paris: UGE 10/18.

Conley, Verena. 1984. *Writing the Feminine: Hélène Cixous*. Lincoln: University of Nebraska Press.

Drapeau, Renée Berthe. 1986. *Féminins singuliers. Pratiques d'écriture: Brossard, Théoret*. Montreal: Triptyque.

Duchen, Claire. 1987. *French Connections. Voices from the Women's Movement in France*. London: Hutchinson.

Dworkin, Andrea. 1987. *Intercourse*. New York: Free Press.

Evans, Mary. 1985. *Simone de Beauvoir. A Feminist Mandarin*. London: Tavistock.

Felman, Shoshana. 1975. "The Critical Phallacy," *Diacritics*, Vol. 2, No. 10 (Winter): 2–10.

Freud, Sigmund. 1925/1985. "Some Psychological Consequences of the Anatomical Distinction Between the Sexes." Pp. 17–26 in Jean Strouse (ed.), *Women and Analysis*. Boston: G.K. Hall.

Gallop, Jane. 1982. *Feminism and Psychoanalysis: The Daughter's Seduction*. London: Macmillan.

Gallop, Jane and C. Burke. 1980. "Psychoanalysis and Feminism in France." In A. Jardine and H. Eisenstein (eds.), *The Future of Difference*. New Brunswick, N.J. and London: Rutgers University Press.

Gallop, Jane and C. Burke. 1985. *Reading Lacan*. Ithaca: Cornell University Press.

Gallop, Jane and C. Burke. 1987. "French Theory and the Seduction of Feminism." Pp. 111–5 in A. Jardine and P. Smith (eds.), *Men in Feminism*. New York: Methuen.

Green, André. 1983. *Narcissisme de vie, narcissisme de mort*. Paris: Minuit.

Grosz, Elizabeth. 1990. *Jacques Lacan: A Feminist Introduction*. New York: Routledge.

Irigaray, Luce. 1974. *Spéculum de l'autre femme*. Paris: Minuit. Trans. G. Gill, *Speculum of the Other Woman*. Ithaca: Cornell University Press, 1985.

Irigaray, Luce. 1977. *Ce Sexe qui n'en est pas un*. Paris: Minuit. Trans. C. Porter and C. Burke, *This Sex Which is Not One*. Ithaca: Cornell University Press, 1985.

Irigaray, Luce. 1979/81. *Et l'Une ne bouge pas sans l'autre*. Paris: Minuit. Trans. H. Wenzel. "And One Does Not More Without the Other," *Signs*, Vol. 7, No. 1 (Fall): 60–7.

Irigaray, Luce. 1984. *Ethique de la différence sexuelle*. Paris: Minuit.

Jardine, Alice and Hester Eisenstein (eds.). 1980. *The Future of Difference*. New Brunswick and London: Rutgers Press

Jardine, Alice and Hester Eisenstein. 1985. *Gynesis. Configurations of Woman and Modernity*. Ithaca: Cornell University Press.

Jones, Ann Rosalind. 1981. "Writing the Body: Towards an Understanding of 'l'écriture féminine'," *French Studies*, Vol. 7: 247–63.

Kristeva, Julia. 1974. *La Révolution du langage poétique*. Paris: Seuil. Trans. N. Waller. New York: Columbia University Press, 1984.

Kristeva, Julia. 1977. *Polylogue*. Paris: Seuil.

Kristeva, Julia. 1983. "Narcisse: la nouvelle démence" and "Notre religion: le semblant." Pp. 131–70 in *Histoires d'amour*. Paris: Denoël. Trans. L. Roudiez, *Stories of Love*, New York: Columbia University Press, 1977.

Kristeva, Julia. 1990. *Les Samouraïs*. Paris: Fayard.

Lacan, Jacques. 1966. *Ecrits I*. Paris: Seuil. Trans. A. Sheridan, New York: Norton, 1977.

Leclerc, Annie. 1974. *Parole de femme*. Paris: Grasset.

Lindsay, Cecile. 1986. "Body/Language: French Feminist Utopias," *The French Review*, Vol. 60, No. 1 (October): 46–55.

Marks, Elaine and Isabelle de Courtivron (eds.). 1980. *New French Feminisms*. Brighton: Harvester.

Millett, Kate. 1970. *Sexual Politics*. New York: Doubleday.

Mitchell, Juliet. 1974. *Psychoanalysis and Feminism*. Harmonsworth: Penguin.

Mitchell, Juliet and Jacqueline Rose. 1982. *Feminine Sexuality. Jacques Lacan and the École freudienne*. London: Macmillan.

Moi, Toril. 1985. *Sexual/Textual Politics*. London: Methuen.

Moi, Toril (ed.). 1986. *The Kristeva Reader*. New York: University of Columbia.

Moi, Toril (ed.). 1987. *French Feminist Thought. A Reader*. Oxford: Blackwell.

Morrison, Andrew P. (ed.). 1986. *Essential Papers on Narcissism*. New York: New York University Press.

Nye, Andrea. 1988. *Feminist Theory and the Philosophies of Man*. New York: Routledge.

Pagès, Irène. 1985. "Simone de Beauvoir and the New French Feminisms," *Canadian Woman Studies*, Vol. 6, No. 1: 60–2.

Date Due

FEB 2 2 1996
Rev. 1
Jan 3/ 97
NOV 2 8 1996
OCT 1 2 1999
OCT 1 8 1999

BRODART, INC.   Cat. No. 23 233   Printed in U.S.A.

UNIVERSITY COLLEGE OF THE CARIBOO LIBRARY
WILLIAMS LAKE

U.C.C. LIBRARY
71898910

HQ 1154 .A685 1992
The Anatomy of gender
c.2   71898910